WILD
FLOWERS

OF BRITAIN AND EUROPE

Margot and Roland Spohn

A&C BLACK
LONDON

Contents

How to Use this Book

For each flower species in this book, you will find details describing the natural habitat, with interesting historical or biological facts and tips about how to use the flowers. Informative illustrations with notes about key features make the flowers easy to identify. The main photograph shows a flower's typical appearance or typical detail. Other illustrations provide more information about significant characteristics, which are essential for identification purposes. The text in the margin provides images and information highlighting details relating to the habitat and key facts of note along with a drawing of a typical flower. If an entire page is devoted to a single flower, the **'Did you know?'** box gives particularly interesting information about this species.

Height (H)
The size indicates the flower's height. Above ground-level height is also given for creeping plants, but without the maximum length of stems growing horizontally.

Month
The month(s) specifies the flowering season. This applies to the main distribution areas of flowers in their natural habitats across Europe.

General information
This section gives interesting information on various topics including usage, history, medicine and biology.

Typical appearance
A large photo gives an impression of an entire plant or character-istic detail, with captions referring to key features.

'Did you know?' box
The box, often contain-ing an image, highlights particularly interesting information about the flower. In many cases, a related species is also featured.

Glo
Trollius
H 30–60

Accordin
to have
presuma
Globeflo
mountai
disappea
dried out.

Common name
Scientific name
Plant family

Form
Is the plant annual, biennial or perennial? Does it over-winter as an herbaceous perennial, shrub or tree? A warning symbol indicating potential danger shows poisonous flowers.

...ver

...buttercup family)
perennial

Habitat
The photo displays the flower in one of its natural habitats. The text describes other habitats and distribution across Europe.

...nd, hobgoblins and sprites were supposed
...flowers as torches. The plant's name is
...rom the spherical shape of the flowers.
...s were once very common in hills and
...owadays, however, the plant has
...olaces, as many wetland meadows have

Habitat Damp to wet-land meadows, lowland fens, alongside streams. Especially in high mountains to altitudes of over 2,000 m. Almost everywhere in Europe.

> protected species in England
> occasionally flowers again in autumn
> mostly grows in loose groups next to one another

Key features
A summary of general information, for instance, about identi-fication, distribution or usage.

mostly 1, occasionally 2–3 flowers at end of stems

flowers 2–3 cm across

spherical flower

10–15 petals

upright stems

Flower
A typical flower is shown with key identifying features. An entire flower head is illustrated for composite flowers.

 239

Colour code
Each of the five main groups is colour-coded by typical flower colour (see page 1).

leaves divided as far as leaf node

sections further indented

Symbol
Silhouettes defining the flower's shape allow for further sub-division of the flower colours (see page 1).

Identification details
The small illustrations show a plant detail, which is crucial for identification purposes. For example, this may include leaves, fruits, more flower details or roots. The captions refer to typical features.

Did you know?
Only small insects reach the flower as pollinators. Three species of flies drink not only the nectar but also lay their eggs in the ovary, where their larvae then feed. However enough seeds are usually left over to ensure the plant's reproduction.

Flower Colours

The flowers featured in this book are arranged by easy-to-identify and characteristic colours, which are colour-coded into five main flower groups. Specialist botanical knowledge is not required, since the colour codes quickly highlight a flower's identity within a group.

Flower colour

The colour code highlights red, white, blue, yellow and green/brown flowers. Most flower species are quite easy to classify within these groups. It is best to assess a flower's typical colour when the petals are fully open.

Changing flower colour

Violet flowers display varying hues from red to blue. If flowers appear more violet-red throughout the flowering season, then they belong to the main red group. If their colour is more violet-blue, they belong to the main blue group of flowers. However, many

A flower is made up of different parts.

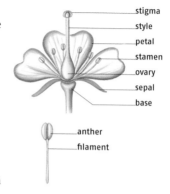

- stigma
- style
- petal
- stamen
- ovary
- sepal
- base

- anther
- filament

petals change colour throughout a flowering season. In these cases or if, when compared, the flowers of a single species display varying petal colours, you are recommended to consult all of the main groups that seem relevant.

The Spring Pea is **reddish-violet** in colour

The Alkanet is **bluish-violet** in colour

Typical Flower Shapes

Shape is one of the most important identifying features of flowers. The colour groups used in this book are therefore also divided into additional subgroups, which are marked by five outlines. The position of each outline in the margin of each page and inside the colour bar symbolises a flower's typical outline and number of petals. The individual subgroups may – or may not – represent a flower's individual parts and varying characteristics, yet this is merely a reflection of the myriad of different flower shapes and appearances.

 Flower with more than five petals or composite flowers

 Flower with **six identical petals**; Wild Tulip

 Composite flower head with **ray or outer florets only**; Chicory

 Composite flower head with **disc florets** only; Safflower

 Composite flower head with **outer ray and disc florets**; Ox-eye Daisy

 Flowers with no more than four petals

Single florets with sepals and petals; Sea Rocket

 Flowers with five petals

Corolla fused together, **tubular and flared tips**; Purple Gromwell

 Corolla fused together, **bell-shaped**; Deadly Nightshade

 Corolla fused together, **flat-faced**; Apple of Sodom

 Bilaterally symmetrical flowers

 Pea-like flower; White Clover

 Labiate; Meadow Sage

 Flower with spur; Common Toadflax

 Orchid-like flower; Fragrant Orchid

Typical Flower Structure

In addition to observing their colour and shape, an important way to identify flowers is to concentrate on how they are arranged on the stems. Some flowers are solitary, whereas others form characteristically structured groups. These flowers are developed in an especially typical fashion when the blooms are fully open or even when the first flowers are already wilting or have in fact died away.

Cluster
Stalked flowers arranged in clusters on a single stem; Tufted Milkwort

Spike
Many dense flowers along the stem to the tip; Hoary Plantain

Branched cluster or raceme
Flowers more or less branched; Common St John's Wort

Club-shaped
Similar to a spike, with the fleshy spadix covered by densely packed florets; Common Sweet Flag

Umbel
Flower stalks arranged more
or less in one tier;
Meadow Cowslip

Flowers in whorls
Flowers more or less
arranged in tiers;
Henbit Dead-nettle

Flower head of tiny umbellules
Stalks of tiny umbellules radiate
from a single point at the end of
the stem; Water Hemlock

Round cluster
All petals tightly clustered at the
top of the stem and more or less
forming a round flower head;
Round-headed Rampion

Typical Forms

Even though flowers have the same basic structure, they manifest quite different plant forms. Key characteristics include longevity and the way in which the plants survive the winter. Annual and biennial herbaceous plants live for just one or two years respectively. During the winter, herbaceous perennials mainly survive underground, with their roots overwintering as rhizomes, bulbs or tuberous roots. By contrast, shrubs and trees survive as woody plants and continue to grow bark, with their trunks, branches and twigs growing upright into the winter sky.

In addition to this classification, as shown in the short features summary for each flower, the direction of growth and branching of the stems also defines a plant's form.

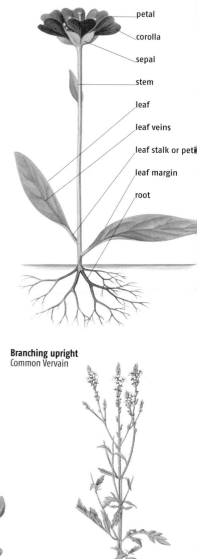

petal
corolla
sepal
stem
leaf
leaf veins
leaf stalk or peti
leaf margin
root

With twining stems
Dodder Thyme

Branching upright
Common Vervain

Stems low or creeping
Creeping Jenny

Upwards-climbing stems
Alpine Gypsophila

With leaf rosette and leafless stems
Common Butterwort

Spreading plant, with runners
Woodland or Wild Strawberry

Cushion
Moss Campion

The Leaves of Flowers

In addition to the flower heads, features of the foliage also qualify as plants' most important characteristics. Apart from the appearance of a single leaf, observing the attachment of the leaves on the stem may be another important means of identification.

Leaf shapes

Different leaf shapes can be classified according to specific basic patterns.

Arrow-shaped
Field Pennycress

Pinnately lobed or pinnatifid (leaflets joined at base)
Wormwood

Pinnate
Jacob's Ladder

Finely divided
Giant Fennel

Linear
Yellow Asphodel

Lanceolate
Canada Goldenrod

Oval
Bastard Balm

Palmate
Bloody Crane's-bill

Heart-shaped
May Lily

Trifoliate
Bermuda Buttercup

Kidney-shaped
European Wild Ginger

Digitate
Large-leaved Lupin

Leaf positions

A few basic features characterise the position in which the leaves are attached to the stems. It is extremely helpful to be aware of these patterns for identification purposes. When observing a plant, concentrate on checking the lower section, rather than the tip of the stem.

Alternate
Warty Spurge

Clasping, in two rows
Fragrant Solomon's Seal

Decussate
Gypsywort

In whorls
Sweet Woodruff

The 'Did you know?' Box

It is difficult for us to imagine our world without flowers. They are a delightful sight and provide basic substances for a spectrum of different products. Moreover, flowers represent an indispensable part of an efficiently functioning natural environment. Often, we scarcely give a thought to the life cycle of each individual species. For that reason, this book gives you general information about each featured flower, along with a selection of other interesting details. If only one species is featured on a single page, more space is given to relevant facts. In this case, a '**Did you know?**' box also highlights especially interesting information.

Medicinal Plants

Flowers are created out of a variety of different chemical substances that help to protect them from foraging animals or to attract their pollinators, for example. Some of these substances are poisonous to humans, whereas others supply the valuable raw materials needed for use as extracts in herbal medicines. Contemporary medicine would be very impoverished without the store of accumulated knowledge about these medicinal plants and their effects. Many healing plants are widely cultivated to meet the high demand for natural remedies.

Cultivated Plants

A long process of cultivation from native wild species produced many naturalised plants that we are familiar with today. Consequently, in many cases the wild plant's similarity with the contemporary varieties can scarcely be recognised.

Did you know?
The origins of lettuce go back to the Prickly Lettuce. Nowadays, this wild species is regarded as the standard plant for cultivating different varieties. In China, the stems of a prickly lettuce cultivar are commonly eaten like green asparagus.

Ornamental Plants

Many wild flowers are so striking and beautiful that, in their wild state, they naturally integrate into manicured gardens. In some cases, horticulturalists specifically cultivated even larger blooms with extra variety and more colours than the wild plants. Whereas wild flowers have developed to ensure their survival by subsequently producing seeds, many cultivated varieties are grown for their beauty alone and no longer produce any seeds at all.

Did you know?
The roots of the Spiny Restharrow are used for their diuretic effect and are helpful in preventing inflammations of the urinary passage. When finely cut, they are used as one of the ingredients for soothing herbal teas recommended for kidneys and the bladder.

Habitats for Animals and Plants

A cleared and cultivated landscape hardly offers wild animals and plants any natural habitat and thus frequently lacks species variety. For that reason, conservationists are committed to preserving or re-establishing natural diversity. Every single flower species has a part to play. For instance, many animals have developed highly specialised survival techniques and rely either on a specific plant or plant family as their natural habitat or as food providers.

Flowers and their Tricks

We may be captivated by colourful and beautifully shaped flowers or marvel at their unique features, but we are even more amazed to learn about the purpose of their clever adaptations. Flowers have developed ingenious solutions to guarantee that they can survive and successfully reproduce in their ideal habitat. They find ways to ensure effective pollination, the farthest and safest distribution of their seeds or the best method to gain essential nutrients.

Did you know?
Claret-coloured or black 'Carrot flowers' at the centre of the umbel help the flower's pollination, because flies visit these florets. In turn, other flies prefer landing on the spot that these insects vacated. Therefore, the dark flowers function like fly traps.

Did you know?
Plants can often be eaten away. For instance, deer graze on young buds and the Scarlet Lily Beetle, a red beetle measuring 6–8 mm, likes to chew through foliage. If you hold these beetles up to your ear, their quiet squeaking noise just becomes audible.

Meadow Rue

Thalictrum aquilegifolium (buttercup family)
H 40–120 cm   May–July   perennial

Habitat Riverside woodlands, woodland ravines, damp meadows, among other tall perennials. Mainly in central Europe and the Alps up to altitudes of 2,300 m.

> attracted to damp soil, rich in nutrients
> foliage similar to the Rue (p. 215)
> attractive in a wild flower garden

The Meadow Rue is a 'painter's flower', destined to be captured by the artist's paintbrush. The flower's most striking parts are not the petals, but its numerous and highly conspicuous stamens. Their scent and colour attract a host of different insects – beetles, flies, bees and bumblebees – eager to collect the pollen.

richly formed, dense florets appearing as branched clusters

roundish to oval leaflets

blue-green leaves

leaves double–triple pinnate

4 small sepals quickly fall away

numerous stamens with reddish or violet filaments

Common Sorrel

Rumex acetosa (knotweed family)
H 30–100 cm   May–July   perennial

Habitat Meadows, pastures, wayside verges, river- and streambanks. Throughout Europe.

> leaves with a sour aftertaste
> especially striking in May and June
> attracted to nitrogen-rich places

The same substances as are present in the Wood-sorrel (p. 117) account for this plant's sour taste. The young leaves are ideal in salads and soups. However, if they are used in excessive quantities, they can cause diarrhoea and vomiting. They may also cause kidney damage.

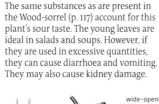

flower head with abundant florets

erect stem

wide-opening male flower

6 yellow anthers

female flower with green or reddish petals

protruding stigmas

pointed apex

arrow-shaped lower leaves

3 roundish leaves around the fruit

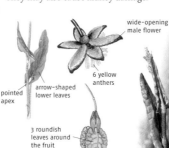

Opium Poppy

Papaver somniferum (poppy family)

H 40–150 cm   June–Aug   annual   ☠

scored capsule yields a milky juice

When thickened, the milky juice of the unripe capsules is the source of the drug commonly known as opium. However, this drug not only unleashes feelings of elation, but can also be addictive. In medicine, opium is regarded as one the most effective painkillers. Individual parts also prevent coughs and alleviate muscle spasms. From the days of antiquity until early modern times, doctors mainly used Opium Poppy or opium and Henbane (p. 235) in operations as an anaesthetic.

Habitat Gardens, weedy patches on rubble, wasteland. Originally from west Asia, occasionally growing wild after cultivation in Europe.

> *varieties also with dazzling red or dense flowers*
> *long-lasting fruits*
> *cultivated since the early Stone Age*

bloom's colour variant

unripe fruit capsule with grey-white coating

4 petals, usually with a dark blotch at the base

stamens in abundance

fat ovary

19

single flower on long stems

with 5–12 stigma rays

fruit capsule more or less spherical

petals up to 10 cm in size

perfoliate leaf, clasping stem

plant blue-green

blue-green foliage, sparse, with waxy coating

Did you know?

Up to 2,000 seeds develop inside every fruit. The ripe Poppy seeds are a popular baking ingredient and no longer contain any poisonous substances. Poppy oil can also be pressed from them.

Common Poppy

Papaver rhoeas (poppy family)
H 30–90 cm   May–July   annual   (☙)

leaves pinnately divided

Habitat *Corn fields, country paths, station sidings, wasteland, also sown on roadside verges for greenery. All over Europe.*

solitary flowers

> petals open early in the morning
> roots grow to about 1 m deep
> warm locations essential in summer

Each flower produces the amazing and immense quantity of about 2.5 million pollen grains. These are high in nutrients and various insects collect them. Every morning, bumblebees in particular often wait for the Poppy petals to open. Flowers emit the most pollen during the morning before 10 am.

numerous stamens

4 petals, up to 4 cm long

often with a black blotch at the base

petals crumpled after opening

opens with pores

broad and oval fruit capsule

Sea Rocket

Cakile maritima (cabbage family)
H 15–30 cm   July–Oct   annual

Habitat *On sandy or shingle beaches inside the tideline. Often grows in sparse groups. Beaches all around Europe.*

> Leaves often with slender sections
> salt-tolerant
> piquant taste

Sea Rocket was among the first flowering plants to inhabit the volcanic island of Surtsey, after its creation as part of Iceland. The upper part of the double-sectioned fruit contains a fibrous air cavity and can be washed far away on the tide. The lower section initially remains attached to the plant, falling to the ground later, where it becomes firmly anchored.

flowers in loose corollas

fleshy leaf

4 pink, purple or white petals, 0.6–1 cm long

4 slender sepals

fruits 1–2 cm long

divided into two sections

Round-leaved Penny-cress

Thlaspi cepaeifolium (cabbage family)
H 5–15 cm   June–Sept   perennial

The Round-leaved Penny-cress is particularly conspicuous because of the unusual places where it is found. It often grows in total isolation, creating a patch of greenery in among shifting debris and rubble. Its long stems grow for several years and creep in among the rubble. When pulled away, they simply root elsewhere and grow into a new plant.

Habitat *Loose, rough limestone rubble. At altitudes of 1,500 to over 3,000 m. Mountains in central and southern Europe.*

> *needs damp under-soil*
> *favourite fodder of Chamois goats*
> *overwinters mostly in green rosettes*

leaves oval, slightly fleshy

umbel-like flower clusters

fruit 4–8 mm long

creeping stems

4 purple petals, 6–9 mm long

21

Great Burnet

Sanguisorba officinalis (rose family)
H 30–150 cm   June–Sept   perennial

The meaning of the plant's scientific name is roughly equivalent to 'absorbing blood'. The plant is rich in tannins. Its roots were once used to arrest heavy bleeding during the menstrual cycle and the foliage was used to treat wounds. The blood-red colour of the flower heads was also interpreted as a sign of the plant's medicinal powers.

flowers in dense, 1–3 cm long clusters

Habitat *Damp and wet meadows, moor and mountain meadows. On fertilised or slightly fertilised soil. Almost everywhere in Europe.*

> *flower heads nod before flowering*
> *noticeable due to pro-found, deep red colour*
> *needs sufficient moisture*

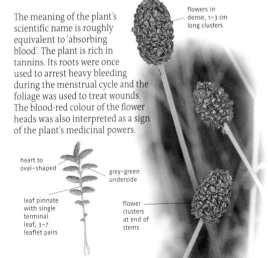

heart to oval-shaped

grey-green underside

leaf pinnate with single terminal leaf, 3–7 leaflet pairs

flower clusters at end of stems

4 dark, brownish-red triangular sepals

Heather

Calluna vulgaris (heather family)

H 30–100 cm   Aug–Oct   perennial shrub

Habitat *Heaths, rough grassland, open pine forests, moors, cliffs. In light places, on low-nutrient, acidic soil. All over Europe.*

> **also known as 'besom or broom Heather'**
> **can transform entire swathes of countryside into a pink sea of flowers**
> **a key component of heaths and moorland**

In areas where Heather is growing, trees can only establish sparse or late growth, unlike on other open ground. Heather roots release substances into the soil, which suppress the growth of various fungi. But this also restricts the growth of trees dependent on co-habitation with the fungi. Bees collect nectar for their 'Heather honey'. Brooms or besoms were once made out of Heather twigs.

petals half as long as sepal

4 mm long, red-violet sepal

22

flowers mostly towards one side

cluster with multiple flowers

leaves overlap in a roof tile pattern

heavily branched

evergreen leaves 2–4 mm long

Did you know?

'Heather' is derived from the Germanic 'haithio' and means 'wild, untilled country'. This is similar to the early name for non-Christians, who were either never reached by the missionaries or else were reached last of all, since as 'heathens' they lived so far out in the countryside.

Alpine Heather

Erica carnea (heather family)
H 15–30 cm   Jan–April   perennial shrub

flowers mostly grow towards one side

Alpine Heather is a popular garden plant and many varieties are cultivated as a winter flowering, low evergreen shrub. Varieties range from yellowish foliage and flowers to white or dark violet blooms. The corollas only fall away long after the flowers have been pollinated. This creates the impression of a long-lasting, flowering plant.

Habitat Frequent garden plant. Grows wild in sunny pine forests in the mountain regions of central and south Europe. Mostly on chalky soil.

> belongs to the **Erica** genus
> flowers already in bud in early autumn
> attracts bees, butterflies and other insects

nodding flowers, in thick clusters

leaves needle-shaped, 6–10 mm long

leaves in whorls of 3–4

sepal shorter than flower corolla

cylindrical to cup-shaped corolla, 5–7 mm long

protruding stamens

23

Fairy Garland Flower

Daphne striata (mezereon family)
H 10–35 cm   May–July   perennial shrub

The low-spreading Fairy Garland Flower is similar to the Alpenrose (p. 41), also known as the 'Alpine Rose' or 'Mountain Rose'. The name of the plant's family derives from Greek mythology: Apollo is said to have transformed the nymph, Daphne, into a bay laurel. And another name for the related species, Mezereon (p. 24), is also 'February Daphne'.

flowers 1–1.5 cm across

leaves up to 2.5 cm long

forming a tuft at the ends of branches

leathery, shiny leaves

Habitat Mountain heathland with low shrubbery, mountain grassland. Altitudes of 1,500 to 2,800 m on chalky soils in the Alps.

> low-spreading plant form
> evergreen foliage
> flowers fragrant like Lilac

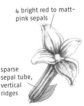

4 bright red to matt-pink sepals

sparse sepal tube, vertical ridges

Mezereon

Daphne mezereum (mezereon family)

H 40–120 cm   March–April   perennial shrub

Habitat Forests with a rich variety of herbaceous plants, shrub above the tree line, rocky wasteland. Nearly all over Europe, up to altitudes of 2,000 m.

> deadly poisonous
> flowers appearing before foliage, heavily scented
> broken-off twigs with unpleasant odour

An alternative name for Mezereon also alludes to its irritable effect and is simply 'Tormented Throat'. The name alludes to the toxins, which are highly potent and contained in the bark and seeds. They can cause an acute strangling sensation in the throat and produce severe inflammation. Even a few berries can cause a fatal shock or breakdown of the circulatory system. Skin contact with the juice can lead to rashes and blisters.

Did you know?

Wagtails and thrushes eat the red fruits, spitting out the kernels again. Evidently, the toxins do not seem to harm these birds.

foliage only on the tips of branches

4 dark pink, occasionally white sepal tips

silky hairs on exterior of sepal tube

24

leaf lanceolate

smooth margin

short leaf stalk

flowers up to 1 cm across, attached directly to branches

bright red fruit, juicy, 0.5–1 cm in size

Great Willowherb

Epilobium hirsutum (Willowherb family)
H 80–150 cm   June–Sept   perennial shrub

Great Willowherb seeds can float undamaged for several weeks on the water's surface. In the 18th century, the hairy down of the seeds of this plant and of the Rosebay Willowherb (p. 26) were used as lining material in eiderdowns and bed covers and for making candle wicks or small ropes. However, the seeds had little value as a source of fabric material, since the fibrous matter could not be spun.

many flowers in the axils of upper leaves

Habitat By streams, edges of ditches, springs. On wet, nutrient-rich and mostly chalky soils. Almost everywhere in Europe.

> plant with ragged hairs
> also tolerates dirty water
> attractive in wild flower gardens

4 slightly notched petals

flower 1–2 cm across, deep pink to purple-red

ovary appears like a thick stalk

elongated fruit, with soft hairs

leaf margin with forward-sloping teeth

leaves resting

Marsh Willowherb

Epilobium palustre (willowherb family)
H 10–50 cm   July–Sept   perennial

When not in flower, the Marsh Willowherb is slightly reminiscent of a Willow branch – just like the other willowherbs. In many localities, people once gathered the flowering stems to arrange in herb bundles, which were consecrated on Ascension Day. These were meant to protect the home from lightning strikes in the event of a thunderstorm.

Habitat Disturbed fens, edges of ditches, wetlands. Mostly on soil with low lime content. Almost all over Europe.

> seeds with hair tufts, resembling nearly all willowherbs
> prefers cool places
> mostly grows in isolation or small groups

leaves only 2–7 mm across

flowers in axils of upper leaves

slightly branched stems

4 petals, 4–7 mm long, deeply notched at the front

ovary appears like a thick stalk

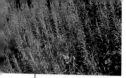

Rosebay Willowherb

Epilobium angustifolium (willowherb family)

H 60–120 cm   July–Aug   perennial

Habitat *Wood clearings, open forest cuttings, storm buffer zones, forest paths, riverbanks. Mostly on soil low in lime. Almost everywhere in Europe.*

> seeds short-lived
> the most conspicuous **Willowherb** variety
> can cover vast areas

According to herbal remedies, tea made from the Rosebay Willowherb is an effective cure for an enlarged prostate. The very young leaves are also suitable as wild vegetables. The flowers are only initially radial and symmetrical. During the flowering season, both the lower petals bend upwards and the lower sepal occupies the vacant space, so the flowers become symmetrical on both sides.

4 petals, up to 1.5 cm long

4 sepals

stigma with 4 star-shaped branchlets

26

fruit inconspicuously 4-sided

lanceolate leaves

upright stem

flowers in terminal clusters

Did you know?

Each plant produces many thousands of tiny seeds, which can fly up to 10 km, thanks to their hairy tufts. This is how the plant quickly colonises new locations in vast quantities.

Water Mint

Mentha aquatica (mint family)

H 20–80 cm   July–Oct   perennial

Water Mint was among the sacred herbs used by the Druids, along with Meadowsweet (p. 116) and Vervain (p. 170). You can also collect the leaves to make herbal tea, although the aroma is not as pleasant as that of Peppermint. Peppermint is not a wild plant, but was first cultivated in England in the 17th century from a cross between Water Mint and Spearmint.

dense flower head, clustered

Habitat *On riverbanks, in ditches, among reeds, on wetlands and moorland meadows. All over Europe.*

> *smells and tastes like Peppermint*
> *resilient to floods*
> *aromatic flowers attract many insects*

hairy plant

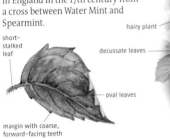

short-stalked leaf

decussate leaves

oval leaves

margin with coarse, forward-facing teeth

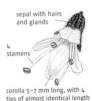

sepal with hairs and glands

4 stamens

corolla 5–7 mm long, with 4 tips of almost identical length

Horse Mint

Mentha longifolia (mint family)

H 50–100 cm   July–Sept   perennial

flower clusters at the top of stems

'Horse' is meant in a derogatory sense, to show the inferiority of this Mint variety in comparison to others. It also refers to the aroma, which is vaguely reminiscent of horse urine. Evidently, this herb was once used to treat horse diseases. It is not suitable as a herbal tea plant. However, the mint is used as a spice in Asian cooking.

Habitat *Riverbanks, wet pastures, ditches, wayside verges. On wet, occasionally flooded ground. Especially in central and south Europe.*

> *downy-white leaf underside*
> *aromatic, similar to Peppermint*
> *attracted to wet locations*

dense, elongated

sharply toothed margin

no leaf stalk

fairly longish leaves, 4–10 cm long

corolla 3–4 mm long, pale lilac to pale red

4 almost identical tips

hairy sepal

Soapwort
Saponaria officinalis (pink family)
H 30–80 cm   June–Sept   perennial   (☻)

Habitat *Weedy patches on riverbanks, country paths, on rocky ground, reservoirs, wasteland. On nutrient-rich soil. Almost all over Europe.*

> **flowers also occasionally white**
> **main root extensive, like root vegetables**
> **aromatic, particularly in the evening and at night**

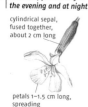

cylindrical sepal, fused together, about 2 cm long

petals 1–1.5 cm long, spreading

28

with three longitudinal veins

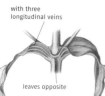

leaves opposite

anther frequently black-violet

If the anthers are a black-violet colour, this is a sign that a parasitic fungus known as 'Smut' has attacked the plants. Instead of containing pollen, the anthers are only filled with fungus pores that insects now transport to other flowers. The plant's roots have medicinal powers, which help prevent catarrh, by liquefying the viscous mucus in the nasal passages. However, in large quantities, the roots are poisonous and can cause nausea and irritate the mucous membranes.

Did you know?
The roots contain substances that form a foamy lather when mixed with water and therefore are ideal as a washing agent. Sections of the roots were once used as soap, especially to wash wool. The plant was cultivated for this purpose in the early 20th century.

flowers in upper leaf axils and at end of stems

erect or upright stem

Rock Soapwort
Saponaria ocymoides (pink family)
H 10–30 cm   April–Oct   perennial (☙)

The Rock Soapwort can develop a mass of flowers, so it is not surprising that it is also popular as an ornamental plant in rockeries. A beneficial characteristic that also helps the plant to colonise rocky areas is its firm underground root system. The stems spread only loosely above the ground.

Habitat Dry slopes, rocky debris, verges, roadside embankments, open forests. Altitudes of up to 2,200 m. Central and south Europe.

> attracts butterflies
> can form extensive dense patches
> flower colours light red to deep purplish-red

leaves up to 3 cm long

flowers in loose clusters

leaves opposite

prostrate stems

petals about 1 cm across

front edge of petals not at all or slightly notched

Alpine Gypsophila
Gypsophila repens (pink family)
H 8–25 cm   May–Aug   perennial

The plant covers rocky scrub like a carpet and helps to stabilise the rubble. Mostly with numerous flowers, the plant attracts flies, bumblebees and butterflies. Although Alpine Gypsophila is native to the high mountain plains, it is also relatively intolerant of cold. The plant overwinters, without any damage, under a protective snow covering, but without snow, the plant will die.

Habitat Chalky rubble up to 2,800 m, stony Alpine riverbanks. In mountains of central and southern Europe.

> delicate appearance
> pink or white flowers
> stems and foliage survive the winter

branched flower clusters overtopping stems

narrow linear, bluish tinge

many upwards climbing, flowering stems

leaves opposite

plant loose and cushion-like

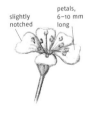

slightly notched

petals, 6–10 mm long

Carthusian Pink

Dianthus carthusianorum (pink family)
H 15–50 cm   June–Sept   perennial

Habitat *Rough grassland, sunny slopes, copses, forest edges. Mostly on chalky soil.*

> aromatic, like cloves, though not related
> requires plenty of heat
> can also grow in cliff crevices

The pink family may have been named not for their colour but after the shape of the flowers which resemble pinking shears. However, 'Carthusian Pink' presumably first referred to the Sweet William, which used to grow frequently in monastery or convent gardens.

up to a total of 30 flowers, not opening simultaneously

dark purple petals, toothed at front edge

flowers 2–2.5 cm across

sepal tube, up to 2 cm long, brownish-red

leaves very slender

leaves opposite, fused together at base

brown-skinned leaves surrounding flower cluster

erect stem

Maiden Pink

Dianthus deltoides (pink family)
H 15–40 cm   June–Sept   perennial

Habitat *Rough grassland and pastures on silicate rock, copses, sandy grassland. On dry soil. Central and north Europe.*

> flowers closed at night
> heat-loving plant
> plant with flowering and non-flowering stems

The Maiden Pink can form dense areas of foliage in suitable places. As with other carnation or pink varieties, this plant is not only endangered because the flowers entice people to pick them, but also because of the fertilising effect of air pollutants. Carnations are also found in white, pink-coloured, red and dense garden varieties. Their fragrant flowers attract butterflies.

solitary flowers, occasionally double at the end of stems

front edge toothed

petals with darker cross-line and white dots

tubular-shaped sepal

flowers 1.2–1.5 cm across

very slender

erect, slender plant

leaves opposite, fused together at base

Corncockle

Agrostemma githago (pink family)
H 40–100 cm   June–July   annual

The Corncockle was once feared because it poisoned flour. It was harvested in among the cereal crops and threshing made the seeds fall out of their fruit capsules, then mixing in with the corn. As the seeds could hardly be distinguished in size from the corn, they were difficult to extract and infiltrated the mill. Alternatively, they reappeared in the fields during the next sowing season. The toxins can cause dizziness, cramps and prove fatal.

Habitat Arable fields, especially for winter cereal, sandy grassland. On humus-rich, sandy or loamy soils. Almost everywhere in Europe.

> flowers attract butterflies
> previously caused mass cases of poisoning
> seeds rarely fall unaided from fruits

narrow, lanceolate to linear

flat silky hairs

leaves opposite

dry sepals preserved

fruit opens atop

seeds black, warty

petals red with 3–4 darker lines

lighter centre

sepal tip longer than corolla

31

petals 3–5 cm across, single flower at the end of twigs

fork-like stems, branching

Did you know?

The Corncockle is now rarely found out in the open fields because of modern techniques of cleaning cereal crops and also due to weed killers. Occasionally, the Corncockle is included in wild flower mixtures.

Ragged Robin

Lychnis flos-cuculi (pink family)
H 30–80 cm   May–July   perennial   (❀)

Habitat Meadows, marshy fields and moorland pastures. On wet or damp nutrient-rich soil. From plains to mountains throughout Europe.

> attracted to damp soil
> petals appear tousled
> attractive in wild flower gardens

The plant's 'ragged' petals make it easy to identify. The spittle of the Cuckoo-spit Insect, commonly called the Meadow Spittlebug, also frequently covers the plant. This explains why the German equivalent for the plant's name also literally means 'Cuckoo Light Pink', as people used to believe that the first cuckoo in spring had spat all over the plants.

flower heads with up to 30 flowers, 3–4 cm across

pink petals, deeply set and in 4 parts

narrow, lanceolate

leaves opposite

narrow tip

Moss Campion

Silene acaulis (pink family)
H 1–5 cm   June–Sept   perennial   (❀)

Habitat Stony grassland, cliff crevices, rocky and chalky slopes. North Europe, the mountains in central and south Europe. In the Alps from approximately 1,500 to 3,000 m.

> forms characteristic cushions with taproot
> also called 'Cushion Pink'
> aromatic flowers

Moss Campion is well adapted to survive in exposed locations, beaten by the wind and snow. Humus is enriched deep within the plant's interior and supplies nutrients as well as storing moisture. In the sunshine, the plant's cushions heat to about 15 °C above the surrounding air temperature. This probably promotes the flowers' development and helps ripen the fruit. The flowers only open during the daytime.

very dense, flat cushions

solitary flowers at the end of stem

leaves slender, 0.5–1.2 cm long

opposite

5 petals, 0.6–1.4 cm long

notched at the front

Red Campion

Silene dioica (pink family)
H 30–90 cm   April–Sept   perennial   (☻)

The male and female flowers grow on separate plants. They especially attract butterflies and bee-flies as pollinators. In May, in the right locations, meadows are often tinged with a red-violet hue and a lavish display of flowers. Only the odd late-flowering bloom appears afterwards.

Habitat Damp meadows and open forests. Almost all over Europe.

> **attracted to nutrient-rich soil**
> **flowers without fragrance**
> **the similar White Campion has white flowers**

leaves opposite, oval

several 1.5–2.5 cm wide flowers in a branching cluster overtopping stems

stems with protruding hairs, up to and over 2 mm long

female flower with globular to oval sepal

petals split

male flower with cylindrical sepal

33

Thrift

Armeria maritima (thrift family)
H 5–50 cm   May–Nov   perennial

Thrift is not only tolerant of salt, but some varieties even colonise soils polluted by toxic heavy metal. The plant then stores the absorbed metals within the basal leaves. The dried flower heads of Thrift also keep their colour and shape in dried flower bouquets. However, as they are a protected species, picking the flowers from plants growing in the wild is strictly prohibited.

Habitat Beach and salt meadows along sea coasts, dry grassland. On sandy or stony, salt-rich soil. North, central and west Europe.

> **grass-like leaves**
> **forms a long taproot**
> **adapted to salt-rich locations**

flowers form a terminal cluster

fairly thick, up to 3 mm across

leaves all basal

dry-skinned leaves beneath flower head

corolla about 5 mm across

funnel-shaped sepal

Common Knotgrass
Polygonum aviculare (knotweed family)
H 5–50 cm   May–Nov   annual

Habitat Paths, verges, cracks in asphalt, cobblestone squares, weedy patches. All over Europe.

> grows flat or upright
> very springy, resistant to footsteps
> attracted to nitrogen-rich soil

Birds like to eat the seeds of the Knotgrass, you will often see sparrows pecking at these plants. People have encountered the manifold forms of the Common Knotgrass since the time of the early Stone Age. Nowadays, the plant occurs around the world in more moderate climates. Seeds easily cling to the soles of shoes, which is how they are transported along country paths.

pink or greenish petals, 2–3 mm long

ridged stems

flowers inconspicuous, nestling at leaf-corners

sheath with translucent, split membrane

leaves 0.5–4 cm long

stems low or climbing upwards

Amphibious Bistort
Persicaria amphibia (knotweed family)
H 30–300 cm   June–Sept   perennial

Habitat Ponds in among other plants, on riverbanks, in marshy pastures, on wet arable land and rocky ground. Throughout Europe.

> very variable in form and location
> flowers pleasantly fragrant
> only forms seeds in damp locations

Amphibious Bistort either grows as a water plant with floating leaves or as a terrestrial plant with erect stems. Either way, it is so flexible that it can adapt from one form to the other. If the rivers run dry, it simply continues growing in its terrestrial form. It is also better than many other water plants at tolerating heavy fluctuations in water levels.

3–5 cm long, about 1 cm thick, cylindrical flower clusters

leaves up to more than 20 cm long, slender-lanceolate

sheath membrane around the stem

short stalk

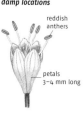

reddish anthers

petals 3–4 mm long

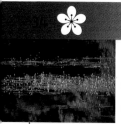

Common Bistort
Bistorta officinalis (knotweed family)
H 30–100 cm   May–July   perennial

The plant is not only attractive to look at, but also useful. The flowers produce a rich source of nectar for insects. Cattle like to feed on the young stems and leaves – incidentally, they also make tasty wild vegetables. In Siberia and Iceland, people used to eat the roasted roots that were rich in starch. The roots were also ground as straightening in flour. In herbal remedies, Common Bistort was used against diarrhoea and throat inflammations.

Habitat *Marshy pastures, riverside forests, riverbanks. From plains to high mountains. Central Europe.*

> *can often cover large areas*
> *attracted to wet soil*
> *also suited for edges of garden ponds*

dense flower clusters at the end of stems

flower cluster 3–6 cm long, 1–2 cm thick

longer protruding stamens

petals 4–5 mm long

🌼 **35**

wavy edge of leaf stems

stem surrounded by a sheath

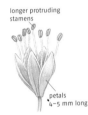

s-shaped rhizome or twisting in serpentine fashion

Did you know?
Years ago, people saw the winding rhizome as a sign of the plant's healing power. Herbal books in the 16th century therefore stated that distilled water made from the plant was effective against poisonous snakebites.

Common Mallow

Malva sylvestris (mallow family)

H 30–100 cm   June–Oct   perennial

Habitat Sunny weedy patches on paths, rocky waste ground, wasteland. Preferably in warm, dry locations. Almost all over Europe.

> flowering over a long period
> petals violet-pink or dark purple
> also called 'Cheese Cakes'

The cake-shaped, flatly squeezed fruits look similar to cheeses. Children especially used to like collecting them while they were still unripe and eat them raw. They taste fairly similar to cabbage. In the 16th century, the Common Mallow was still regarded as a medicinal plant for all types of ailments. Today, the foliage and petals are only used for dry, tickly coughs and to prevent laryngitis. The dark petals are also suitable for colouring foodstuffs.

notched front edge

noticeably darker veins on petals

petals 2–2.5 cm long

36

upper leaves divided to about mid-way, with 3–7 leaflets

haired

can also flower dark purple

2–6 flowers each in leaf axils

Did you know?

Rust-coloured blisters often cover the Mallow's foliage. These are left by a rust fungus. Plants infested with this fungus will not die, but no longer look very attractive.

Hoary Rock-rose

Cistus incanus (rock-rose family)
H 30–100 cm   April–June   perennial

The leaves and branches of a subspecies are used to make 'Rock-rose tea', which should prevent heart and circulation ailments and generally improve the immunity system. Extracts also help prevent sore throats. At least, this has proved to be the case in laboratory testing, where the plant was shown to prevent flu viruses from multiplying – a property that might enhance its importance in future.

Habitat Sparse forests and shrub around the Mediterranean, except in France and Spain.

> suited to dry conditions
> reminiscent of a rose from a distance
> only flowers from morning to early afternoon

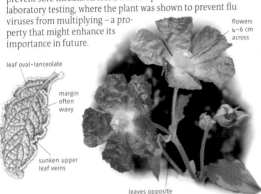

flowers 4–6 cm across

leaf oval-lanceolate

margin often wavy

sunken upper leaf veins

leaves opposite

5 crumpled petals

numerous stamens

🌸 37

Scarlet Pimpernel

Anagallis arvensis (primrose family)
H 5–30 cm   June–Oct   annual

The Scarlet Pimpernel was once thought to be an effective medicinal plant for treating mental afflictions. The flowers open about 9 am in the morning and close again in the afternoon by 3 pm at the latest. Since the petals also close again when the sky is overcast and when rain is on the way, the plant was also commonly regarded as a weatherglass.

Habitat Weedy patches in arable fields, gardens, roadside verges, on rocky ground. On nutrient-rich soil. All over Europe.

> often spreading along roadside verges
> fruits deflexed towards ground
> needs plenty of light

solitary flowers on long stalks in leaf axils

a rare variant with blue petals

haired filaments

oval to lanceolate

leaves opposite

divided almost to the base in up to 6 mm long tips

wheel-shaped corolla

Purple Cyclamen
Cyclamen purpurascens (primrose family)

H 5–15 cm   June–Sept   perennial

Habitat Broad-leaved forests on limestone. In mountains of central and southern Europe.

> leaves evergreen
> tuberous root mostly protruding from soil
> a protected plant everywhere, should not be uprooted!

In antiquity, the plant was among the ingredients used in aphrodisiacs and, in fact, this was fairly dangerous. The Greeks and Romans also cultivated these herbaceous plants near their villas, in the belief that this protected them against the fatal effect of their poisonous potions. Yet the plant's poisonous effect can itself cause suffocation.

upper surface with dark green mottled pattern

roundish tuberous bulb

petal tips up to 2.5 cm long, curving backwards

toothed margin

38

leaves kidney to heart-shaped

solitary flowers, nodding

Did you know?
The Silver or Pewter-leaved Cyclamen that grows wild in Bulgaria and on the Crimea flowers in March. Nearer to home, this plant is popular in gardens as an ornamental attraction.

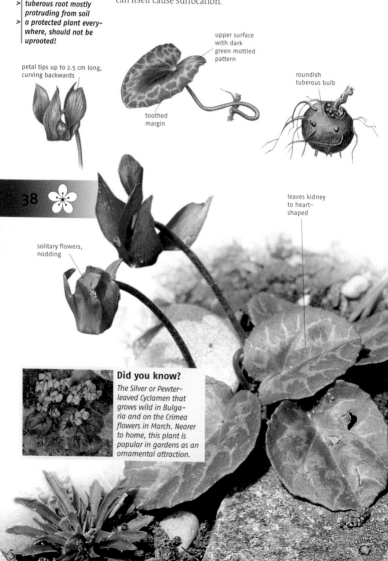

Sea Milkwort
Glaux maritima (primrose family)
H 3–20 cm   May–Aug   perennial

The Sea Milkwort is well adapted to salty locations. The leaves have special glands, which simply eject the poisonous salt it absorbed underground. Glaux was already the English name of a plant in antiquity that was meant to increase the milk yield of cattle.

Habitat *Salty grassland with damp, sandy soil along coastlines all around Europe.*

> *flowering pink, red or white*
> *appears grey-green from a distance*
> *tolerates soil with high salt content*

fairly dense foliage

solitary flowers, slightly concealed in leaf axils

slightly leathery

leaves longish-oval, up to 1.5 cm long

sepal takes over display feature of missing petals

flower up to 5 mm long

filaments mostly red

39

Bird's-eye Primrose
Primula farinosa (primrose family)
H 10–30 cm   May–July   perennial

The Bird's-eye Primrose can only thrive in exposed locations. If planting is too dense, it disappears, since then rosettes that grow close to the ground cannot find enough light. The yellow ring at the apex of the flower tube signals to insects, especially butterflies, the route to the flower's nectar.

Habitat *Marshy moorlands, moorland pastures, stony grassland. Alpine foothills, Alps, north Europe, Pyrenees.*

> *only faintly aromatic*
> *recognisable by the white powder on leaf undersides*
> *requires lots of moisture*

3–15 flowers forming an umbel

dense white dusting underneath

all leaves in one rosette

leafless stem

corolla wheel-shaped, up to 1.5 cm in size

yellow ring

deeply notched tips

Alpine Rock Jasmine
Androsace alpina (primrose family)
H 1–5 cm   June–Aug   perennial

Habitat *Rocky cliffs and crevices as well as glacial moraines above the tree line. In the Alps on silicate-rich rock.*

> tolerant of wind and cold
> occasionally also white flowers
> mainly visited by flies

The Alpine Rock Jasmine is one of the flowering plants that grow the highest in the Alps, growing at altitudes of up to approximately 4,200 m. In locations that are partially exposed to the wind, the plant's form is highly beneficial: in the interior, the flat cushions, which grow up to 30 cm, can retain valuable humus stores that also absorb water after rain.

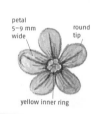

leaf oval to lanceolate

flat cushions out of small rosettes

petal 5–9 mm wide

round tip

yellow inner ring

leaves 3–10 mm long

40

Orpine
Sedum telephium (stonecrop family)
H 30–80 cm   July–Sept   perennial

Habitat *Edges of copses, stony waste ground, spinneys, country paths, arable fields, cliffs. Mostly on stony soil nearly every-where in Europe.*

> heat-loving, requires sunshine
> attractive ornamental plant for gardens
> tubers and young leaves edible

The leaves and roots can store water, so the plant is very hardy and resilient throughout sustained dry periods. Years ago, Orpine had to live up to numerous prophesies: if the plant was hung up to dry and continued growing, this was seen as a sign of hope for a long life ahead or of a sick patient's recovery. This was also a good omen for a fairytale happy ending.

abundant flowers, less than 1 cm in size

petals pink, dark violet or yellowish-green

fleshy leaves, 2–10 cm long

thick, root vegetable and swollen storage roots

thick, umbel-like flower head

ovaries consisting of 5 parts

sparse plant

Alpenrose
Rhododendron ferrugineum (heather family)
H 70–150 cm   June–Aug   perennial shrub   ☠

In some parts of the Alps, the shrubs are known as 'Mountain Pasture Rush'. 'Rush' in this case is a general term for low scrub and probably does not refer to an audible rushing sound in the wind or an intoxicating effect. Tea made from the leaves leads to nausea, cramps and can even be heart-stopping. The flowers of many rhododendron varieties are also poisonous. If bees collect nectar from them, the toxins even permeate their honey.

Habitat Among trees at the forest limits, heathland with dwarf shrubs on acidic soil above the tree line. Mountains in central and southern Europe.

> leaves evergreen, underside with rust-brown scales
> can form giant groups
> requires snow covering in winter

Did you know?
The Hairy Rhododendron looks alike and grows on chalky soil in similar places. Both sides of the Hairy Rhododendron's leaves are green and hairy at the margin. Each of these varieties suffers without snowfall in winter, since the protective snow cover is missing.

bell-shaped corolla, with 5 blunt tips

with brightly spotted glands

41

flowers about 1.5 cm long overtopping branches

upper side of leaves shines dark green

Purple Saxifrage
Saxifraga oppositifolia (saxifrage family)
H 1–5 cm   April–July   perennial

Habitat Stony scrub, rubble, stony mountain grassland. Preferably on damp soil. From the tree line up to over 3,500 m. North Europe, mountains in central and southern Europe.

> most conspicuous saxifrage
> forms bright and vibrant cushions
> one of the more common flowering plants in the extreme north

Since the flowers are already established the previous year, this variety quickly flowers after the snow has melted. Often, the flowers appear so early that no insects are active. In this case, the flowers are self-pollinating. Opened blooms tolerate temperatures of −15 °C. In contrast, the young leaves are more sensitive and only come into bud later. Once they are fully opened, the leaves tolerate temperatures of up to −40 °C.

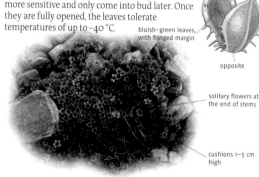

bluish-green leaves, with fringed margin

opposite

solitary flowers at the end of stems

cushions 1–5 cm high

flower up to 2 cm in size

oval petals

Marsh Cinquefoil
Potentilla palustris (rose family)
H 30–100 cm   June–July   perennial

Habitat Marshes, moors, ditches. On wet, often flooded and fairly acidic soil. From the plains to mountainous regions. Central and north Europe.

> requires a cool climate
> also reproduces when stems are snapped off
> often grows directly at the water's edge

Marsh Cinquefoil fruits slightly resemble strawberries. In many regions, children actually once collected them to eat. Animals also feed on them while grazing, excreting any of the undigested kernels and so making sure of the plant's dispersal. Additionally, the released seed kernels may also float away on water currents.

a few flowers on upright stem, up to 2.5 cm in size

sepal encasing fruit

many styles

dark purple sepal and flower corolla

underside of leaves bluish-green

abundant stamens

5–7 pinnate leaflets

Water Avens

Geum rivale (rose family)
H 30–70 cm   April–July   perennial

The styles are still attached to the fruits, which are elongated and form hooks that cling like burrs to animals and so are dispersed. Herbal remedies once used the roots of the Water Avens against diarrhoea and inflammations of the mouth and throat.

Habitat *Wetland pastures, ditches, streams, riverside woodlands, moorland pastures. On wet soil. Throughout Europe, mountainous regions in the south.*

> **attracted to nutrient-rich areas**
> **requires cool, damp climate**
> **forms dense clusters**

large, mostly three-part terminal leaflet

erect stem, densely haired

lower leaves occasionally pinnate

fruitlets resembling a wig

bell-shaped flower

purple-brown sepal

petals pink to yellowish

43

Sweet Briar

Rosa rubiginosa (rose family)
H 100–300 cm   June–July   shrub

When its leaves are rubbed, the Sweet Briar produces the unmistakeable aroma of fresh apples, a fragrance that is released of its own accord in early summer. The poetic saying 'a rose between two thorns', is perhaps more aptly rendered as – 'a rose between two spines'. Unlike thorns, these defensive features are not created out of transformed leaves or twigs, but only out of a skin-like membrane and can be broken off, without damaging the branch.

Habitat *Copses on rough meadows, field hedgerows, woodland edges, embankments, rocky slopes. On moderately dry, mostly chalky soil. Throughout Europe.*

> **easily recognisable by the fragrant apple aroma**
> **prefers warm locations**
> **fruits suitable for tea**

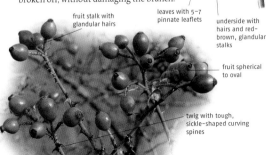

fruit stalk with glandular hairs

leaves with 5–7 pinnate leaflets

underside with hairs and red-brown, glandular stalks

fruit spherical to oval

twig with tough, sickle-shaped curving spines

flower 2.5–4 cm in size

sepals longer than petals

Dog Rose
Rosa canina (rose family)
H 100–300 cm   June   shrub

slender oval fruit, sparse

Habitat Hedges, woodland edges, verges, copses in open pastures, trees in open fields, wasteland. Throughout Europe.

> also planted on slopes
> fragrant flowers
> spines assist the plant to climb

The fruits or rosehips produce aromatic, pleasantly acidic tea and a purée that is rich in Vitamin C. In Germany, the old German name for the flower hips was 'butt', which used to be the word for 'barrel' and denotes a short, squat shape. The Germanic peoples dedicated the Dog Rose to Freya or Frigg, the love goddess, who was also a symbol of the soul's life after death.

leaf with 5–7 pinnate leaflets

sparse, often bluish-green

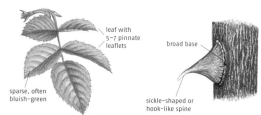

broad base

sickle-shaped or hook-like spine

abundant stamens

petals light-pink, slightly heart-shaped

44

petals 4–5 cm across, light pink or also white

leaf upper-side, dark green

Did you know?
Unusual reddish growths are often seen on the Dog Rose. People used to call these features 'Rose apples' or even 'Robin's pin cushions'. Actually, they are galls, where the larvae of the gall-forming wasp eat and later pupate.

Common Stork's-bill

Erodium cicutarium (crane's-bill family)
H 10–60 cm   April–Oct   annual or biennial

flower head on long, hairy stalk

The fruitlets can be used as moisture gauges: when rolled up, the 'bill' indicates 'dry'; and when opened out, it signals 'wet'. The movement that occurs as the flower absorbs moisture is also visible to the naked eye. If this occurs in a fruit lying on the ground, the seed anchors itself in the soil – the plant's way of ensuring an ideal spot is found for germination.

pinnate leaf, with indented leaflet

fruitlets with a 3–4 cm long 'bill'

Habitat Sparse weedy patches on sandy areas, arable fields, wasteland, in vineyards, on pathways. All over Europe.

> attracted to sandy soil
> pioneer plant in exposed areas
> requires heat in summer

pink petals less than 1 cm long

hairy sepals

veins usually darker

45

Bloody Crane's-bill

Geranium sanguineum (crane's-bill family)
H 15–50 cm   June–Aug   perennial

fruit 3–4 cm long

The plant's name may have various origins: flower colour, autumnal colour or the blood-red colour of the sliced rootstock. The roots contain large quantities of tannins. These were once used to arrest blood flow. More recent investigations show that extracts of the roots prevent the spread of flu viruses.

leaves palmately divided

sections divided into 2–3 points

protruding above the next leaf

single flowers

Habitat Margins of dry copses and forests, cliffs, rough grassland, slopes. Especially in central and southern Europe.

> heat-loving
> attracts bees as pollinators
> also a lusciously flowering ornamental garden plant

petals up to 20 mm long, vibrant and deep crimson red

mostly with shallow notches at the front

Herb Robert
Geranium robertianum (crane's-bill family)
H 20–40 cm   May–Oct   annual

Habitat *Woods, ravines, floodplains, walls, cliffs, hedges, stony places, station precincts, wasteland. Nearly all over Europe.*

> **often also grows in towns**
> **whole plant often red in sunny locations**
> **very strong and characteristic fragrance to the touch**

Due to a special centrifugal mechanism, the seeds can fly for distances of over 3 m and almost up to 2 m high. Therefore the plant occasionally also grows on mossy trees or in the forks of branches. The plant's aroma is unpleasant to most living creatures and was commonly used to ward off moths.

flowers mostly double on shared stalk

very restricted roots, offers little support

leaf stalks do not die off and support the plant

petals about 1 cm long, usually with 3 long stripes

leaves palmately divided, almost to the base with 5–7 leaflets

Common Centaury
Centaurium erythraea (gentian family)
H 10–50 cm   July–Sept   annual

Habitat *Sunny wood clearings, semi-dry grassland, dry copses. Especially in central and southern Europe.*

> **requires a lot of sunshine**
> **bitter taste**
> **especially attracts butterflies**

The names 'Centaury' and *centaurium* express the almost priceless value that was ascribed to this medicinal plant in days gone by; 'cent-' is a Latin prefix that refers to 100 – in this case 100 gold pieces. Of the many ailments that the herbaceous plant was reputed to treat, nowadays only the digestive cure has proved effective.

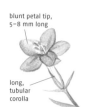

blunt petal tip, 5–8 mm long

long, tubular corolla

many flowers on a spreading flower head or raceme

leaves opposite, slightly fleshy

no leaf stalk

Chiltern Gentian

Gentianella germanica (gentian family)

H 5–40 cm   June–Oct   biennial

Although the Chiltern Gentian and the Autumn Gentian belong to the same species, they could easily be mistaken for two entirely different ones. The Chiltern Gentian flowers in spring and summer; it is a slightly branching plant, with longer sections of stems dividing the foliage. This is the county flower of Buckinghamshire, although now officially classed as an endangered species. The equally rare Autumn Gentian is heavily branched, compressed and with up to 50 flowers on clusters. In spite of the short time until winter, the autumn-flowering Autumn Gentian still produces ripe seeds.

Habitat Rough grass-lands and pastures on chalky soil, especially in low mountain ranges. In sunny locations in Britain and Europe.

> occasionally also with white flowers
> tastes very bitter
> very diverse forms

upwards-facing, abundant flowers

trumpet-shaped flower, corolla tube about 3 cm long

long fringes at entry

47

leaves opposite, oval, pointed

slightly branching stems

Did you know?

The Field Gentian is similar to the Chiltern Gentian, but its flowers have four pointed petal tips. It grows in the low mountain ranges of Europe and up to altitudes of 2,800 m.

Oleander
Nerium oleander (periwinkle family)
H 100–400 cm   July–Sept   shrub

Habitat Around the Mediterranean growing wild on river- and streambanks, occasionally on dried-up stream beds, often planted along motorway verges.

> upright form, often spreading
> very resilient to exhaust fumes
> grown as pot plants in central Europe

Without flowers, the shrub is vaguely reminiscent of a willow tree. The flowers, which can also be white, pink and double in the cultivated varieties, are especially fragrant in the evenings. They also attract moths such as the Oleander Hawk-moth, whose caterpillars survive on the leaves of this shrub. Evidently, these creatures are unaffected by the strong toxins that are detrimental to the heart – indeed, for humans, the plants can prove fatal.

fruit up to 10 cm long, elongated, pod-like

leaves leathery, up to 15 cm long

conspicuous main vein

lighter underside

petals with fringes

flowers about 5 cm across

several flowers in umbel-like flower heads

Purple Lettuce
Prenanthes purpurea (daisy family)
H 50–150 cm   July–Aug   perennial

Habitat Forests, woodland clearings, woodland paths. More usual in shady locations. Central and southern Europe.

> plant has grey-green appearance
> contains milky juice
> requires fairly high humidity

This species can easily prove deceptive, leading to confusion especially because of the sparse petals on the flower head, which can be mistaken for a solitary flower with only a few petals. This lettuce variety only grows in the wild, in contrast to other lettuces, which are cultivated for green salads.

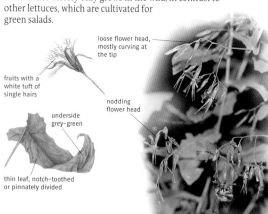

loose flower head, mostly curving at the tip

nodding flower head

composite flower heads with 2–5 ray florets

fruits with a white tuft of single hairs

underside grey-green

thin leaf, notch-toothed or pinnately divided

Common Comfrey
Symphytum officinale (borage family)
H 30–100 cm   May–July   perennial   🐝

In antiquity, Common Comfrey was already used to heal wounds. From the Middle Ages, it was also considered useful for healing broken bones and broken legs. Nowadays, it is proven that the plant helps soothe all kinds of injuries from minor bruises and pulled muscles to crushing wounds or sprains. It also helps broken bones to mend more quickly. However, as the plant also contains substances in varying quantities that may cause damage to the liver and cancer, only officially tested and approved medicines should be used.

Habitat *Riverbanks, verges, wetlands, ditches, riverside woodlands. On damp to wet soil, especially on low-lying sites. Almost all over Europe.*

> **flowers yellowish white, purple or red-violet**
> **entire plant densely covered in rough, spiny hairs**
> **also known as 'Bone-set'**

sepal with long, pointed tips

corolla 1–2 cm long, cylindrical

49

flower heads inrolled before flowering

upright stem

roughly haired

leaf broad-lanceolate

Did you know?
Only bee-flies can reach the nectar with their long proboscis. Bumblebees, which have short proboscises, must bite or pierce the corolla's tube sideways. From here, they commit 'daylight robbery' of the flowers' nectar, as they fail to pollinate them.

Summer Pheasant's-eye

Adonis aestivalis (buttercup family)

H 20–60 cm   May–July   annual

Habitat *Arable fields, wayside banks and verges. On chalky, mostly stony soil. As far as the low mountain ranges in central and south Europe.*

> *flowers open in sunshine*
> *heat-loving*
> *occasionally with yellow flowers*

Greek mythology recounts how the Summer Pheasant's-eye was created from the blood of the handsome youth, Adonis. Aphrodite transformed her lover into this flower after he was killed on the hunt by a wild boar. Since the middle of the Bronze Ages, the plant has been found growing as a weed among cereal crops. Today, it is exceptionally rare.

single flowers, up to 3.5 cm in size

leaves, pinnately divided

usually 6–8 petals

fruit comprised of many nutlets

leaf tip up to 1 mm across

black blotch at base

Garden Anemone

Anemone coronaria (buttercup family)

H 10–45 cm   Feb–April   perennial

Habitat *Rocky areas, scrubland, cultivated land, exposed olive groves, fallow areas. Around the Mediterranean.*

> *the plant's juice also acts as a skin irritant*
> *requires lots of light*
> *without sepals, unlike the similar Persian Buttercup*

The plant forms a tuberous root, so it can last through the dry summers that are common to its native habitat. The Romans already delighted in the sheer beauty of this flower's blooms. Beyond the Mediterranean, the Garden Anemone is popular as an early-flowering garden plant. In late winter, this plant beautifully adorns cut flower arrangements.

solitary flowers, up to 6.5 cm across

flowers also violet, blue or white

5–8 petals

base often lighter

abundant dark stamens

stems with 3 leaves, triple pinnate, deeply lobed

Garden Peony
Paeonia officinalis (peony family)
H 30–60 cm   May   perennial ☠

In Greek mythology Paeon, the healing God, used a peony flower to heal the wounds of Hades, God of the Underworld. For a long time, the roots were also used as a cure for gout. Burrs from the seeds used to be hung around babies' necks when they were teething – a custom that can hardly have had a soothing effect and was even potentially fatal because of the toxins. Each flower produces about 3.6 million grains of pollen – a record in the plant kingdom.

Habitat Dry slopes, dry shrubbery on limy soil up to heights of 1,700 m. Southern Europe, southern Alps.

> flowers around Whitsuntide
> partially naturalised from garden cultivation in Central Europe
> fragrant flowers

Did you know?
Varieties of the Garden Peony, with dense flower heads, are often grown in gardens. These flowers' stamens have been transformed into petals.

5–10 pink to dark red petals

abundant stamens

51

petals up to 12 cm across

smooth leaf margin

tuberous roots

red and black seeds

leaves divided at base

fruit capsule opens in sections

Purple Loosestrife
Lythrum salicaria (purple loosestrife family)
H 50–100 cm   July–Sept   herbaceous perennial

Habitat *Wet pastures, meadow ditches, pond edges. On damp to wet, nutrient-rich soil. Almost everywhere in Europe.*

> *leaves opposite or in whorls of 3*
> *often grows in dense clusters*
> *suitable for a garden pond*

The Purple Loosestrife's style and stamens come in three possible forms. The style may be short with medium-long and long stamens. Alternatively, the style may be medium-long, with short and long stamens. A third variation is a long style, with short and medium-long stamens. Charles Darwin examined this phenomenon, observing that most of the seeds form when pollen from the anthers of one flower comes into contact with another flower with styles of the same length.

6 violet-red petals, over 1 cm in length

style short

style medium-long

style long

dense flower spikes at the end of the stem

lanceolate leaf, similar to the Willow

occasionally with shorter side spikes

upright stem

52

Did you know?

The Purple Loosestrife contains tanning agents, which help prevent diarrhoea and enteritis. Herbalists and healers already knew this at about the time of antiquity. In the 19th century, the roots were used in massive quantities to prevent the spread of cholera epidemics in England.

House-leek

Sempervivum tectorum (stonecrop family)
H 15–50 cm   July–Sept   perennial

Once, people believed that the House-leek acted as a lightning conductor, so they consecrated the plant to the god of thunder, Jupiter, known as Thor in Norse legends. Charlemagne, the Holy Roman Emperor, even issued a decree to cultivate the House-leek by planting on the rooftops of his estates. Scholars from the 16th century onwards liked to mock the plant's magical powers, but the plant still grows on many rooftops today, even if this is only for decorative purposes.

Habitat *Cliff stretches, walls, roofs. In warm, dry, sunny locations up to altitudes of 2,800 m. Central and south Europe.*

> stores water
> the main rosette forms subsidiary rosettes, dying off after the flower
> an ancient plant with magical powers

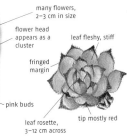

many flowers, 2–3 cm in size

flower head appears as a cluster

leaf fleshy, stiff

fringed margin

12–16 petals

pink buds

leaf rosette, 3–12 cm across

tip mostly red

Cobweb House-leek

Sempervivum arachnoideum (stonecrop family)
H 5–15 cm   June–Sept   perennial

The 'cobwebs' that stretch across the leaf tips are actually spun by the plant itself. Young leaf tips resting close together also stick to each other a little and, when they grow, the sticky parts 'spin threads'. The glistening hairs protect from the sun's rays in dry, sunny locations.

Habitat *Cliff crevices, open, fallow mountain grasslands, cliff heads, tops of walls. Mountains in Central and south Europe up to altitudes of 3,000 m.*

> in sunny locations, plant often tinged red
> separated leaf rosettes put down roots, ensuring reproduction
> tolerates arid conditions

leaf-covered, upright stem with flowers

lanceolate leaves forming dense rosettes

cobweb-like hairs spreading across leaf tips

6–12 crimson-red petals

petal 1–2 cm across

Greater Burdock
Arctium lappa (daisy family)
H 80–150 cm   July–Aug   biennial

Habitat *Weedy patches on scrub, station sidings, country paths, gates, riverbanks, disturbed woodland groves. Central and south Europe, southern Scandinavia.*

> **burr-like fruits often cling to withered plants in winter**
> **leaves up to 50 cm long**
> **similar Woolly Burdock has flower heads dusted with cobweb-like coverings**

purple-red disc flowers

spherical capsule

sepals with hooked tip

54

Burdock fruits cling to animals roaming past or to people's clothing and may be transported over long distances. Without realising, passers-by have probably sown the plant in all sorts of places, plucking the fruits from their clothes and casting them away. Extracts from the roots help prevent skin irritations and dandruff. In Japan, the plant is also cultivated as a vegetable. The fleshy roots can be prepared like Black Salsify.

several composite flowers forming a loose flower head

stalked composite flowers, up to 4.5 cm across

broad, triangular leaves

underside sparse downy grey

thick storage root

Did you know?

The reverse hooks on the burr fruits of the Greater Burdock were the inspiration for Velcro. In 1951, Georges de Mestral, the Swiss inventor, patented this fastener. A French name for the Burdock, dating at least from the 19th century, is 'Bouton de Soldat' (Soldier's Button), which shows that the idea already existed beforehand.

Hemp-agrimony

Eupatorium cannabinum (daisy family)

H 50–150 cm July–Sept perennial

In Germany, the plant was also known as the 'Kunigunde Herb', probably because it was consecrated as a healing plant of Saint Kunigunde, Queen consort to the Holy Roman Emperor, Henry II. (11th century). Herbal remedies once recommended the plant for ailments of the liver and gall bladder and to treat wounds. Today, the plant is only used in homeopathic dilutions, because it causes liver damage and may even cause cancer if used in too large quantities.

Habitat Wood clearings and margins of damp forests, riverbanks, ditches, embankments. On damp soil all over Europe.

> forms large groups
> attracts lots of bees and butterflies
> slightly similar to Wild Marjoram (p. 80)

abundant umbel-like flower heads

toothed margin

styles protruding a long way

small composite flowers, each with 4–6 disc florets

leaves opposite

palmately divided into 3 or 5 leaves

Common Adenostyles

Adenostyles alliariae (daisy family)

H 50–120 cm July–Aug perennial

The Common Adenostyles can grow up to heights of 2 m in nutrient-rich locations. The basal leaves grow to sizes of up to 50 cm. This made them good material to use as toilet paper for anybody outdoors – hill climbers and hikers probably still make use of them today! If the plant is not in flower, it is easy to confuse with the Butterbur (p. 56).

Habitat Mixed forests, perennial areas above the forest line up to about 2,600 m, banks of streams. On wet soil. In the Alps and mountains in central and south Europe.

> leaves grey, downy undersides
> lower leaves reminiscent of the Butterbur (p. 56)
> despite similar appearance, unrelated to Wild Marjoram (p. 80)

protruding styles

pink disc floret, with 4 points

surrounding hairs

flower heads protruding high above the leaves

many small composite flowers, each with 3–6 disc florets

Butterbur
Petasites hybridus (daisy family)
H 15–100 cm   April–May   perennial

Habitat Banks of streams and rivers, wet meadows, floodplains. On good drainage, damp soil, gravel and rubble. Almost everywhere in Europe and in the mountainous regions in the south.

> with giant, umbrella-like leaves
> requires high humidity
> flowering before green foliage emerges

composite flower, up to 1 cm in size

reddish, occasionally white disc florets

In the Middle Ages, people thought that this unpleasant smelling plant could ward off the plague. Healers or medical practitioners therefore dosed patients with the plant in the form of powder or dissolved in wine. The effect was to induce heavy perspiration, which could cause the body to emit toxins. Masks worn in front of the face to protect against the plague often contained coarsely crushed Butterbur. Nowadays, medicines containing Butterbur are used to treat acute pain in the urinary tract or even as a preventative cure against migraine.

rhizomes thickened, tuberous

fruit-bearing cluster up to 1 m in height

fruits with surrounding hairs

full-grown leaves up to 90 cm across

cluster with up to more than 100 composite flowers

stem with scaly leaves, tinged with violet

Did you know?
If you collect Butterbur, make sure that you do not use it in herbal remedies. First, the plant's dangerous toxins must be extracted using a special process.

Musk Thistle

Carduus nutans (daisy family)
H 30–100 cm   July–Sept   biennial

Musk Thistle's flowers have a sweet, slightly musky and aromatic fragrance. They attract insects in droves. The young flower heads used to be eaten like artichokes and were cooked along with the young shoots and leaves.

composite flowers
3–6 cm across,
mostly nodding

leaves with
triangular,
thorny
sections

leaf
margins
running
down the
stem

stem with leaves
almost to the top

Habitat *Weedy patches on paths, quarries, embankments, on rubble sites and heavily grazed, rough pastures. Almost everywhere in Europe.*

> **fruits with single hairs**
> **spiny leaves deter overgrazing**
> **attracted to nitrogen-rich places**

sepal casing with stiff,
backwards-curving thorns

purple disc flowers

57

Woolly Thistle

Cirsium eriophorum (daisy family)
H 80–180 cm   July–Sept   biennial

A leaf rosette is produced in the first year. You can easily recognise the plant by the distinctive appearance of the leaves. The shoots that push through in the second year were once savoured as vegetables, just like the young flower heads, which used to be eaten like artichokes. 'Friar's Crown' is also another popular name for this prickly thistle, as the flower head looks like a monk's head with bald crown.

spherical or oval-shaped
flower cluster

sepals
whitish,
hairy

branching
stems

sturdy thorns

leaf sections alternately facing
tip or base

Habitat *Weedy patches in heavily grazed, rough pastures, verges, edges of copses, spinneys, up to altitudes of over 2,000 m. Central and south Europe.*

> **fruits with long, feathery hairs**
> **needs sufficient heat**
> **ideal for buttonholes or wedding flower arrangements**

purplish to violet-blue
disc florets

thorny
capsule,
with a dense coating of
white, cobweb-like hairs

Creeping Thistle
Cirsium arvense (daisy family)
H 60–120 cm   July–Sept   perennial

Habitat *Weedy areas, arable fields, country paths, scrub, spinneys, wasteland. On nutrient-rich soil. Throughout Europe.*

> *often simultaneously flowers and produces fruits*
> *scattered all over the world due to cereal cultivation*
> *salt tolerant*

The Creeping Thistle is not popular with farmers, as the plant's roots grow up to 3 m underground. Ploughing or tilling the soil only encourages the root sections to spread. For some time, scientists have been searching for a way to combat them, without using weedkillers and organically developing a fungus that only attaches itself onto this plant.

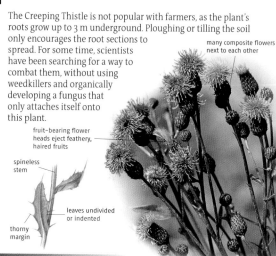

many composite flowers next to each other

fruit-bearing flower heads eject feathery, haired fruits

purple disc flowers

spineless stem

composite flower up to 2 cm long

capsule spherical to oval

leaves undivided or indented

thorny margin

58

Brown Knapweed
Centaurea jacea (daisy family)
H 20–150 cm   June–Nov   perennial

Habitat *Meadows, pastures, rough grassland, wayside embankments. On nutrient-rich soil in light locations. Almost everywhere in Europe.*

> *tough stems*
> *attracts bees and butterflies*
> *the similar Greater Knapweed has pinnately lobed leaves*

Brown Knapweed is not exactly the favourite fodder of grazing cattle due to the high tannin content. That is why this plant is invariably left standing while all other plants have already been eaten. In some mainly Catholic regions of northern Europe, the plant is still bound in herb bundles that are consecrated on Ascension Day.

composite flower head 2.5–4 across, solitary flower overtopping stems

sepal with roundish, slit, brown appendages

outer ray flowers heavily enlarged

with 5 points

brown sepal, with leaves arranged like roof tiles

oval to lanceolate leaf

smooth margin or slightly toothed

Milk Thistle

Silybum marianum (daisy family)
H 20–150 cm   June–Sept   annual to biennial

In antiquity, the Milk Thistle was already used as a medicinal plant and as a vegetable. The fruits are meant to help treat muscle strains and snake bites. When boiled, the leaves produce a cabbage-like vegetable. The roots can be prepared like Black Salsify and the young flower heads like artichokes. The white patches on the leaves were interpreted in the Middle Ages as the milk of the Virgin Mary.

Habitat *Wasteland and cultivated ground. Requires plenty of nutrients and warmth. Around the Mediterranean.*

> *characteristically blotched foliage*
> *one of the most well-known thistles in the Mediterranean*
> *portrayed on many images of the Virgin Mary*

composite flower head up to 8 cm across

sepals with stiff thorns

59

upper leaves with long thorns, up to about 1 cm in length

overwinters with leaf rosette

solitary composite flowers, with long stalks

leaves conspicuously white, marbled

thorny, lobed margin

Did you know?

In the Middle Ages, the plants fruits were called 'poking seeds' and were believed to cure a stitch in one's side. Nowadays, doctors enthuse about their beneficial effect on the liver. A substance extracted from them is even used as an antidote for cases of poisoning from false death cap mushroom.

Cotton Thistle

Onopordum acanthium (daisy family)

H 30–250 cm   July–Aug   biennial

Habitat Weedy patches an refuse sites and rocky deposits, quarries, embankments, wayside verges. Central and south Europe.

> silver appearance from a distance
> one of the major composite flower species
> flower base edible, like artichokes

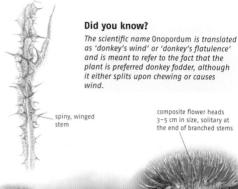

purple disc florets

spherical sepal, cobweb-like

stiff thorns, growing apart

spiny, winged stem

Thistles, especially the Cotton Thistle, which is also known as the 'Scotch Thistle', are Scotland's national flower. According to legend, in the Middle Ages they were said to have contributed to the end of the Vikings' attacks on Scotland. When the Vikings crept up to a Scots settlement through the thistle fields, their cries of pain alarmed the inhabitants, so that they were alerted and could rush to defend themselves.

Did you know?

The scientific name Onopordum *is translated as 'donkey's wind' or 'donkey's flatulence' and is meant to refer to the fact that the plant is preferred donkey fodder, although it either splits upon chewing or causes wind.*

composite flower heads 3–5 cm in size, solitary at the end of branched stems

Orange Hawkweed

Hieracium aurantiacum (daisy family)
H 20–50 cm June–Aug perennial

One interpretation of the name implies that many varieties of hawkweed only grow on cliffs that are accessible to hawks. An ancient folklore relates that hawks are supposed to coat their eyes with the plant's juice, if they lose the power of sight. Orange Hawkweed is one of the few hawkweeds that are fairly easy to identify. Most other species are yellow-flowering.

2–25 composite flower heads together

each 2–3 cm in size

with many, mostly light hairs

leaves spatula-shaped, soft

Habitat *Rough mountain grasslands and mountain pastures. Also on park lawns, roadside embankments, station sidings. North Europe, mountains in central and south Europe.*

> **hollow stems**
> **mostly growing in groups with many rosettes**
> **often growing wild as an ornamental plant and garden escape**

orange-yellow to brown-red ray florets

sepal mostly with blackish hairs

✳ **61**

Golden Hawk's-beard

Crepis aurea (daisy family)
H 5–30 cm June–Sept perennial

In sunny weather, the Golden Hawk's-beard creates a brilliantly colourful shimmer above flower-filled grasslands in the mountains and especially attracts butterflies, but also beetles, flies and bumble-bees as pollinators. In dull weather conditions, the flower heads remain closed up. People once used extracts of the flowers to colour butter and cheese yellow.

toothed to pinnately lobed leaf

only 1 flower head per stem

Habitat *Mountain meadows and pastures, stony mountain grasslands from the tree line up to 2,900 m. Mountains in central and south Europe.*

> **leaves reminiscent of the Dandelion (p. 257)**
> **plant contains milky juice**
> **beautiful plant for rockeries**

orange-red ray florets

composite flower up to 4.5 cm in size

Salsify

Tragopogon porrifolius (daisy family)
H 20–120 cm   April–July   annual to biennial

grass-like, linear leaves

Habitat *Fallow areas, rocky deposits, wayside verges, grassy locations. Growing wild in south Europe. Wild escape from early cultivars in central Europe.*

> composite flower head, only opened in the mornings
> also called 'Purple Goat's Beard'
> plant contains milky juice

Salsify was planted in central Europe as a root vegetable until the end of the 16th century. Later, it grew less popular and the Black Salsify took its place, as the roots of this vegetable are still appetising even if taken from flowering plants. To harvest the root of Salsify, the flower must be severed from the tap root, which can grow up to 30 cm in length.

purple to wine-red ray florets

composite flower head 7–8 cm across

mostly 8 green sepals

Flowering Rush

Butomus umbellatus (flowering-rush family)
H 50–150 cm   June–Aug   perennial

Habitat *Banks or bankside areas of still, standing or slowly flowing, nutrient-rich waters and dykes. Almost everywhere in Europe.*

> grass-like leaves, up to over 1 m long
> heat-loving
> also planted near ponds

The Flowering Rush has a long, slender and flexible flower stalk. If found in deeper wetlands, the plant does not flower and forms ribbon-shaped leaves. These were once used to produce baskets and mats. Nurseries cultivate the plants for decorative and ornamental purposes to grow by garden ponds.

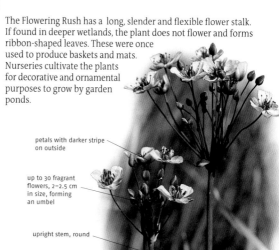

petals with darker stripe on outside

up to 30 fragrant flowers, 2–2.5 cm in size, forming an umbel

upright stem, round

3 shorter and 3 longer, pink to white petals

Martagon Lily

Lilium martagon (lily family)
H 40–100 cm   June–July   perennial

The flowers attract all kinds of moths that hover above the flower heads while drinking nectar. Other butterflies have difficulty clinging on to the oily coating on the petals. The golden-coloured bulb was once regarded as important. Alchemists in the 16th century used the bulbs in their experiments to produce gold. It was also supposed to be adorned as a charm around the necks of teething babies. Supposedly also an effective cure for haemorrhoids.

Habitat Woodlands with herbaceous undergrowth, copses, mountain meadows up to about 2,400 m. On chalky soil in partial shade. Mountains in Europe.

> buds often chewed away by deer
> early plant used in magic
> turban-like flowers, with evening fragrance

Did you know?

Plants can often be eaten away. For instance, deer graze on young buds and the Scarlet Lily Beetle, a red beetle measuring 6–8 mm, likes to chew through foliage. If you hold these beetles up to your ear, their quiet squeaking noise just becomes audible.

6 to up to 4 cm long, light purple petals with dark blotches

red anther

63

scales, in roof tile pattern

flower cluster with up to 10 pendent flowers

yellow bulb

upright fruits

petals roll upwards

leaf with parallel veins

Fritillary
Fritillaria meleagris (lily family)
H 15–30 cm   April–May   perennial

pendent flowers on gently curving stalks

Habitat *Untreated floodplains or wetland meadows that are not cut back before early June. Central and south Europe.*

> **grass-like leaves**
> **also known as 'Guinea Hen Flower'**
> **occasionally white flowering with yellowish veins**

The Fritillary, also commonly known as Snakeshead Fritillary, has an unusual and distinctive pattern and chequered markings on the flowers. The inside of each petal has a long vertical groove that is rich in nectar and designed to attract bees and bumblebees. Fritillaries are becoming increasingly endangered in the wild, as their preferred habitats are disappearing.

bell-shaped corolla, chequered like a chessboard, purplish red with white blotches

solitary flowers, rarely 2 to 3, up to 4 cm

grooves on inner side of each 6 petals

Chives
Allium schoenoprasum (lily family)
H 10–40 cm   June–Aug   perennial

Habitat *Found in the wild on damp rocky deposits in the mountains. Growing wild on sand banks and gravel alongside rivers. Throughout Europe.*

> **forms dense clumps with basal leaves**
> **also cultivated as herbal seasoning as well as found in the wild**
> **typical onion aroma**

Chives also grow in the wild in Asia and North America, as far as the Arctic. In Central Europe, they have been cultivated as a herbal seasoning since the late mediaeval period. They contain aromatic wild onion and mustard oils and are rich in Vitamin C. Cut back the clumps of Chives in your garden about three times a year. Bulbs can be dug up in wintertime to grow in pots on the window ledge.

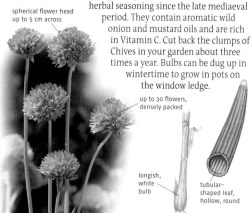

spherical flower head up to 5 cm across

up to 30 flowers, densely packed

petals about 1 cm long

stamens shorter than the corolla

longish, white bulb

tubular-shaped leaf, hollow, round

Meadow Saffron

Colchicum autumnale (lily family)

H 5–40 cm   Aug–Nov   perennial   ☠

The entire plant contains the highly toxic chemical colchicine and is therefore shunned by grazing animals. Poisoning can cause cramps, paralysis or prove fatal. Colchicine prescribed in precise quantities was used for a long time in medicine as a standard treatment for severe gout. Nowadays, other treatments are available. In plants, the chemical affects the genetic distribution and is therefore suitable to cultivate high-performance varieties, such as apples, bananas and citrus fruits

Habitat Pastures with reeds and rushes, damp meadows, rough meadows, orchards, riverside woodland glades. On nutrient-rich soil. Central and south Europe.

> reminiscent of a crocus
> only flowers emerge in autumn
> leaves and fruits appear in spring

leaves with parallel veins

8–25 cm long

fruits between leaves

bulb deeply embedded in ground

6 purple, pink or whitish 4–6 cm long flower tips

upright flowers, visible part up to 20 cm long

※ **65**

Did you know?

The Kolchis region is located on the Black Sea's eastern coast. According to Greek mythology Medea, a mixer of poisons, lived there. The saga recounts how several drops of her poisonous drinks split out onto the earth and grew into Colchicum, the Meadow Saffron.

long, thin flower tube emerging directly from the ground

Hollowroot
Corydalis cava (fumitory family)
H 10–35 cm   March–May   perennial

Habitat Sparse deciduous and woodland ravines, riverside woodlands, orchards, copses. Especially in central Europe.

> older bulbous roots are hollow inside
> attracted to nutrient-rich soil
> flowers often also white

The white appendages on the seeds are very nutritious and attract ants, which drag the seeds to their nests in order to detach this part from the seeds, only to transport the remainder out of the nest again. This is how the seeds arrive several hundreds of metres from the parent plant. In the spur, the flowers are full of sweet nectar.

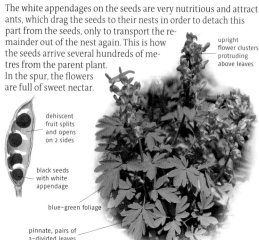

upright flower clusters protruding above leaves

dehiscent fruit splits and opens on 2 sides

black seeds with white appendage

blue-green foliage

long spur

flower 1–3 cm long

hood-like cover over stamens

pinnate, pairs of 3-divided leaves

Common Fumitory
Fumaria officinalis (fumitory family)
H 15–30 cm   May–Oct   annual

Habitat Weedy patches on arable fields, in gardens, vineyards, exposed locations on building sites and other wasteland. All over Europe.

> flowers mostly self-pollinating
> attracted to nutrient-rich places
> frequently found growing in large groups

Presumably, the name 'Fumitory' is related to the fact that large groups of this plant look grey from a distance, virtually as though smoke were billowing out of the ground. When cut back, the plants also give off weak, acidic vapours that burn like smoke in one's eyes. Medicines containing Common Fumitory alleviate cramps related to complaints of the gall bladder, stomach and intestines.

flowers in terminal clusters of 10–50

bluish-green foliage, often with a reddish tinge, finely divided

dark purple at the front

short, sack-like spur

0.5–1 cm long flower

fruits spherical, green

Spiny Restharrow

Ononis spinosa (pea family)
H 30–60 cm   June–July   perennial, shrub

The Spiny or Prickly Restharrow used to be regularly harvested, although the thorns make it difficult to collect the plants from pastures. People compared the thorns to a rake that stems and other grass blades cling to, hence the origin of the name 'Harrow'.

Did you know?

The roots of the Spiny Restharrow are used for their diuretic effect and are especially helpful in preventing inflammations of the urinary passage.

Habitat *Rough grassland and pastures, wayside verges, forest margins, embankments, weirs. On warm, chalky soil. In central and South Europe.*

> forms a long taproot
> attracted to soil with poor yields
> often left standing in pastures because of thorns

roundish upper petal

1–2 cm long, typical pea flower

67

flowers pink to light, violet-red growing in 1s and 2s in leaf axils

twigs with thorns

short hairs

toothed margin

leaves lanceolate

stiff branches

Goat's-rue
Galega officinalis (pea family)
H 60–120 cm June–Aug perennial

Habitat *Fallow areas, reveres, stations, quarries, roadside verges, ditches. On damp, nutrient-rich soil. South and central Europe.*

> rather sensitive to frost
> leaves vaguely reminiscent of the Rue (p. 215)
> also an ornamental plant

typical pea flower, about 1 cm long

all petals roughly the same length

Animals that feed on Goat's-rue are said to yield more milk. It is possible that the name is related to the use of the plant for animal fodder. However, it is also plausible that the addition of the prefix 'Goat's' was simply to distinguish the plant from the Rue (p. 215). In traditional medicine, the plant is considered to lower the sugar content in the blood. However, there is no specific scientific evidence to support this.

cylindrical fruit, 2–5 cm long

light-purple flowers, slightly nodding, in loose clusters

Alpine French Honeysuckle
Hedysarum hedysaroides (pea family)
H 10–30 cm July–Aug perennial

Habitat *Mountain pastures, stony mountain grasslands, dwarf shrub heathlands from 1,500 to over 2,800 m.*

> Mountains in central and south Europe
> very long taproot
> rather bitter tasting
> typical pea flower, purple-red, approximately 2 cm long

oval leaflets

pendant flowers

Alpine French Honeysuckle is among the most valuable plants for animal fodder and found in the mountains. It is rich in proteins and is the favourite fodder of both grazing cattle as well as wild game in the mountains. However, the plant will suffer if overgrazing occurs, so mountain farmers in many places prefer to produce hay in the plant's habitat.

flower cluster 2–5 cm long

pinnate leaves with 9–19 leaflets and single terminal leaflet

Red Clover
Trifolium pratense (pea family)
H 15–40 cm   June–Sept   perennial

For many centuries and at least since the 18th century, instead of allowing an arable field to lie fallow, farmers frequently sowed Red Clover. This not only provides an abundant and valuable store of cattle fodder, but also simultaneously improves the soil (see box). More recently, plant-based herbal remedies have also discovered Red Clover, since extracts are said to help alleviate symptoms associated with the menopause.

Habitat *Meadows, pastures, wayside verges, planted on arable fields in various cultivars. Found all over Europe.*

> *a very common Clover variety*
> *attracted to nutrient-rich soil*
> *attracts bumblebees*

1–4 spherical to oval-shaped flower heads overtopping stem

light crimson to fleshy red, 1–2 cm long typical pea flower

 69

flower heads more or less encased by uppermost leaves

trifoliate leaf

leaflet often with arrow-shaped, white marking

Did you know?
The roots grow up to 2 m below ground and have small bulbous growths, where bacteria live. The bacteria absorb nitrogen from the atmosphere and make this nutrient available to the plant. At the same time, they also fertilise the soil with the substance.

Crimson Clover
Trifolium incarnatum (pea family)
H 20–40 cm   June–Aug   annual

Habitat Scrub, fallow arable fields, roadside verges and slopes, arable fields. Areas with mild winters.

> originates from around the western Mediterranean
> clover with striking flower colour
> included in wild flower seed mixes

Cultivation of Crimson Clover dates back at least to the 19th century. The clover not only helps create nutrient-rich soil, but is also a source of green cattle fodder that is full of goodness. However, cultivation has been on the decline for some time now, although this bright crimson clover species is occasionally re-sown on roadside embankments.

3–6 cm long flower head, 1.5–2.5 cm across

stalked flower head

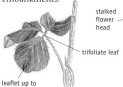

brilliant red, 1–1.5 cm long typical pea flower

trifoliate leaf

sepal hispid or with stiff hairs

leaflet up to 3.5 cm long, hairy

70

Alpine Clover
Trifolium alpinum (pea family)
H 5–20 cm   June–Aug   perennial

Habitat Rough mountain grasslands, mountain lawns and pastures, in among dwarf shrubs from the tree line up to about 2,700 m. Mountains in central and south Europe.

> flowers especially fragrant in sunshine
> a large-flowering clover

The Alpine Clover's taproot grows underground up to more than 1 m deep, supplying the plant not only with nutrients, but simultaneously preventing wild animals from ripping up the delicate plant, often from stony soil, as chamois goats and marmots frequently graze on the softly fragrant Alpine Clover.

over 2 cm long, typical pea flower

terminal flower head with 3–15 flowers

leafless stem

slender leaflet, up to 7 cm long, sparse

trifoliate leaf

Crown Vetch

Securigera varia (pea family)
H 30–60 cm   June–Aug   perennial

The pinnate leaflets have a limb at their base and turn upwards in a 'sleeping position' at night-time. The plant contains substances that are beneficial for the heart, although nowadays, it is no longer used in herbal remedies. Symptoms of poisoning include severe nausea and cramps. In extreme cases, the plant may even prove fatal.

5–20 nodding flowers in clustered flower head

pinnate leaf, with single terminal leaf

conspicuously ridged stem

Habitat Wayside and roadside embankments, station cuttings and roadside embankments, quarries, semi-arid grasslands, light copses, forest margins. In central and south Europe.

> occasionally also almost white flowering
> mostly spreading form with prostrate stems
> attracts bees

1–1.5 cm long, red typical pea flower

flower stalk longer than sepal

71

Sainfoin

Onobrychis viciifolia (pea family)
H 30–60 cm   May–July   perennial

Sainfoin was originally found growing in south-eastern Europe. From the 16th century onwards, the plant was cultivated in central Europe as protein-rich animal fodder and often left to grow wild. Although the plant does not tolerate direct grazing, it can prove a valuable supply of hay. Nowadays, it virtually has no agricultural usage any longer. Instead, farmers much more frequently plant corn, Lucerne (p. 187) or Red Clover (p. 69).

20–50 flowers form a dense, upright cluster

15–29 oval, short-stalked leaflets

leaves pinnate, with single terminal leaf

toothed edge

fruit 6–8 mm long, with network veins

Habitat Semi-arid grasslands, pathways, embankments. On warm, moderately dry limy soil in sunny locations. Almost everywhere in Europe.

> roots grow up to 4 m deep
> improves soil
> fruits become attached to animals

1–1.5 cm long, pink typical pea flowers

dark stripes

Spring Pea

Lathyrus vernus (pea family)
H 20–40 cm   April–May   perennial   (☺)

Habitat Forests, especially beech forests with rich herbaceous undergrowth. Mostly on chalky soil. Almost everywhere in Europe.

> * leaves pinnate, without tendrils
> * striking bloom due to early flowering season
> * attractive in wild flower garden

The colour of the flowers depends on their acidity content and changes quite noticeably, depending on the flower's age. The juicy liquid in the bud is acidic, which explains the red colour pigment. Once the flower opens, however, the cell juice is neutral, giving a red-violet and blue colour. When the flower finally withers, it is alkaline like soap and the flower colour changes to turquoise.

3–7 flowers forming a long-stalked cluster

1–2 cm long, typical pea flower, early flowers red-violet

bloom a blue to turquoise colour in late-flowering stage

Tufted Milkwort

Polygala comosa (milkwort family)
H 15–25 cm   May–June   perennial

Habitat Sunny, rough grassland and pastures, wayside reveres. On moderately dry, in summer mostly lime-rich soil. In central and south Europe.

> * flowers reminiscent of pea-like flowers
> * flowers of the similar Common Milkwort are mostly blue
> * attracted to poor soil

The Tufted Milkwort usually flowers two weeks before Whitsun. The typical, fringed attachment at the tip of the flower serves as a landing pad for insects and is presumably also intended to feign stamens and signal a source of available nourishment. However, as a reward for their visit, the pollinators can drink sweet nectar.

15–30 flowers at the end of each stem forming clusters

1–2.5 cm long, linear-lanceolate

cluster often appears tufted atop

leaves alternate

2 wing-like, 4–7 mm long petals growing sideways

striking, fringed appendage

several stems

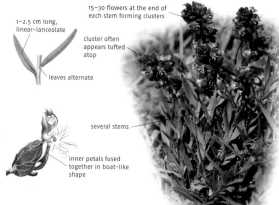

inner petals fused together in boat-like shape

Dittany

Dictamnus albus (rue family)

H 60–120 cm   May–June   perennial   ☠

On hot days, the plant emits oils in substantial quantities of essential vapours from the leaves' glandular hairs and oil vacuoles. On calm days without any wind, this even forms a vaporous cloud hanging over the plant, which can even be ignited or is self-igniting. The plant is therefore also known as 'Burning Bush'. However, as with flambéd dishes, no damage is caused to the plant.

Habitat *Sunny, rocky, shrub-lined slopes, light, dry forests and forest margins. On dry, rough, mostly lime-rich soil in central and south Europe.*

> *intense aroma of lemon and cinnamon*
> *skin contact with juice can cause blisters*
> *needs lots of heat*

terminal flower clusters

flowers 4–5 cm across

5 rose-coloured petals with dark veins

10 long, curving stamens

73

leaves pinnate with single terminal leaf and 7–11 leaflets

upright stem

5-part fruit with glandular hairs

Did you know?

The 'Burning Bush' in the Bible was not Dittany, but probably the 'Alexandrian Senna' or 'True Senna', related to the pea family. Its yellow flower clusters are faintly reminiscent of flames.

Indian Balsam

Impatiens glandulifera (balsam family)

H 50–250 cm   July–Aug   annual   (✸)

Habitat *Riverside woodlands, damp forests, riverbanks. Prefers shady locations with high humidity. Almost everywhere in Europe.*

> **flowers intensely fragrant**
> **ripe fruits split when touched**
> **grows very rapidly**

Indian Balsam is native to the Himalayas. It was first sown in Dresden around 1837 as an attractive ornamental plant and later in numerous gardens all around Europe. From here, it rapidly spread to grow in the wild. Nowadays, the plant partly forms dense groups on riverbanks and in riverside woodlands and is increasingly suppressing the native flora by colonising these habitats, taking over from native plants. Conservationists therefore battle with the plant in many locations.

leaf petiole with stalked glands

fruit 3–5 cm long, club-shaped

fruit sections inrolled

black seeds

5 petals of varying sizes

broad hood

greenish, curved spur

racemes with 5–20 flowers, up to 5 cm long

fruits and flowers often present simultaneously

leaves deeply toothed

Did you know?

Indian Balsam guarantees dispersal of its seeds by an explosive, spinning mechanism. Substantial tension builds up within the fruits that lead them suddenly to explode of their own accord or when touched. The seeds then disperse, flying up to distances of 7 m.

Red Dead-nettle

Lamium purpureum (dead-nettle family)
H 15–45 cm   March–Oct   annual

The Red Dead-nettle grows very rapidly and each year up to four generations of plants can be produced. The plants even flower in winter, if conditions are favourable. The nutlets of the fruits have a nutritious, oily body, which attracts ants that ensure the dispersal of the seeds.

whorl-like flower heads with pea flowers up to 1.7 cm in size in leaf axils

4-edged stems

leaves opposite

leaves 1–2.5 cm long, roundish, soft hairs

margin roughly toothed

upper lip curved, hood-like

keel or lower lip with large, lightly marked middle section

Habitat *Sparse weedy patches on arable land, in gardens, vineyards, alongside paths, rocky deposits, wasteland. All over Europe.*

> leaves often tinged red in sunny places
> attracted to nitrogen-rich soil
> often found growing in groups

Spotted Dead-nettle

Lamium maculatum (dead-nettle family)
H 15–60 cm   April–Sept   perennial

The flowers conceal rich stores of nectar deep within their base, consisting up to approximately 40 per cent of sugar – no wonder that bumblebees like visiting the flowers so frequently. Smaller bumblebees, whose proboscis is too short, bite into the flower tube sideways on. These holes then also enable honeybees to draw out the nectar with their proboscis.

Habitat *Weedy patches, riverside woodlands, forest edges, ditches, hedgerows, wayside verges, fences. In semi-shady locations. Central and south Europe.*

> when flowerless, slightly reminiscent of a Common Stinging Nettle (p. 289)
> attracted to nutrient-rich soil
> attractive in wild flower gardens

oval leaf, with hairs

irregularly toothed margin

leaves alternate

star-shaped sepal with 5 teeth

after flowering, encloses 4 tiny fruitlets

whorl-like flower clusters

4-edged stem

upper lip curved, hood-like

2–3 cm long, purple pea flower

white, red-spotted lower lip

Common Hemp-nettle
Galeopsis tetrahit (dead-nettle family)
H 10–70 cm   June–Oct   annual

Habitat Weedy patches on arable fields, rocky deposits, wood clearings, on country pathways, fences, wasteland. From flatlands to the high mountains. All over Europe.

> teeth-like, winged petals are characteristic
> attracted to nitrogen
> also known as 'Day Nettle' due to spiny sepals

hood-like upper lip

patterned lower lip, with 2 hollow teeth-like wings

sepal with 5 spiny, bearded teeth

The teeth of the Common Hemp-nettle flower serve as a 'crash barrier' for insects about to land. If animals brush against the hard, spiny sepals during the fruit season, they cling on to their coats. The elastic stems curve, finally springing backwards and spinning the fruits out of the sepals in the process.

oval to broad lanceolate leaves, 1.5–4.5 cm across

toothed margin

with bristles and glands

thickened stem beneath foliage

several whorls above each other

6–15 flowers on each cluster, in dense whorls

pea flowers, 1.5–2 cm long

76

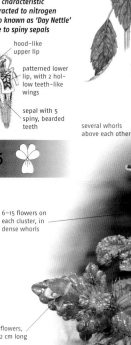

Did you know?
The Red Hemp-nettle is commonly found on gravelly places and rough stone between railway tracks, yet also in quarries. The leaves are only 2–5 mm across and the flowers resemble those of the Common Hemp-nettle.

Black Horehound
Ballota nigra (dead-nettle family)
H 30–100 cm   June–Sept   perennial

The flower of the Black Horehound has a pungent odour; it is also sometimes called the Stinking Horehound for this reason. In traditional medicine, the plant is recommended as an antidote for stomach complaints, symptoms of the menopause, restlessness and whooping cough.

leaves opposite

hairy plant

Habitat *On weedy patches by waysides, fences, on rocky ground, especially in villages. Especially in central and south Europe on warm ground.*

> **dark green plant, frequently almost black**
> **unpleasant aroma when crushed**
> **attracted to nitrogen**

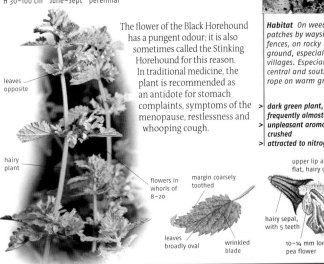

flowers in whorls of 8–20

margin coarsely toothed

leaves broadly oval

wrinkled blade

upper lip almost flat, hairy outside

hairy sepal, with 5 teeth

10–14 mm long pea flower

Wall Germander
Teucrium chamaedrys (dead-nettle family)
H 15–30 cm   July–Aug   perennial

Herbalists once recommended this fragrant herbaceous plant as an antidote for digestive complaints, gout and the fever. However, after it emerged that the plant is also responsible for cases of poisoning and damage to the liver and even jaundice, it is wise not to use Wall Germander as a medicinal plant.

leaves oval, slightly rough

irregularly toothed margin

flowers in axils of upper, often red-violet leaves

Habitat *Cliffs, sunny slopes, dry grassland and forests. On warm, dry, mostly chalky soil with poor nutrients. In central and south Europe.*

> **plant pleasantly aromatic when crushed**
> **requires lots of heat**
> **mostly grows in groups**

no upper lip

keel or lower lip with 5 points

1–1.5 cm long, pink pea flower

Bastard Balm

Melittis melissophyllum (dead-nettle family)
H 20–50 cm   May–June   perennial

Habitat Open forests, forest margins, sunny copses. Often on stony soil in semi-shady, warm locations. In central and south Europe.

> requires heat
> when dried, an aroma vaguely reminiscent of Woodruff (p. 98)
> conspicuous, large pea flowers

The plant may contain sweet nectar, but as the name suggests, this is nothing but a deceptive ploy. The sugary nectar is hidden so deep within the flower's long tube that the honeybee is unable to reach the nectar because of its surprisingly short proboscis. Only bumblebees and butterflies can extract it.

leaves decussate

flowers in axils of upper leaves

flowers mostly towards one side

leaf 3–9 cm long, oval

margin with regular, coarse teeth

3–4.5 cm long, pink or white pea flower

long tube

lower lip with red-violet blotches

Betony

Betonica officinalis (dead-nettle family)
H 30–100 cm   July–Aug   perennial

Habitat Moorland and rough mountain meadows, heaths. On damp soil in slightly warmer locations. Especially in central and south Europe.

> leaf pairs very far apart
> attracted to soil with poor yields
> long flowering, attracts many insects

In antiquity, Betony was highly prized as a medicinal plant, which was believed to protect against epidemics and evil spells. During the 16th and 17th century, people believed that the herb could be used to treat almost any ailment. The plant contains tannins, which can be an effective antidote to treat cases of diarrhoea.

dense, spike-like flower cluster overtopping stem

1–1.5 cm long, dark-pink pea flowers

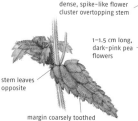

upper lip almost flat

narrow tube

3-part lower lip

stem leaves opposite

margin coarsely toothed

Hedge Woundwort

Stachys sylvatica (dead-nettle family)
H 30–100 cm   June–Sept   perennial

This species is one of the few flowering plants that still produce blooms in the shady forest. If pollinators and insects do not visit the flowers, they can be self-pollinating.

Habitat Woods, copses, woodland springs, woodland paths. On damp to wet, nutrient-rich soil. Almost everywhere in Europe, in mountainous regions in the south.

> *flowers noticeably dark*
> *leaves similar to nettles*
> *unpleasant smell when crushed*

margin with coarse, pointed teeth

plant with stiff, hispid hairs

leaves stalked

many loosely tiered flower whorls overtopping stems

dark, brown-red pea flower, 1–1.5 cm long

smaller upper lip

lower lip with distinctive pattern

79

Motherwort

Leonurus cardiaca (dead-nettle family)
H 30–100 cm   June–Sept   perennial

This herbaceous plant is said to act as an antidote for heart complaints – a healing remedy dating from the 15th century. Nowadays, Motherwort is still used in traditional medicine to treat nervous heart conditions. More recently, the plant was also occasionally cultivated because bees are attracted to the rich food supply.

Habitat Weedy patches along waysides, walls, hedgerows, gardens, fences, especially in villages. On nutrient-rich soil. Almost everywhere in Europe.

> *forms several, erect, unbranched stems*
> *requires warmth*
> *also called 'Lion's Tail'*

dense flower clusters in upper leaf axils

leaves opposite

leaf deeply cleft with 3–7 lobes

upright, slightly hood-like upper lip

numerous hairs on the outside

pea flower, about 1 cm in size

Wild Marjoram
Origanum vulgare (mint family)
H 20–60 cm   July–Sept   perennial

Habitat Edges of copses, dry grassland, light, warm woods and spinneys, embankments. Almost everywhere in Europe.

> herbal aroma when crushed (excellent for pizza toppings)
> flowers attract numerous insects
> requires heat in summer

red-violet anthers protruding from the flower

4–7 mm long pea flower

3-part lower lip

Marjoram native to Europe can also be used as herbal seasoning. However, what is commercially available as 'Oregano' generally contains leaves and flowers of different Wild Marjoram varieties and related species. These highly aromatic plants are native to the Mediterranean. In folklore, Marjoram was among those plants used to ward off evil spirits and to frighten the devil.

dense, clustered flower head overtopping stem

red-tinged stem

branched opposite

leaves longish or oval, up to 3 cm long

Did you know?
The closely related Marjoram is also an aromatic herb, which is especially recommended for seasoning meats. However, the plant is intolerant of cold and therefore occurs less frequently in northern Europe.

Large Thyme

Thymus pulegioides (mint family)
H 5–40 cm   June–Oct   perennial

The plants often colonise anthills, as the fruitlets are transported by ants to their nests. Large Thyme has a soothing effect on the nasal passages and is an excellent herbal remedy to treat catarrh because of its ether-based essential oils. However, it is used less frequently for this purpose than Garden Thyme (see below).

Habitat Rough grassland and pastures, embankments, cliffs, anthills. Pioneer plant found all over Europe and up to 2,000 m in the mountains.

> herbal aroma, sometimes even scent with a hint of lemon
> evergreen leaves
> requires heat and sunshine

dense, clustered flower heads over-topping stem

more flowers in whorls below

stem heavily 4-edged

short hairs on edges

leaves up to 2 cm long and 1 cm across

small upper lip

broad 3-part lower lip

purplish-pink pea flower, approximately 6 mm long

Garden Thyme

Thymus vulgaris (mint family)
H 10–30 cm   April–July   perennial

In ancient times, the Greeks used to burn thyme in sacrificial rituals in a similar way that we burn incense today. The plant's name is also derived from this custom (the Greek, 'thyein', means 'to smoke'). Thyme used to be regarded as a symbol of death, since people believed that the souls of the dead would turn into the blooms of sweetly fragranced flowers. Today, the plant is used in cough medicine and as herbal seasoning.

Habitat Sunny shrub and dry places on limestone. Grows wild in the western Mediterranean as far as Italy, otherwise cultivated.

> plants mostly in tight groups
> often cultivated as a medicinal plant and for herbal seasoning
> with a characteristic aroma

flowers forming dense heads

leaves opposite

downy white underside

margin curled inwards

less than 1 cm long

woody plant

whitish to pink lipped pea flower, 4–6 mm long

3-part lower lip deeply cleft

Foxglove

Digitalis purpurea (figwort family)

H 40–150 cm   June–Aug   biennial, herbaceous perennial

Habitat Woodland pathways, forest clearings, mountain woodlands, spinneys. On soil with low lime content in sunny to semi-shady locations. Especially in west Europe.

> often grows in groups
> deadly poisonous
> blotches of colour on flowers look like anthers and attract bumblebees

corolla light to dark crimson red, with globular tube

inside with dark, white-edged blotches

long clusters with up to over 100 flowers

long leaf stalk

downy grey underside

leaves oval

According to Nordic mythology, elves adorn themselves in hats made from Foxglove flowers when they dance in the moonlight. Though poisonous, this is a highly effective medicinal plant and, if prescribed by doctors in the right dosage, it can alleviate specific heart conditions. In the late 18th century, William Withering, a doctor and botanical researcher, discovered the beneficial effect of digitalis on the heart. Before then, the plant was only used to treat abscesses and ulcers.

pendant flowers, 3.5–5 cm long

Did you know?

The terminal flower sometimes has an unusual appearance. For this so-called 'pelory', the flower parts become so changed that their form almost resembles a large saucer-shaped flower.

Field Cow-wheat

Melampyrum arvense (figwort family)
H 15–50 cm   June–Sept   annual   (☹)

The fruits contain black seeds
that are shaped just like wheat
kernels and are about the same
size. If they get into flour or
bread, they impart a bluish hue.
The scientific name *Melampyrum*
is derived from Greek 'melas'
meaning 'black' and 'pyros'
meaning 'wheat'.

leaves tinged
purple-red if
close to flower
head

*Habitat Cereal fields,
edge of copses, sunny
hedgerows, country
paths. Found mostly on
dry, nutrient-rich soil
almost all over Europe.*

> *conspicuous from a long
distance*
> *seeds transported by
ants*
> *occasionally found in
wild flower mixtures*

conspicuous flower spikes
overtopping stems

2-lipped violet-red
flower, 2–2.5 cm long

middle section
yellow to
yellowish-
white

upper leaves with long,
narrow teeth

Toothwort

Odontites vulgaris (figwort family)
H 10–45 cm   May–Oct   annual

flowers
approximately
1 cm long

flower spikes
growing to
one side,
with leaves

As with many herbaceous plants belonging
to the figwort family, Toothwort is a parasitic plant. However, it also has foliage
enabling carbohydrates to form independ-
ently. To absorb water and nutrients it
grows special sucking roots, sinking
them into the roots of nearby
grasses. It extracts vital minerals
from the grasses by mustering
substantial suction power. This
is why if plants are picked, they
wither away rapidly after only a
few minutes.

*Habitat Wayside
verges, woodland
paths, pastures. Warm
locations in summer,
also in places with
substantial footfall.
Everywhere in Europe.*

> *semi-parasitic*
> *tolerant of ground with
high salt content*
> *mostly in smaller groups*

lanceolate, mostly
toothed

long side
branches,
growing
apart

leaves opposite

protruding
stamens

2-lipped
flower,
hood-shaped
upper lip

lower lip with
3 points

Red Bartsia
Lathraea squamaria (figwort family)
H 10–30 cm   March–May   perennial

Habitat Riverside woodlands, woodland ravines. Mostly in small groups from the flatlands to low mountainous regions, almost everywhere in Europe.

> fleshy plant, without foliage
> grows in shade or semi-shade
> requires damp to wet soil

Red Bartsia survives as a parasite on perennial plants, mainly on alder, hazel and poplar. It sinks sucker roots into the roots of these plants and extracts all the things that they require to grow and flourish: water, nutrient salts and organic substances. This means Red Bartsia does not need any light and can also grow in very dark places deep within the forest.

sepals resembling petals

dense flower clusters, growing to one side

2-lipped flower, 1.5–2 cm long, light pink to light violet

pale, scale-like leaves

84

Whorled Lousewort
Pedicularis verticillata (figwort family)
H 5–20 cm   June–Aug   perennial

Habitat Wet mountain grasslands, low, stony meadows and pastures in the Alps from altitudes of 1,000 to 2,800 m.

> leaves growing on stems in whorls of 3–4
> requires damp soil
> especially attracts bumblebees

Surplus liquid from infusions of lousewort plants were once used as a treatment for lice and other parasites living on humans and cattle. There are about 600 different lousewort species around the world, with more than 20 of them surviving in the Alps. All the plants are semi-parasitic. They have foliage, in order to produce carbohydrates, but they absorb water and mineral salts from host plants, by attaching themselves to their roots.

flowers forming a dense flower head

hood-shaped upper lip, upright

2-lipped flower, about 1.5 cm long, purple-red

leaf heavily pinnate

margin toothed

plant often tinged red

Bedstraw Broomrape

Orobanche sp. (broomrape family)
H 20–50 cm   June–July   annual to woody perennial

Bedstraw Broomrape survives as a parasite. Every variety taps into the roots of a specific group of host plants. The plant absorbs water and all other nutrients from these hosts by using powerful, sucker roots. In the Mediterranean, some Broomrape varieties are also feared, because they cause damage to cultivated plants.

Habitat Plants graft onto roots of various cultivars and wild plants. Almost everywhere in Europe.

> plant completely without foliage
> could be mistaken for an orchid
> withers after flowering

loose to moderately dense flower spike

flowers facing all sides

stem noticeably thickened at base

upper lip often with a rounded corner at front

2-lipped flower, up to 3.5 cm long, light yellow to dark red

85

Red Valerian

Centranthus ruber (valerian family)
H 30–80 cm   May–July   perennial

Only the proboscis of butterflies is long and thin enough to reach through the tubular flower and find the nectar contained in the spur. Red Valerian is a rewarding plant to grow in sunny locations as a garden perennial. Its roots were previously used on occasions for insomnia, as with Common Valerian (p. 128).

Habitat In south Europe, on sunny walls, cliffs and on rubble. Cultivated as a decorative plant in central Europe and growing wild in warm locations.

> leaves slightly blue-green
> also with white flowers
> requires sufficient heat

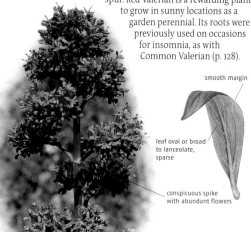

smooth margin

leaf oval or broad to lanceolate, sparse

conspicuous spike with abundant flowers

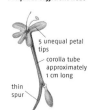

5 unequal petal tips

corolla tube approximately 1 cm long

thin spur

Bear's-breech
Acanthus mollis (bear's-breech family)
H 40–90 cm   April–Aug   perennial

Habitat Copses, fallow and wasteland in the western and central Mediterranean, in the wild as a garden escape.

> leaves can be up to 1 m long
> grows in clusters
> the related Bear's Breeches has thistle-like thorns

The flowers are constructed so that only strong bumblebees and related insects can reach the nectar at their base. To do so, they have to force their way through the firm canopy formed by the upper sepal lobes and the flower's lower lip. Nurseries occasionally provide the stately, robust plants that also grow in central Europe as park and garden perennials.

upper sepal lip protruding above flower

lobed lower lip of corolla

toothed leaf beneath flower

violet-red sepal lobes

dense, cylindrical flower spike

flowers about 4 cm long

leaf soft, characteristically indented and toothed, without thorns

Did you know?
Acanthus *leaves* were already used in antiquity as the pattern for decorative finishes on columns. Today, you can still see the Acanthus *leaf* on many buildings as a decorative embellishment.

Marsh Gladiolus

Gladiolus palustris (iris family)
H 30–50 cm   May–June   perennial

The scientific name *Gladiolus* (Latin for 'a small sword') refers to the typical leaf shape of the tuberous plant. The large-flowered gladioli that are popular as cut flowers and grown in gardens are a cross between a number of different, mostly African species.

Habitat Swamps and moorland pastures, wet pasture areas on slopes. On damp or occasionally flooded ground. In Central and southeast Europe.

> intolerant of fertiliser
> increasingly rare in the wild
> the similar Field Gladiolus grows on arable fields in the Mediterranean

tuberous root, up to 2 cm in size

network-fibrous casing

flowers forming loose spikes, curving to one side

6 petals, up to 3 cm long

fused together at base forming a curving tube

87

Fragrant Orchid

Gymnadenia conopsea (orchid family)
H 25–60 cm   May–Aug   perennial

up to 15 cm long, dense, cylindrical spike with up to 140 orchid flowers

The long, thin flower spur is a clue as to this orchid's pollinators. They are the butterflies and moths that easily reach inside the tubular flower with their thin proboscis. The flower is less than 1 mm across and the insects can extract nectar that is highly visible in reflected light. At twilight, in many places, the plants have a particularly intense fragrance.

Habitat Moorland pastures, rough grassland, open forests. Arid as well as damp, mostly chalky soil. Nearly everywhere in Europe.

> flowers with intense fragrance
> occasionally also with white flowers
> a protected plant, as with all orchids

upright leaves, 1–2 cm across, green

leaved stem

lip wider than long

very long, thin deflexed spur

Early-purple Orchid

Orchis mascula (orchid family)
H 15–50 cm   May–June   perennial

Habitat *Rough mountain pastures, semi-dry grassland, light forests, riverside woodlands, quarries. Throughout Europe.*

> **leaves also without blotches**
> **characteristic upright spur**
> **also called 'Dead Man's Thumb'**

The tuberous roots that always grow in pairs have a similar appearance to human testes. In the first century B.C., the Greek scholar Dioskurides described how consuming these roots could influence the sex of a woman's unborn child ('orchis' = 'testes'). In the early 19th century, the popular belief was that the roots of the Early-purple Orchid acted as an aphrodisiac.

loose, uniform spike with 20–70 flowers

upright spur

purple-red flower

3-part lip, 10–12 mm long

leaves broad to lanceolate, mostly with dark blotches

stems often dark at the top

88

Military Orchid

Orchis militaris (orchid family)
H 25–45 cm   May–June   perennial

Habitat *Rough grassland, embankments, moorland meadows, floodplains, light copses. On chalky, humus-rich soil in slightly warmer locations. Almost all over Europe.*

> **often grows in groups**
> **shunned by cattle**
> **conspicuous from a long distance**

hood pale pink to ashen grey, lighter than lip petal

cylindrical, dense spike with 20–50 flowers

The Military Orchid is among the more common orchids. It can colonise newly cleared locations such as roadside embankments or reservoirs. In these places, it often appears long before other orchid varieties.

light green upper leaves clasping stem

half-spherical hood with red veins inside

3-part lip, 1–2 cm long

middle lobes divided at front

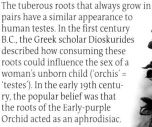

Heath-spotted Orchid

Dactylorhiza maculata (orchid family)
H 10–60 cm   May–Aug   perennial

As with other orchids, the Heath-spotted Orchid also forms seeds that are as fine as dust and enclosed within a loose casing. The seeds are so excellently adapted to dispersal on the wind that they can fly up to a distance of 10 km. However, they hardly contain any reserve minerals and only produce a tiny seedlet. For the seed to grow, the plant must co-habit with fungus.

Habitat Damp rough grassland, heathland moors, heaths. On wet or damp, mildewy soil rich in humus. Almost everywhere in Europe.

> flowers and shape very variable
> non-fragrant
> pollinators unrewarded with nectar

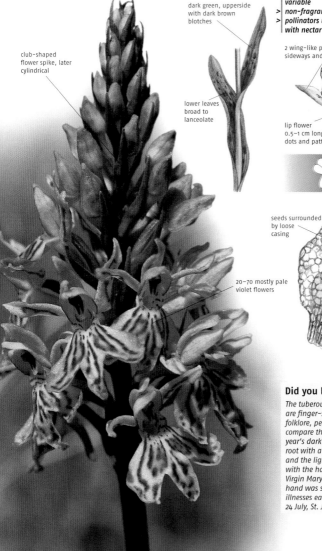

club-shaped flower spike, later cylindrical

dark green, upperside with dark brown blotches

lower leaves broad to lanceolate

2 wing-like petals, sideways and apart

lip flower 0.5–1 cm long, with dots and patterns

89

20–70 mostly pale violet flowers

seeds surrounded by loose casing

dust-fine seeds

Did you know?

The tuberous roots are finger-shaped. In folklore, people used to compare the previous year's dark tuberous root with a devil's hand and the light, new root with the hand of the Virgin Mary. The light hand was said to cure illnesses each year on 24 July, St. John's Day.

Garlic Mustard
Alliaria petiolata (cabbage family)
H 20–100 cm April–June annual

Habitat *Shady weedy patches at forest edges, hedgerows, in gardens, parks. From flat plains to low mountain ranges. Almost everywhere in Europe.*

> *shoots grow early in year*
> *attracted to nitrogen-rich places*
> *easily recognisable by aroma when crushed*

If you like garlic, you can crush or finely chop the tender young leaves of Garlic Mustard and use them for seasoning in yoghurt or quark dressings and salads. The taste and smell is similar to garlic and the leaves are also rich in Vitamins A and C. You can also freeze the leaves either chopped or whole. Dried leaves tend to lose their aroma.

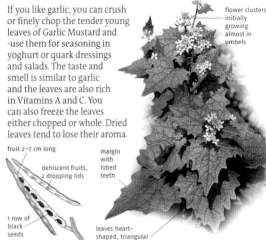

flower clusters initially growing almost in umbels

flower 0.6–1 cm across

4 petals of equal size

fruit 2–7 cm long

dehiscent fruits, 2 drooping lids

1 row of black seeds

margin with lobed teeth

leaves heart-shaped, triangular

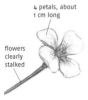

Sea-kale
Crambe maritima (cabbage family)
H 30–75 cm May–June perennial

Habitat *Sand dunes in coastal regions, rocky beaches, prefers nitrogen-rich locations. Sea coasts almost everywhere in Europe.*

> *unmistakably cabbage-like aroma*
> *fruits dispersed by the sea*
> *rarely growing wild and should not be picked if found*

Sea-kale can be used as a vegetable and is also cultivated for this purpose in England and France. The scientific name is derived from the Greek 'krambos', which means something like 'shrunken in' or 'shrivelled'. Perhaps, leaves of the Sea-kale were compared to other common cabbage varieties.

fruit with thick seed coat

round, 8–14 mm long fruits

smaller, narrower upper leaves

dense flower heads with abundant solitary flowers

waxy, blue-green and fleshy

4 petals, about 1 cm long

margin heavily notched

flowers clearly stalked

large basal leaves

Horseradish

Armoracia rusticana (cabbage family)

H 60–120 cm   May–July   perennial

Horseradish is native to south-eastern Europe, where it has been cultivated since ancient times and frequently grows in the wild. When grated, the roots are suitable for use as seasoning in salads, sauces and with meat – although the sharp taste is not to everyone's liking. The taste is finest when freshly grated. In medicine, the plant is used for its properties as a killer of bacteria as well as an antidote for cramps and the beneficial effect of its substances on the circulation.

Habitat Weedy patches, paths, scrubland, roadside verges, wasteland, river banks. On nutrient-rich soil. Almost everywhere in Europe.

> also known as 'Red Cole'
> roots with hot, spicy aroma and taste
> especially grows near villages

Did you know?

In the Middle Ages, Horseradish was among the only hot and spicy herbs, in addition to mustard, which people could afford. Pepper, on the other hand, was an expensive luxury product, because it was imported over land to Europe from India.

4 white petals

petals 5–9 mm in size

91

flowers in clusters

upper leaves smaller than basal leaves

lanceolate

bluntly toothed

leaves fairly thick, glossy

long-stalked leaves

wavy margins, bluntly toothed

thick, fleshy to woody roots

very large basal leaves

Watercress

Nasturtium officinale (cabbage family)
H 20–80 cm   May–Oct   perennial

Habitat *In streams, ditches and springs with clear, cool, flowing water. From the plains to high mountains, all over Europe.*

> can also live submerged in water
> anthers always yellow
> hollow stems, can be compressed

4 inverted, oval petals

initially white, later also pale purple

yellow anthers

92

Watercress contains mustard oils and Vitamins A and C as well as significant quantities of minerals. It makes savoury, slightly peppery and very healthy salad or vegetables. However, take care thoroughly to clean the cress, as water snails and other aquatic animals are often hidden away in the foliage. Watercress has been cultivated in Europe since the Middle Ages. In Thuringia in eastern Germany, from the 16th century, the plant was especially cultivated in Watercress beds (cress gardens), so that it could be harvested in the winter months when vitamins were scarce.

spreading flower clusters

spike-shaped fruits

leaf pinnate with single terminal leaf

1–5 pairs of pinnate leaflets

larger terminal leaves

sparse leaves, slightly fleshy

square-edged stem

Did you know?

Large Bitter-cress is easy to confuse with Watercress, but it has violet anthers and its stems are not hollow. People used to harvest this plant, although unlike Watercress it has a very bitter taste and is not as appetising.

Common Whitlowgrass
Erophila verna (cabbage family)
H 3–15 cm   March–May   annual

The plant colonises soils with poor nutrient values, where cultivars do not fully develop. Common Whitlowgrass is therefore a sign of poor yielding soil. A common belief used to be that an abundance of flowering Common Whitlowgrass was a sign of a bad harvest.

white memb-
rane remaining
intact on
opened fruit

numerous
seeds

5–12 mm long
fruits

leafless
stem

lanceolate
leaves forming
a basal rosette

young fruits
frequently
with remnants
of petals

Habitat *Arable fields, pathways, walls, railway platforms, flat roofs, sparse rough pasture, sandy grassland, pebble and wasteland. Found throughout Europe.*

> **short-living plant**
> **leaves wither even before fruit ripens**
> **very variable in size**

divided about up
to the middle

2–5 mm long petals

93

Shepherd's-purse
Capsella bursa-pastoris (cabbage family)
H 2–70 cm   Jan–Dec   annual or biennial

Shepherd's-purse gained its name from the similarity of its heart-shaped fruits with the shoulder bags of shepherds in mediaeval times. In China, the herbaceous plant is also used as a vegetable. In Europe, it is used as a medicinal plant to treat an irregular menstrual cycle and nose bleeds.

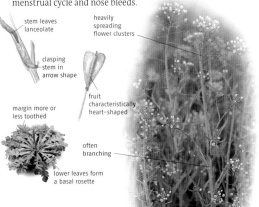

stem leaves
lanceolate

clasping
stem in
arrow shape

margin more or
less toothed

heavily
spreading
flower clusters

fruit
characteristically
heart-shaped

often
branching

lower leaves form
a basal rosette

Habitat *Weedy patches on arable fields, rocky places, wasteland, in gardens, on pathways. From plains to the high mountains. Throughout Europe.*

> **attracted to nitrogen**
> **requires lots of light**
> **also flowers and bears fruit in the snow**

4 white petals,
about 3 mm long

4 upright
sepals

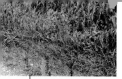

Field Penny-cress

Thlaspi arvense (cabbage family)
H 10–50 cm   April–Aug   annual

Habitat Weedy
patches on arable
fields, vineyards, on
scrubland, wasteland.
On nutrient-rich soil,
throughout Europe.

> faint aroma of onion
  when crushed
> easily recognisable by
  typical fruits
> very common

The Field Penny-cress derives its name from its coin-shaped
fruits. Their broad margin is carried by the wind, breaking open
the ripe fruits and ensuring that the seeds are scattered far
and wide. The seeds were once pressed
for fuel and cooking oil, while the
radish or mustard-tasting leaves
were used to season salads and
soups.

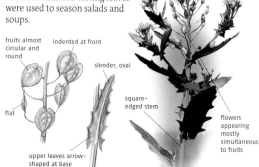

flowers in
clusters

fruits almost
circular and
round

indented at front

slender, oval

square-
edged stem

flat

flowers
appearing
mostly
simultaneous
to fruits

upper leaves arrow-
shaped at base

slightly rounded at front or
slightly notched

4 white
petals,
3–4 mm
long

94

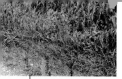

Flax-leaved Daphne

Daphne gnidium (mezereon family)
H 50–200 cm   June–Oct   perennial   ☠

Habitat Dry woodlands
near coasts, forests,
Mediterranean region.

> frequently flowering
  simultaneously and
  bearing fruits
> leaves survive for a full
  year
> not to be plucked, as
  the juice can be a skin
  irritant!

Daphne, the scientific name, translates as 'bay tree'. This reference
alludes to the fact that some species of the plant have evergreen
foliage, similar to the bay tree. In Greek mythology, Daphne was a
tree nymph, with whom Apollo fell in love, so
Zeus transformed the nymph into a shrub.

flower clusters
overtopping
twigs

leaves arranged
in spirals

leaf 2–5 cm
long, bare,
leathery

blue-green
underside

shiny red
berry fruits

corolla with 4 points

hairy

Caper

Capparis spinosa (caper family)
H 30–150 cm   April–Oct   perennial

Capers were known in antiquity as an effective substance against sciatica and cramps as well as a spice. Both the closed flower buds as well as the caper fruits can be marinated and preserved in salt, vinegar or oil. They each have a piquant, slightly peculiar aroma. When marinated, the fruits – also known as caper berries – taste more intense. Capers are used in all kinds of Mediterranean dishes.

Habitat *Cliffs, walls, wasteland, fallow arable land, roadside verges, Mediterranean region.*

> **especially cultivated in France and Spain**
> **flowers only opened for a few hours**
> **slightly climbing plant**

with a clear point

leaves alternate

leaf broad, elliptical

ovary long, stalked

profusion of stamens

flowers 4–5 cm across

95

fleshy fruit capsule

stalked flowers in leaf axils

Did you know?

The short-lived flowers even play a role in the Bible. In the Book of Proverbs, Solomon describes a growing Caper bush as an image of the ephemeral and of growing old.

Enchanter's-nightshade
Circaea lutetiana (willowherb family)
H 20–70 cm   June–Aug   perennial

Habitat *Forests, woodland paths, copses, wetland meadows. On damp soil. Almost everywhere in Europe.*

> *attracted to nutrient-rich soil*
> *also flowers in the shade*
> *flowers especially attract hoverflies*

Enchanter's-nightshade has club-shaped fruits. Their small hooks mean that they easily cling to animals and also people's clothing, so they may be dispersed over long distances. Perhaps the rather uncanny way in which the fruits attach themselves to garments without being noticed explains the name 'Enchanter's-nightshade', or at least the scientific genus of *Circaea*. In Greek mythology, Circe was an enchantress or witch.

flowers in a loose cluster

fruits 3–4 mm long

dense, with hook-like bristles

hairy

leaves opposite

2 petals, 2–4 mm long

deep, 2-part

96

Dwarf Cornel
Cornus suecica (dogwood family)
H 5–25 cm   May   perennial

Habitat *Moors, heaths with low shrubs. On peaty soil. In north Europe, north Germany*

> *leaves coloured red in autumn*
> *underground, creeping rhizome*
> *needs cool summers*

Of the few habitats where the Dwarf Cornel is still found today in central Europe, most are considered to have been formed in the Ice Age. During the last Ice Age, the plant was widely dispersed. Closely related to this attractive perennial are plants that grow in shrub or tree form.

leaves oval to longish

no leaf stalk

arching leaf veins

fruit clusters at end of stems

4 white or cream-coloured leaves with petal-like appearance

actual flowers tiny, brownish

Hoary Plantain
Plantago media (plantain family)
H 10–45 cm   May–Sept   perennial

Plantago is derived from the Latin 'planta', which means sole of the foot. With leaves pressed close to the ground, the foliage is slightly reminiscent of footprints and the plant also tolerates being trampled upon. If the leaves or leaf stalks are torn apart, thin threads remain standing. These are vascular bundles that are responsible for the transport of water or other chemicals. In this plant, they are easy to pull off.

Habitat Semi-dry grasslands, rough meadows, pastures, grassland areas, pathways, roadside verges. Mostly in sunny locations. Almost all over Europe.

> **mostly in well-trodden places**
> **flowers pleasantly fragrant**
> **nuisance on mown lawns, where grass dies beneath the rosette**

5–9 longitudinal veins

very short leaf stalk

leaves forming a basal rosette

purple filaments, long and protruding

4 white petal tips

flowers about 4 mm long

97

spike lengthens during flowering season

leafless stems

flowers in a dense spike

Did you know?
The seeds of all plantain varieties become sticky when wet and then cling particularly well to the soles of shoes. This is how the Greater Plantain arrived in North America. The Indians called the plant 'white man's footstep', as it grew everywhere that white men reached.

Woodruff

Galium odoratum (bedstraw family)
H 15–30 cm   May–June   perennial   (image)

Habitat *Deciduous and mixed forests with good herbaceous undergrowth. In shady locations. Almost everywhere in Europe.*

> one of the frequent, conspicuous broadleaved forest plants
> ideal low spreading plant
> also suitable for use in fragrance pillows

The typical aroma of Woodruff only develops when the plant is picked, about to wither or to be dried. During this process, the aromatic substance courmarin (similar to vanilla flavouring) is created. Plants that are just about to flower are especially aromatic. Woodruff can be consumed in liquid form, for instance, in summer punch, but in too large quantities, it can cause headaches and light-headedness.

branched flower heads protruding above upper leaves

upright stem, unbranched

leaves in whorls of 6–9

trumpet-shaped corolla

4 pointed tips

lanceolate, 2–4 cm long

coarse at margin

fruits out of 2 spherical half-nutlets

covered in hook-like bristles

98

Hedge Bedstraw

Galium mollugo (bedstraw family)
H 25–100 cm   May–Sept   perennial

Habitat *Meadows, forest edges and copses, wayside groves. Mostly on nutrient-rich soil. All over Europe.*

> species with many varieties
> conspicuous due to abundant flowers
> gains support from other plants

In some areas, Hedge Bedstraw was also once known as 'Wild Madder'. The roots contain a red dye substance. Pre-treating wool with Alum salt together with this dye can turn the wool a shade of red, so that the colour is also non-fading. Bedstraw roots were once also used to colour Easter eggs.

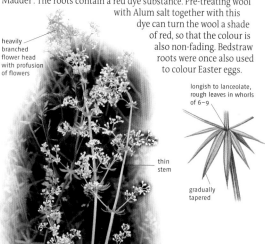

heavily branched flower head with profusion of flowers

longish to lanceolate, rough leaves in whorls of 6–9

corolla with 4 flat, beard-like pointed tips

thin stem

flower 3–5 mm in size

gradually tapered

Cleavers

Galium aparine (bedstraw family)
H 60–200 cm   June–Oct   annual

The plant's thin stems are too weak to grow upright without support. However, they stick almost everywhere due to specially formed hairs. This is how they easily climb up other plants and low vegetation or grow in profusion over fences in order to reach the light. Animals and people may tear off parts and unwittingly carry them away, thus assisting new plants to establish in other locations.

Habitat Weedy patches at edges of hedges, forest margins, riverbanks, arable fields and scrub, also in villages or towns. Everywhere in Europe.

> attracted to nitrogen-rich locations
> fruits and entire shoots 'cleave' to garments
> also popularly known as 'Goosegrass'

entire plant covered in bristles

fruits consisting of 2 half-nutlets

flowers about 2 mm in size

petal white or greenish, with 4 flat, pointed tips

99

stems with backward-curving bristles

inconspicuous flowers

leaves in whorls of 6–8

margin and leaf vein with backward-directed hispid or stiff hairs

Did you know?

Almost everyone has accidentally transported the fruits back home with them on socks or shoelaces or picked them out of their dog's coat en route. The fruits' tiny backward-directed hooks provide an efficient means of transport for this inconspicuous plant.

Water Plantain

Alisma plantago-aquatica (water plantain family)

H 30–100 cm   July–Aug   perennial   (🐝)

Habitat *Flat, flooded lakesides, ponds, slow-moving stretches of water, ditches, in among reeds and rushes. Throughout Europe.*

> plant mostly protruding out of water
> also suitable for garden ponds
> flowering stems without leaves

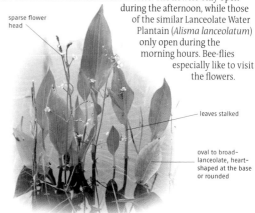

sparse flower head

The plant and, in particular, its burning and tangy-sharp juice are skin irritants that can cause blisters. The flowers only open during the afternoon, while those of the similar Lanceolate Water Plantain (*Alisma lanceolatum*) only open during the morning hours. Bee-flies especially like to visit the flowers.

leaves stalked

oval to broad-lanceolate, heart-shaped at the base or rounded

flowers about 1 cm in size

3 white to light pink petals, slightly toothed

3 green sepals

100

Frogbit

Hydrocharis morsus-ranae (frogbit family)

H 15–30 cm   June–Aug   perennial

Habitat *Mostly floating between plants in stagnant or gently flowing freshwater and lakes. Throughout Europe.*

> requires sufficient heat in summertime
> needs water with nutrients
> leaves slightly reminiscent of a small Water-lily

The notches in the leaves at the base look as though something has taken a bite out of them. As frogs often like to collect insects from among the plants, people once believed that frogs were eating them, so the plant was named 'Frogbit'. At the most, however, frogs will only catch small insects resting on the leaves.

heart-shaped, 1.5–6 cm in size

flowers protruding above water

leaf with long stalk

leaves float on water's surface

3 white, roundish petals

flower 1–1.5 cm in size

Water Soldier

Stratiotes aloides (frogbit family)

H 15–45 cm   May–Aug   perennial

Beneath the flowers, the leaves resemble the claws of a crab and the plant is also known as 'Crab's Claw'. Another name is 'Water Aloe', which refers to the similarity of this plant with Aloe species that are partially used as a medicinal plant. Stratiotes means 'sword-bearer' and the name is derived from the shape of the leaves. In late autumn, the plants sink to the bed of the river or lake, where they overwinter.

Habitat *In mostly stagnant, nutrient-rich water of craggy tarns and backwaters in protected baylets and bank sides. Almost everywhere in Europe.*

> can form mass colonies
> also known as 'Water Aloe'
> both male and female plants

2 toothed, rough leaves beneath the flowers

leaf fleshy, triangular in cross-section

3 roundish petals

flowers about 2 cm in size

101

lanceolate or sword-shaped leaves, 10–40 cm long

sharply toothed margin

semi-submerged leaf rosette

Did you know?

The Green Hawker dragonfly only lays its eggs on this plant and depends on finding a sufficiently large Water Soldier colony.

Bog Arum
Calla palustris (lords-and-ladies family)
H 15–30 cm   May–Sept   perennial

Habitat Banks of ponds, forest pools, meres, moors. Preferably in shady locations. In north and central Europe.

> also planted out in ponds
> often grows in dense groups
> flowers with an unpleasant aroma, attract carrion flies and small beetles

Calla is a derivation of the Greek 'kallos', meaning beauty, and refers to the conspicuous, white tall leaf, which sits directly beneath the flower spike. The snaking rhizome is rich in starch and the plant used to be fed to pigs. In Russia, the starch was used in flour and also to make bread dough. The plant contains sharp, burning substances that are skin irritants and can cause severe rashes.

flower spikes, about 2 cm long with tiny flowers

leaf-like tall hood, white inside

scarlet red berries, approximately 5 mm in size

in abundance and tightly packed

102

leaves rounded, 4–10 cm in size

Did you know?
The florist trade offers cultivars called 'Calla' lilies, which are cultivated from related African varieties of the Bog Arum. These also grow in the wild in southern Europe on the Canary Islands and on Madeira.

Arrowhead

Sagittaria sagittifolia (water plantain family)
H 30–100 cm   June–Aug   perennial

The plant overwinters with bulbs that emerge in autumn. These are very nutritious and have a nutty flavour when cooked. In China, Arrowhead is cultivated for food and the plant used to be cultivated in Europe. In traditional medicine, the bulbous roots used to be regarded as suitable for treating wounds. They were also reputed to be an effective antidote against fear of water.

flowers above each other, in whorls of 3

Habitat Mostly in slowly flowing, nutrient-rich rivers and ditches and edges of ponds. Almost everywhere in Europe.

> swamp and aquatic plant
> can also survive submerged
> named after the leaf shape

leaves noticeably arrow-shaped

walnut-sized bulbs in mud

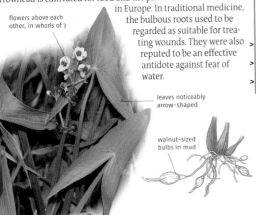

flowers 1.5–2.5 cm in size

3 white petals, tinged red at base

 103

May Lily

Maianthemum bifolium (lily family)
H 5–20 cm   May–June   perennial 🕱

The sweet-tasting berries are poisonous to humans. However, birds can eat them without difficulties and ensure dispersal of the seeds. The plant only establishes itself in low, shady positions, although in the mountains, the May Lily is more tolerant of light and also grows on pastures. Only the flowering plant has two leaves, as non-flowering stems only form one leaf.

glossy yellow to red, often dotted berry fruits

1–5 cm long flower cluster

heart-shaped leaves

veins running in curve-like form

flowering plants, mostly with 2 leaves

Habitat Broadleaved and coniferous forests with poor species variety, moors, mountain meadows. In shady locations. Especially in central and north Europe.

> tiny flowers, yet with a pleasant fragrance
> characteristic leaf shape
> non-flowering plants only with 1 leaf

4 white backwards-curved petals, 2–3 mm long

Aconite-leaved Buttercup
Ranunculus aconitifolius (buttercup family)
H 20–50 cm   May–July   perennial

Habitat Banks of streams, springs, well-manured and damp pastures, open and damp forests. In mountain regions, up to altitudes of over 2,000 m. Mountains in central and south Europe.

> mostly on silica soil (sand, weathered granite)
> the similar Large White Buttercup grows on chalky soil

Grazing cattle avoid the Aconite-leaved Buttercup, but the plant flourishes if the ground is fertilised with cow dung. It therefore spreads prolifically in locations that are well covered with manure, often forming large groups near mountain huts on upland pastures. Flies that are attracted to the white flowers find a source of sweet nectar at the base of the petals.

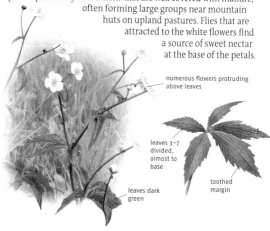

numerous flowers protruding above leaves

leaves 3–7 divided, almost to base

toothed margin

leaves dark green

flowers 1–2.5 cm in size

5 white petals

104

River Water-crowfoot
Ranunculus fluitans (buttercup family)
H 50–600 cm   June–Aug   perennial

Habitat In streams and rivers with gentle to rapid currents and oxygen-rich water. Especially in central Europe.

> creates magical white carpets of flowers in rivers
> requires cool water
> leaves only submerged

The sprawling areas of River Water-crowfoot are appreciated by fish and used as spawning places. The plant's finely divided, drooping leaves are ideally adapted to flowing water. The leaves only offer light resistance to the current, so that instead of being damaged, they are gently washed about while afloat. At the same time, the plant absorbs nutrient salts and gases from the water's surface.

solitary flowers protruding from water

stems and leaves flowing in water

leaves 10–30 cm long

white petals, yellow at base

flowers up to 3 cm in size

long tip, drooping, thread-like

Christmas Rose

Helleborus niger (buttercup family)

H 5–25 cm   Dec–March   perennial   ☠

The black-brown roots used to be dried, ground into powder and employed in the production of snuff. The roots were also thought to help with mental illness and melancholy as well as act as a diuretic. However, in the 16th and 17th century, herbalists knew about the plant's poisonous nature and advised its use only with extreme caution. The plant was later utilised as medicine for heart complaints and as a uretic. Nowadays, due to the risk of poisoning, the plant is hardly ever used.

Did you know?

In the year 600 B.C., a variety of the hellebore played a crucial role in the siege of the Greek city of Kirrha. Solon, the besieger, ordered the roots of the plant to be scattered in the river supplying the city with drinking water. The city's occupants suffered from severe diarrhoea and were thus unable to fight.

Habitat *Deciduous forests, pine forests, copses. On chalky soils. Often used as decorative plants in gardens. Found in the Alps, mountains and in southeastern Europe.*

> also known as 'Black Hellebore'
> also similar species and crosses in gardens
> petals or sepals remain on plant after flowering

flowers 5–10 cm in size

numerous stamens

overlapping petals

leaves divided, pedate

leathery, green throughout the winter

1–2 flowers per stem

105

American Pokeweed

Phytolacca americana (pokeweed family)
H 100–350 cm   July–Oct   herbaceous perennial or shrub

Habitat Wasteland, previously cultivated areas. In nutrient-rich, warm, light locations. Around the Mediterranean.

> originates from America
> occasionally a garden plant in central Europe
> fresh berries have a laxative effect

The black-red fruits contain an intensive red, harmless colouring substance, which quickly turns pale when exposed to light. It was once used especially to colour red wines that were considered too light, which is why the plant was especially cultivated in the wine-growing regions. Early on, however, this deceptive practice was frowned upon. The French Sun King, Louis XIV, is even reputed to have decreed the death penalty as punishment for the practice.

flowers with 10 stamens

conspicuous ovary

petals about 2.5 cm in size

106

leaves mostly 10–20 cm long

smooth margin

stems often tinged red

fruits in hanging clusters

shiny black ripe fruits

Did you know?

In recent years, a pokeweed species has become important in Africa, as the plant is an antidote and cheap way of treating bilharzia, a dangerous tropical disease that freshwater snails pass on to humans. When scattered in the water, pokeweed berries kill the snails.

Glacier Mouse-ear Chickweed

Cerastium uniflorum (pink family)
H 2–6 cm   July–Aug   perennial

Chickweed varieties have horn-shaped, curving fruit capsules. Of all the species that occur in Europe, the Glacier Mouse-ear Chickweed is found highest up in the mountains – the plant grows up to altitudes of about 3,500 m.

Habitat Cliff debris, silica deposits. Mostly above the tree line. Found in mountains from the Alps to the Carpathians.

> grows above rubble and anchors the stone
> attracts insects
> cushions noticeable from a long distance

forms dense lawns

leaves oval

1 flower on each stem

densely haired

petals 10–16 mm long

petals divided to the middle, almost split in 2 segments

107

Greater Stichwort

Stellaria holostea (pink family)
H 15–30 cm   April–May   perennial

The stiff leaves, which often curve backwards, find support amongst each other or from other plants, so the Greater Stichwort can grow quite tall, despite the very slender stems. This attractive, spring-flowering plant with abundant white flowers is also suitable for growing on margins of copses in perennial wild flower gardens.

Habitat Sparse forests with a rich store of herbaceous plants on the forest floor, hedgerows, forest edges, woodland paths. Almost everywhere in Europe.

> often grows in larger groups
> requires sufficient light
> fragile stems

forked, branching

elongated tip

slender to lanceolate

leaves opposite

sparse flower heads

divided into 2 segments, up to about the middle

petals concealing sepals

Common Chickweed
Stellaria media (pink family)
H 3–40 cm   Jan–Dec   annual

Habitat *Weedy patches in gardens, on arable fields, wasteland, on pathways, riverbanks, in flowerpots. All over Europe.*

> - **weed occurring world-wide**
> - **attracted to nitrogen-rich locations**
> - **good green fodder for caged birds**

Each flower produces a fruit, even if the plant is not visited by insects. Ideally, a plant can therefore produce up to 15,000 seeds. If the plants are uprooted, their seeds even ripen on the compost heap. However, this species is not merely a weed, but may also be used as vegetables or in salads and is also a preferred source of food for birds.

flowers in leaf axils

deeply divided into 2

sepals about 3 mm long

oval leaves

petals at least as long as sepal

stem with hairs downwards along one side

creeping or climbing upwards stems

108

Bladder Campion
Silene vulgaris (pink family)
H 15–50 cm   May–Sept   perennial

Habitat *Stony waste ground, quarries, wayside verges, embankments, station gravel, arid pastures. Everywhere in Europe.*

> - **also known as 'Maiden's Tears'**
> - **pioneer plant**
> - **flowers mostly pointing in one direction**

This species is named after the striking and unusual sepal, which remains on the plant even after flowering. The wind can then take hold of the plant, shaking the seeds from the capsules.

Wild vegetables can be prepared from the leaves and young shoots.

stalked flowers forming a loose flower head

longish, pointed to a tip

sepal heavily swollen

highly visible veins

petals divided into 2 sections

leaves opposite

Japanese Knotweed

Fallopia japonica (knotweed family)

H 100–200 cm   July–Sept   perennial

Japanese Knotweed was first introduced in European parks around 1825 as a decorative leafy plant. In 1847, the plant was even awarded a gold medal in the Netherlands as an 'interesting new plant'. It was also cultivated as cattle fodder and to anchor sloping ground. However, the species was soon found growing in the wild and became a nuisance weed. It grows very rapidly and scarcely tolerates any other plants nearby. In this way, it can eliminate native plants covering large areas from the banks of rivers and streams.

Habitat Planted, growing wild or established on riverbanks and riverside forests. On wet, nutrient-rich soil. Almost everywhere in Europe.

> originates from east Asia
> can form sprawling, dense groups
> suppresses native plants

Did you know?

Fragments of roots can easily be washed away in winter, thus ensuring the plant's dispersal. In winter, only the roots of this perennial survive and therefore riverbanks populated by the Japanese Knotweed are extremely susceptible to erosion.

5 greenish, white petals

stalked flower

often arranged in 2 rows

5–13 cm long

flowers in 3–10 cm long spikes

broad, oval

leaves alternate

109

conspicuous spikes with winged fruits or samaras

Round-leaved Sundew

Drosera rotundifolia (sundew family)
H 5–20 cm   July–Aug   perennial

Habitat *Upland moors, acidic low moorlands, damp heathland. On wet soil with very poor nutrients, chalk-free and acidic peat. Found almost throughout Europe.*

> **threatened by the destruction of moorlands**
> **insect-catching plant**
> **sticky leaves**

Numerous droplets on the tentacles glisten like the morning dew and presumably inspired the beautiful name. In fact, the droplets are a sticky mucus that contains digestive enzymes. If a small insect lands on the leaves, it will become attached to the plant. The animals' movements alert the tentacles, which close over the insect after one or two minutes.
The prey is digested by secreted enzymes and absorbed by the tentacles. This is how the plant gains a rich store of life-giving nitrogen.

upper side with long, reddish hairs, with glands at tips (tentacles)

roundish leaf blade

leaf stalk 1–3 cm long

5 individual petals

5 sepals

Did you know?

The English Sundew or Great Sundew is much more rare and has upright standing, longer leaves. The eye-catching varieties that are available in florists' originate from Africa or Asia.

leaves form a basal rosette

prostrate

One-flowered Wintergreen

Moneses uniflora (wintergreen family)
H 5–10 cm   May–July   perennial   (☠)

In the Tyrol, the One-flowered Wintergreen is also popularly known as 'Gschamigs Maderle' or 'Bashful Maid' because of the flower that is slightly drooping towards the ground. If this species is also found elsewhere – apart from the mountainous region in the Tyrol – it is probably due to increased cultivation of fir and spruce forests.

nodding flower

always only 1 terminal flower per stem

round blade, up to 2 cm in size

margin finely serrated

Habitat Coniferous forests. In the shade on mossy soil. Especially in north Europe and the mountains of central Europe.

> **dependent on coniferous population**
> **mostly found growing in sparse groups**
> **evergreen leaves**

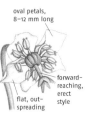

oval petals, 8–12 mm long

flat, out-spreading

forward-reaching, erect style

111

White Stonecrop

Sedum album (stonecrop family)
H 8–20 cm   June–Sept   perennial

The White Stonecrop is well adapted to its plant locations. Its fleshy leaves store water and are covered in a thick wax coating in order to prevent water evaporating from them. If they break off or segments of the shoots are trodden upon, they can easily take root and grow into new plants.

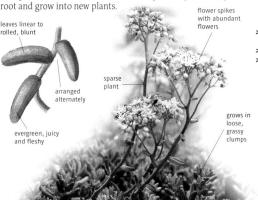

leaves linear to rolled, blunt

arranged alternately

sparse plant

evergreen, juicy and fleshy

flower spikes with abundant flowers

grows in loose, grassy clumps

Habitat Pioneer on cliffs, walls, gravel roofs, dry grassland, stony wasteland. Almost everywhere in Europe.

> **requires plenty of sunshine**
> **low-maintenance plant**
> **previously known as 'Small Houseleek'**

reddish anther

petals more conspicuous than sepals

Meadow Saxifrage
Saxifraga granulata (saxifrage family)
H 15–30 cm   May–June   perennial

leaves lobed, toothed

Habitat *Meadows, rough grassland, grassy banks, gravel roofs. On soil with low lime content. Almost everywhere in Europe.*

> *a saxifrage that mostly does not grow on stony places*
> *leaves also green in winter*
> *also known as 'Bulbous Saxifrage'*

In the Middle Ages, people believed that the brown bulbs that look similar to small stones were a sign that the plant could help to 'break the stone' causing discomfort to patients suffering from gallstone and kidney stone complaints. Another interpretation of the name is that it is derived from the plant's preferred location seen growing in rock crevices.

flowers in racemes

petals, 10–17 mm long

slender, reversed, oval

base of plant with roundish reproductive bulbs

long stems

112

Livelong Saxifrage
Saxifraga paniculata (saxifrage family)
H 10–40 cm   May–July   perennial

Habitat *Cliff crevices, cliff heads and cliff grassland in the mountains of Europe. On dry, mostly chalky rocky soil.*

> *often forming large groups*
> *grows in the sun or semi-shade*
> *evergreen leaf rosettes*

Tiny dimples are set between the leaf tooths and actively emit water. As Livelong Saxifrage grows on chalky soil, this water is high in limestone content that it has to deposit somewhere. After the water has evaporated, the chalky deposit is left just as it remains on household taps. This deposit forms as small scales, which will be washed away again by the next rain shower.

loose flower racemes

leaves 1–3 cm long, blue-green, leathery

basal leaves arranged in a rosette

margin finely toothed

several rosettes together forming flat cushions

flowers 0.8–1.5 cm in size

white petals, often with red spots

Grass of Parnassus

Parnassia palustris (saxifrage family)

H 10–25 cm   July–Sept   perennial

The yellowish heads within the flower gleam as though they were damp with nectar and could provide insects with sugar-rich juice. In reality, however, they are dry. The cup-like flowers not only look attractive to flies due to their promised food supply, but the sun's rays are also trapped within the flower and, with a similar intensity, the light is reflected as though caught in a parabolic mirror. As a result, a super-heated resting place is created.

Habitat *Low-lying moorlands, marshy moors, moorland meadows, wet rough grassland and rough slopes. Up to altitudes of over 2,500 m. Found almost everywhere in Europe, in the south, only in the mountains.*

> **flowers often protruding above surrounding plants**
> **mostly growing in groups**
> **requires damp conditions**

flower 1–3.5 cm in size

5 stamens

petals white with darker, inset veins

113

solitary flowers on long stem

a branching formation in front of each petal with gleaming flower head

heart-shaped leaves

long leaf stalk

Did you know?

In some areas of Germany, the plant is popularly called 'Students' Rose', probably because it flowers when the long summer holidays end and students return to their studies.

White Bryony
Bryonia dioica (bryony family)

H 200–400 cm   June–Sept   perennial, climbing plant

Habitat Hedges, fences, scrubland, country paths. On nutrient-rich soil in warmer locations. Found in central and south Europe.

> plants can be male or female
> roots have unpleasant odour
> a confusion species is Black Bryony, also with red fruits

White Bryony contains substances that severely irritate the skin and mucous membranes. Symptoms of poisoning are dizziness, vomiting, colic, diarrhoea, kidney damage and cramps. The roots were once used as a quite dangerous laxative. The plant is also said to help prevent fever, gout and strokes. A cutting from the root is said to extract splinters and thorns from wounds, in preference to applying sticking plasters.

Did you know?
In the Middle Ages, racketeers and charlatans carved the roots, which are often strangely shaped, into human-like figures and sold them as valuable, lucky charms made from mandrake roots (p. 165). But this trick was practised on pain of death.

climbing stems with tendrils

brush-like hairs

5 yellowish-white petal tips with green veins

male flowers up to 1.8 cm size

114

female flowers smaller than 1.8 cm, greenish

thickened ovary

red, 5–8 mm berries

leaves lobed with five points

Buck's-beard

Aruncus dioicus (rose family)
H 80–150 cm   June–July   perennial

You can use the young shoots as a vegetable. Buck's-beard seeds are extremely light and therefore even the slightest breath of breeze can carry them away from the plant's natural habitat, which is often in sheltered places. The species is suitable as a decorative plant for more shady and woody gardens and in cut flower sprays.

up to 50 cm long flower racemes

oval partial leaflet

leaves up to 1 m long, pinnately compound in 2s and 3s

Habitat *Woodland ravines, shady, damp mountain woodlands, especially in valleys with streams. From the plains to mountainous regions – found in the mountains of central Europe.*

> *male and female plants*
> *ornamental plant in gardens and parks*
> *in Germany, a protected wild plant*

male flowers with 20–30 stamens

flowers 2–4 mm in size

115

Wild Strawberry

Fragaria vesca (rose family)
H 5–20 cm   May–June   perennial

Wild Strawberries have a much more intense flavour than cultivated strawberries. You can easily identify their taste in mixed berry or forest fruits jam. The plants available for gardens are cultivated from this wild species and produce strawberries every month over a longer period.

flowers on long stalks

fleshy, red fruit

leaves in 3s

hairy stem

margin coarsely serrated

Habitat *Spinneys, open woods, woodland paths, forest edges, slopes as far as high mountains. Found throughout Europe.*

> *often covers large areas*
> *attracted to nitrogen-rich soil*
> *sugar content of fruits up to 10 per cent*

5 white, roundish or oval petals

Meadowsweet
Filipendula ulmaria (rose family)
H 50–150 cm   June–Aug   perennial

Habitat *Ditch edges, wetland pastures, dykes, streams, springs, riverside copses, riverside meadows and woodlands. Everywhere in Europe.*

> *flowers with a strong almond-like fragrance*
> *suitable for fragrant flower bouquets*
> *often growing in large groups*

Meadowsweet was once used to sweeten honey wine. The flowers soothe fevers due to colds and similar complaints. During the first half of the 19th century, salicin – a substance that acts as an antidote for colds – was extracted from the plants. Nowadays, the salicin acid that is derived from this process and similar artificial substances created in the laboratory are amongst the most important medicines offering pain relief as well as soothing inflammations and the fever.

fruits winding in spirals

Did you know?
The commercial name for 'aspirin', widely used for pain relief, is derived from Spiraea ulmaria, *the old scientific name for Meadowsweet.*

numerous long stamens

yellowish-white petals, 2–5 mm long

abundant flowers

flower head with characteristic elongated side twigs

leaves pinnate, with single terminal leaf

5–11 pinnate pairs

very small partial leaflets inbetween

leaf pairs 2–8 cm long

Wood-sorrel

Oxalis acetosella (wood-sorrel family)

H 5–12 cm   April–May   perennial   (☻)

The acidic taste of all sorrel species is due to oxalic acid (the old name for the acid derived from sorrel) and its potassium salts (sorrel salts). If taken in large quantities, these substances can upset the stomach and even aggravate kidney stones. Sorrel salts used to be used as a bleaching agent and to remove stains caused by blood and rust spots. Wood-sorrel can still grow in locations that only have 1 per cent daylight, so that you can usually find the plant growing in the darkest part of the forest and at cave entrances.

Habitat Forests. On fresh to damp, mildewy soil. In the mountains up to altitudes of over 2,000 m. Throughout Europe, only in the mountains in the south.

> a shade-loving, flowering plant
> often forms large groups
> sour-tasting

Did you know?

The 3 partial leaves are connected to the leaf stalk by limbs and undergo different movements. At night and in the sunshine, they droop downwards in a 'sleeping position', whereas in diffused light they stay in a horizontal position.

5 petals, mostly with violet veins

5 green sepals

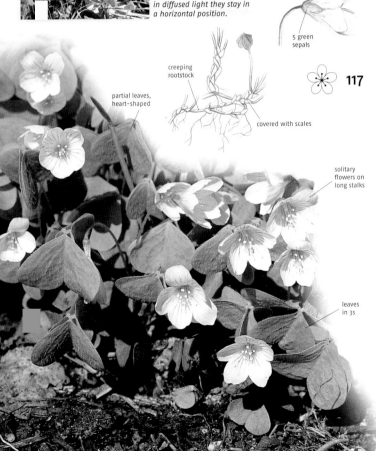

partial leaves, heart-shaped

creeping rootstock

covered with scales

117

solitary flowers on long stalks

leaves in 3s

Astrantia

Astrantia major (carrot family)
H 30–90 cm   June–Aug   perennial

Habitat Copses, mountain meadows, riverside and woodland ravines, forest margins. Mountains in central and south Europe, in the Alps up to altitudes of over 2,000 m.

> requires cool, damp climate
> grows solitary or in loose clusters
> also as a self-standing ornamental plant

The star-shaped flower head is typical for the Astrantia. The scientific name is derived from the Latin word 'aster', meaning star. For shady, damp gardens, there are also varieties with even more attractive umbels and striking foliage.

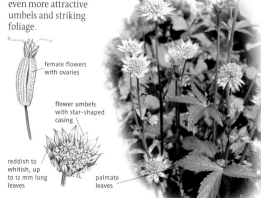

female flowers with ovaries

flower umbels with star-shaped casing

male flowers tiny, white or reddish

reddish to whitish, up to 12 mm long leaves

palmate leaves

Cow Parsley

Anthriscus sylvestris (carrot family)
H 60–150 cm   May–Aug   perennial

Habitat Fertilised meadows, wayside verges, grassy glades. From lowland plains to high mountains. Throughout Europe.

> attracted to fertilised soil
> flowering before similar species with white umbellules
> attracts plenty of insects

In spring, Cow Parsley often transforms heavily manured meadows, along with the Meadow Buttercup (p. 218), into white-yellow oceans of flowers. In contrast to Garden Chervil, the plant has quite an unpleasant odour when crushed and is not suitable as a herb. If combined with sunlight, the juice can cause skin reactions that resemble sunburn.

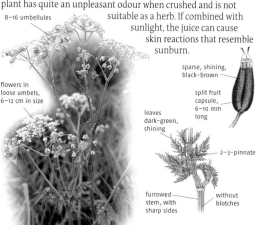

8–16 umbellules

flowers in loose umbels, 6–12 cm in size

sparse, shining, black-brown

split fruit capsule, 6–10 mm long

leaves dark-green, shining

2–3-pinnate

flowers about 4 mm in size

sparse petals

furrowed stem, with sharp sides

without blotches

Hemlock

Conium maculatum (carrot family)

H 80–180 cm   June–Sept   biennial   ☠

Cases of poisoning with this plant, which has an odour a little like mouse urine, cause a burning sensation in the mouth, distorted vision and paralysis. Death occurs through paralysis of the respiratory system, mostly when the victim is still conscious. In antiquity, those condemned to death were given a chalice filled with Hemlock. The most famous victim of this death sentence was the Greek philosopher, Socrates.

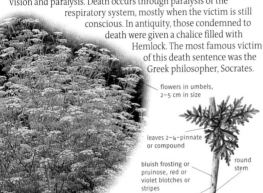

Habitat *Weedy places in ditches, scrub, wayside verges in rural villages. In warm locations in summer. Almost everywhere in Europe.*

> often grows in groups
> attracted to nitrogen-rich soil
> characteristic blotches on stem

flowers in umbels, 2–5 cm in size

leaves 2–4-pinnate or compound

bluish frosting or pruinose, red or violet blotches or stripes

round stem

sparse plant

flowers about 3 mm in size

5 white petals

119

Caraway

Carum carvi (carrot family)

H 30–80 cm   May–July   biennial

Caraway seeds have already been found at the sites of pre-historic lake dwelling settlements and the assumption is that Caraway was already used as a herbal seasoning even in those early days. In addition to the aromatic taste, the plant is also appreciated as an aid to digestion. Caraway alleviates cramps and wind as well as symptoms of gastroenteritis and the feeling of being bloated.

Habitat *Meadows and pastures especially in low mountain regions and high peaks, way-side verges. On mode-rately nutrient-rich soil. Almost everywhere in Europe.*

> prefers cooler climate
> unripe crushed fruits also with a characteristic fragrance
> often flowers again in August/September

split fruit capsule 3–3.5 mm long

umbels with 8–16 umbellules, stalked with different lengths

leaves single or double pinnate

fruit halves curved, ribbed

slender sections

lowest pinnate side leaflets forming a cross

bare

flowers about 3 mm in size

petals white or reddish, broad to heart-shaped

Cowbane

Cicuta virosa (carrot family)
H 60–120 cm   July–Sept   perennial

Habitat Banks of tarns, silty lakes, ditches. Grows standing in level water or on wetlands. Especially in north and central Europe.

> often stands in level water
> characteristic rootstock
> pleasant, spicy fragrance when crushed

The plant's aroma used to lead to repeated cases of poisoning, as people often mistook the plant for celery, parsnip or parsley. In the German state of Prussia, there was even a ruling that ordered the plant to be uprooted. The toxins in the plant can cause cramps, unconsciousness and ultimately prove fatal.

umbels with 8–20 rich, rather curved umbellules

margin with forward-directed teeth

pinnate leaf, linear-lanceolate

bare plant

flowers about 2 mm in size

yellow-brown secretion

hollow inside, mostly with inner chambers

rootstock bulbous-like, thickened

leaves 2–3-pinnate

120

Ground-elder

Aegopodium podagraria (carrot family)
H 50–90 cm   June–July   perennial

Habitat Damp woods, forest margins, riverbanks, gardens, parks. In partial shade. From low plains to high mountains. Almost everywhere in Europe.

> also known as 'Goutweed'
> often forms mass colonies
> attracted to nutrient-rich soil

Sometimes the plant is also known as 'Goutweed' and in traditional medicine, it is used in herbal teas for rheumatic pains and gout. Externally, the pressed plant can be used to prepare compresses against haemorrhoids. The young stems and leaves are also suitable for use in soups and vegetables.

flower umbels 4–7 cm across

leaves pinnate in threes or double pinnate

bare plant

long runners, growing deep underground

dense standing, fresh green leaves

flowers about 3 mm in size

Wild Carrot

Daucus carota (carrot family)

H 30–100 cm   June–Sept   biennial

The old Germanic tribes already knew the carrot as a cultivated plant. While the roots of the wild variety are thin and not very nutritious, cultivars that are propagated from the wild plants form strong roots. Garden carrots must also be harvested the first year, as the next year, their roots turn hard and woody. They are rich in carotin, which the body turns into vitamin A and they also contain vitamins B and C as well as sugar.

Did you know?

Black 'Carrot flowers' at the centre of the umbel help the flower's pollination, because flies visit these florets. In turn, other flies prefer landing on the spot that these insects vacated. Therefore, the dark flowers function like fly traps.

Habitat *Meadows, wasteland places, wayside verges, quarries, station precincts. Preferably on dry, mostly chalky soil. Almost everywhere in Europe.*

> *requires light, sunny locations*
> *dried fruit patches remain throughout winter*
> *also attractive in wild flower gardens*

flowers about 3 mm in size

petals white or cream coloured

121

dense flower umbels 5–10 cm across

surrounded by conspicuous leaves

leaves with slender tips

sunken in the middle

umbel closed up in fruit season

Wild Angelica
Angelica sylvestris (carrot family)
H 80–150 cm   July–Sept   woody perennial

strongly curved flower umbels, 8–20 cm across

Habitat *Riverside woodlands, damp forests, riverbanks, wetlands, wayside verges. From the plains to the mountains. All over Europe.*

> tastes and smells only slightly herbal
> requires partial shade
> withered stems often visible throughout winter

The reference in the name to 'angels' is derived from the highly acclaimed healing powers of the related Garden Angelica (*Angelica archangelica*). In the old days, Wild Angelica root was used as a vegetable and occasionally also to produce candied stems. As a medicinal plant, it was used to treat coughs and stomach complaints. Nowadays, the species is no longer used.

branched

2–3-pinnate leaf

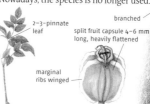

split fruit capsule 4–6 mm long, heavily flattened

marginal ribs winged

petals white to reddish

flowers about 2.5 mm in size

base swollen, globular

leaves up to 60 cm long

122

Hogweed
Heracleum sphondylium (carrot family)
H 50–150 cm   June–Sept   perennial

enlarged external petals of outer flowers

Habitat *Meadows, wasteland patches, ditches, forest margins. On fresh, nutrient-rich soil. Throughout Europe.*

> grows in mass colonies on fertilised meadows
> leaf shape with multiple forms
> fruits dispersed on the wind

The enlarged petals of the outer flowers enhance the spectacular show of the umbels, making them especially. attractive to insects. After contact with the Hogweed, similar skin complaints can emerge as for the Giant Hogweed (p. 123). However, usually, these reactions are not as severe.

sparse split capsule, 6–10 mm long

slice-shaped with broad wings

umbels 10–20 cm across

furrowed stem, bristly hairs

petals deeply notched

leaves conspicuously large, compound or simply divided

Giant Hogweed

Heracleum mantegazzianum (carrot family)

H 200–350 cm July–Sept perennial

Giant Hogweed is originally native to the Caucasus, from where around 1900, it was transported to central Europe as a garden plant. The plant was popular as an attractive decorative feature for verges and parks. Beekeepers also appreciated the plant as a source of sustenance for bees. Nowadays, in many places, the Giant Hogweed has become a nuisance weed. It suppresses the growth of native plants due to its size and its poisonous substances make it difficult to deal with this plant.

Habitat *On riverbanks, roadways, spinneys. Often as a solitary plant. Native almost everywhere in Europe.*

> *also known as 'Cartwheel Flower'*
> *a majestic, umbel-flowered species found in central Europe*

umbels up to 50 cm in size

petals deeply notched

123

stem up to 10 cm thick

leaves deeply 3–5-divided

withered stems and umbels often preserved for a long time

Did you know?

If plant juice comes into contact with the skin in full sunlight, this causes inflammation; the skin turns red and forms blisters, like a burn wound. The blisters take quite a long time to heal and the skin is often discoloured with brown pigmentation.

leaves up to 1 m long

White Swallow-wort

Vincetoxicum hirundinaria (milkweed family)
H 30–120 cm   May–Aug   perennial   ☠

Habitat Forest margins, open pine forests, stony scrubland, cliffside lawns. Mostly on chalky soil. Almost everywhere in Europe.

> forms dark green clusters
> requires lots of heat and sunshine in summer
> can reach water deep underground

The White Swallow-wort is an anchor plant on loose rocky deposits, as its roots grow very deeply and firmly. People used to extract fairly long, firm fibres from the stems. The plant contains toxins, which can lead to cramps and paralysis.

unbranched stems

leaves opposite

flowers in tufts in leaf axils

leaf oval to lanceolate, long with pointed tip

3–5 cm long fruit pods

seeds with silky-shining hairs

almost divided to the base into 5 tips

corolla 3–8 mm in size

stamens and stigma in central profusion

124

Dodder
Cuscuta epithymum (dodder family)
H 20–60 cm   July–Sept   annual

Habitat Overruns other plants with its stems, especially Thyme, broom Heather and Gorse varieties. Almost everywhere in Europe.

> parasitic plant without foliage
> without foliage or roots
> several similar varieties

Silks, which grow in an almost cocoon-like or web form and cling firmly to other plants, were once associated with witches and devil's spells. They were therefore also called devil's twine or witches' yarn. Dodder grafts onto neighbouring plants and extracts all their moisture and carbohydrates.

entwining around host plant

thread-like stem

pale plant, mostly with a reddish tinge

flowers in dense tufts

flowers in small tufts

sepal with 5 triangular tips

corolla bell-shaped, up to 5 mm long

Thorn-apple

Datura stramonium (nightshade family)

H 30–120 cm   June–Oct   annual   🐝

The Indians already knew the effect of the Thorn-apple's poison. Depending on the dose, this can cause hallucinations, severe intoxication, drowsiness or death by respiratory paralysis. This is why the Indians also used the plant for rituals, but also for acts of revenge. If applied regularly, the Thorn-apple can permanently impair health.

margin notched, toothed

solitary flowers

leaves up to 20 cm long

bursts open with 4 sections

fruit capsule, with dense spines

Habitat *Weedy patches on rocky scrub deposits, refuse dumps, on waysides. Attracted to nitrogen-rich soil and salt-tolerant. Especially in south Europe.*

> originally native to central America
> flowers open in the evening and last for about 1 day
> flowers with unpleasant odour

5 pointed tips

corolla 6–10 cm long, trumpet-shaped, folded

sepal with 5-edged tube

Hedge Bindweed

Calystegia sepium (bindweed family)

H 100–300 cm   June–Sept   perennial   🐝

The tips of the shoots twist in an anti-clockwise direction, winding around plants, picket fences etc. They can complete one revolution in about two hours. The plant is an ideal choice as foliage for adorning garden fences or gates. However, it can spread profusely, so the brightly coloured, cultivated Morning Glory is better suited for this purpose.

leaves heart or arrow-shaped

solitary flowers

leaves alternate

Habitat *Riverbanks, riverside woodlands, hedgerows, wayside verges. On damp, nutrient-rich soil. Throughout Europe.*

> flowers also opened at night time, only closed during bad weather
> especially attracts moths

corolla wide, trumpet-shaped, up to 5 cm long

sepal about 1 cm long

margin backward-curving

Field Bindweed

Convolvulus arvensis (bindweed family)

H 20–80 cm   June–Sept   perennial

Habitat *Arable fields, vineyards, gardens, scrub, wayside verges, wasteland. Almost everywhere in Europe.*

> **flowers only opened for 1 day, from about 7 am to 2 pm**
> **roots and runners grow up to more than 2 m deep**
> **requires lots of light**

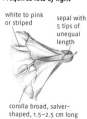

Field Bindweed is regarded as a nuisance weed, twining around other plants and even strangling them. Even herbicides cannot completely eliminate them. After pulling out the weeds, the plant almost always grows back again, as the underground parts can virtually never be removed. The smallest fragments develop again into new plants.

leaves spear-shaped, 3–6 times longer than wider

stems thin, creeping or twining

up to 1–2 flowers in leaf axils

white to pink or striped

sepal with 5 tips of unequal length

corolla broad, salver-shaped, 1.5–2.5 cm long

126

Bogbean

Menyanthes trifoliate (bogbean family)

H 15–30 cm   May–July   perennial   (🔬)

Habitat *Silty ponds, small lakes, fens, peaty areas, wetlands. North and central Europe, in the mountains in south Europe.*

> **very bitter tasting**
> **clover-like leaves, yet unrelated to the clover species**
> **mostly in locations with poor limestone content**

As with many other bitter-tasting plants, Bogbean used to be prescribed for fevers, in spite of the fact that it contains no substances that soothe high temperatures. Tea made from the plant whets the appetite and helps digestion. The plant's wild habitats are protected, but many locations are endangered by schemes to build on flood plains.

dense flower clusters

leaflets inversely oval-shaped, up to 10 cm long

leafless flower stalk

tips densely coated in hairs

sepal with 5 tips

salver-shaped corolla, about 15 mm across

leaves sparse, in 3s

Spiked Rampion

Phyteuma spicatum (bellflower family)

H 30–80 cm   May–July   perennial

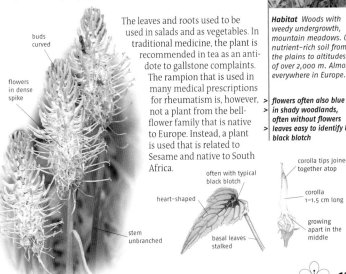

buds curved

flowers in dense spike

The leaves and roots used to be used in salads and as vegetables. In traditional medicine, the plant is recommended in tea as an antidote to gallstone complaints. The rampion that is used in many medical prescriptions for rheumatism is, however, not a plant from the bellflower family that is native to Europe. Instead, a plant is used that is related to Sesame and native to South Africa.

Habitat *Woods with weedy undergrowth, mountain meadows. On nutrient-rich soil from the plains to altitudes of over 2,000 m. Almost everywhere in Europe.*

> *flowers often also blue in shady woodlands, often without flowers*
> *leaves easy to identify by black blotch*

often with typical black blotch

heart-shaped

stem unbranched

basal leaves stalked

corolla tips joined together atop

corolla 1–1.5 cm long

growing apart in the middle

127

Dwarf Elder

Sambucus ebulus (honeysuckle family)

H 60–150 cm   June–July   perennial

Anyone who collects wild berries should not confuse the Dwarf Elder for Elder, which is edible. The fruits of the Dwarf Elder are even poisonous when cooked and can cause nausea, vomiting, diarrhoea, dizziness and heart complaints. The Elder has woody stems and branches, while the Dwarf Elder is not a woody plant.

Habitat *In among other perennials in spinneys, on woodland paths, railway embankments and slopes, floodplains. Almost everywhere in Europe.*

> *unpleasant odour*
> *attracted to nitrogen-rich soil*
> *often forming large groups*

umbels, slightly curving in racemes

toothed margin

leaves pinnate, with single terminal leaf

leaves up to 30 cm long

black drupes, 5–7 mm in size

purple-red anthers

fruit stem with red branchlets

stem not woody

flat-faced corolla tip

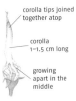

Common Valerian
Valeriana officinalis (valerian family)
H 40–100 cm   May–Aug   perennial

Habitat *Damp meadows, riverbanks, ditches, damp forests. On damp to wet soil. Almost everywhere in Europe.*

> very variable species
> flowers with a different aroma to dried roots
> fresh plants repellent to cats

In the Middle Ages, valerian was used to treat the Plague. The odour of the roots was supposed to drive out witches and evil spirits and was also used to keep away the moths. In the mid-18th century, an English doctor introduced the plant for the first time into medical practice for use as a sedative. Since then, the plant has proved effective in the treatment of nervous conditions and insomnia. Beauty products such as soap with Alpine varieties of this plant contain extracts of aromatic roots of the related Celtic Valerian (*Valeriana celtica*).

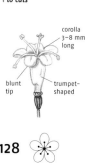

corolla 3–8 mm long

blunt tip

trumpet-shaped

128

abundant flowers, umbel-like, tightly packed

forked raceme

leaves pinnate, with 7–29 pinnate pairs and single terminal leaf or pinnately divided

fruits with 10–14 feathery bristle

leaves opposite

Did you know?
The root contains several medicinal substances. However, the penetrating odour, which is almost like sweaty feet, only emerges when the root is dried. Tomcats get excited by this odour, which they sense as a signal of cats 'on heat'.

White Water-lily
Nymphaea alba (water-lily family)
H 50–250 cm June–Aug perennial ☠

The White Water-lily belongs to the record-holders among native European flora for the longest leaf and flower stalks (up to 3 m) and largest flowers. Tissues in the stalks that are filled with air ensure that the leaves and flowers absorb sufficient water. The Water-lily is named after the Nymphaea – water nymphs and nature goddesses in Greek mythology.

Habitat Ponds, backwaters, still lakes. In standing water of a depth of 1–3 m, or in very gently flowing water. Almost everywhere in Europe.

> *also suitable in gardens*
> *flowers only open during daytime*
> *water-repellent wax layer on leaf upperside*

7–12 cm large flowers floating on water's surface

leaf indented at base

abundant petals, arranged in spiral shape

rough, floating leaves

abundant stamens

129

Chickweed Wintergreen
Trientalis europaea (primrose family)
H 5–20 cm May–July perennial

Chickweed Wintergreen used to be common when the climate was colder. Today, its habitats are relics left over from the Ice Age. The name alludes to the shape and tonal hue of the foliage and an alternative name is 'European Starflower'.

leaves up to 5 cm long

Habitat Mossy spruce forests, birch moorlands, wetlands. On poor, acidic soil. In north and central Europe.

> *needs semi-shade*
> *non-flowering plants similar to Dog's Mercury (p. 294)*
> *forms loose groups*

solitary flowers

entire margin

star-shaped flower corolla, 1.2–1.5 cm in size

most leaves grouped in whorl-like clusters

7 pointed tips

Wood Anemone
Anemone nemorosa (buttercup family)
H 10–25 cm   March–May   perennial

Habitat *Deciduous and coniferous forests, copses, mountain meadows. On fresh to damp soil. Almost everywhere in Europe.*

> *attracted to rich nutrient sources*
> *can also cover wide areas in spring*
> *plucked plants rapidly wither*

As a spring-flowering plant, the Wood Anemone uses favourable light conditions in the forest, before the trees take on foliage and cast everything else in shade. In May or June, after the fruits ripen, the plant already withdraws its upper parts to survive below ground until the following year. It reproduces not just by dispersal of seeds, but also via underground branching systems. It is entirely possible that a group of 100 flowering stems actually belongs to a single plant.

fruit from abundant, 1-seeded nutlets

3-part leaf, bare

6–8 white petals or pink-coloured on the outside

many stamens

no sepal

flowers solitary, 1.5–4 cm in size

130

3 leaves to a stalk

Did you know?
At night-time and during dull weather, the flowers close up and droop downwards. As soon as it turns light, they open again. At the same time, the flower petals grow, so that the flowers gradually become bigger.

Snowdrop Anemone
Anemone sylvestris (buttercup family)
H 15–35 cm   April–June   perennial   ☠

The flowers are not brilliant white because of any colour pigment, but due to their light-filled intersections that reflect the light. If the flowers are firmly pressed, air is expelled so that the tissue appears glassy. Pollen from this anemone is easy for insects to reach and for bees, flies and beetles to collect. The long-haired fruitlets are on upright stalks, so that the wind can easily take hold of them and blow them away.

Habitat *Open pine and deciduous forests, woodland verges, embankments, semi-dry grassland. Mostly on chalky soil. Central Europe.*

> *requires lots of heat and light*
> *entire plant with hairs*
> *should not be picked*

mostly a large, solitary flower, 3–7 cm in size

leaves palmately divided

6 or also only 5 petals

no sepals

long hairs on outside

131

fruitlets long and with white hairs

3 leaves to a stalk

Did you know?
Another species of anemone grows in the mountains of central and south Europe and is known as the Narcissus-flowered Anemone. It has slightly smaller flowers that always grow in clusters of 3–8.

Mountain Avens
Dryas octopetala (rose family)
H 5–15 cm   May–Aug   shrub

upperside
dark green

crenate
leaf margin

Habitat *Cliffside rocky deposits, stony areas, open pine forests. North Europe and mountains in central and south Europe, up to altitudes of about 2,500 m.*

> ground-loving dwarf shrub
> can live up to 100 years
> also in stony gardens

This plant was common in Germany at the end of the last Ice Age or the Pleistocene period (from Greek meaning 'most' and 'new'). Deposits from this period – also known as the Younger Dryas age, hence, the plant's scientific name – preserved masses of fibres from the Mountain Avens. The flowers turn towards the sun creating a parabolic mirror effect as their centre warms a few degrees above the outside temperature. This is how insects find a space to keep warm.

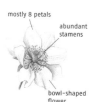

mostly 8 petals

abundant stamens

bowl-shaped flower

flowers solitary, 2–4 cm in size

white, woolly leaf underside

Common Iceplant
Mesembryanthemum crystallinum (dew plant family)
H 20–80 cm   Feb–July   annual or biennial

Habitat *Salty waste areas in coastal regions, salty marshes. In sunny locations. Introduced from South Africa in the 18th century. Around the Mediterranean.*

> flowers only open in strong midday sunshine
> also known as 'Crystalline Iceplant'
> excellent at water storage

This plant used to be cultivated to extract baking soda (sodium carbonate). It was quite suitable for this purpose, as it not only absorbs water from salty ground, but also from salts. The plant then deposits these minerals in its mucus-rich tissue. Fine delicatessens sometimes stock Common Iceplant for salads or as a vegetable. Recently, some skincare products also contain extracts of this plant.

plant covered with glittering, transparent bubble-like cells

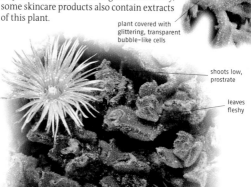

flowers 2–3 cm across

abundant petals

abundant stamens

shoots low, prostrate

leaves fleshy

Daisy

Bellis perennis (daisy family)
H 5–15 cm   Jan–Nov   perennial

At night-time and during cool weather the composite flower heads are closed up. Petals grow on the outside especially for this purpose and by doing so depress the outer, ray florets. Small fruits are dispersed on the wind and washed away from the flower heads in the rain or cling to animals in wet conditions. In addition, earthworms eat the fruitlets and excrete them while still intact. The flower heads make a pretty garnish around salads and, if preserved in vinegar, are edible as a homemade substitute for capers (p. 95).

Habitat Lawns in domestic gardens and parks, meadows, pastures. On nutrient-rich soil in light locations. Almost everywhere in Europe.

> often forms large groups
> also flowers in winter
> one of the most well-known wild flowers

Did you know?

Especially in spring, nurseries sell different cultivated varieties of Daisy, with larger and denser composite flowers. These flowers have more outer or ray florets, which range in colour from white to red.

yellow disc florets

white, pink-tipped outer ray florets

solitary composite flower head, 1.5–3 cm in size

133

small fruitlets

arched capitulum

leafless stem

basal leaf rosette

sepal-like bracts

closed flower head

Oxeye Daisy

Leucanthemum vulgare (daisy family)

H 20–70 cm   June–Oct   perennial

Habitat *Meadows, pastures, semi-dry lawns, arable fields, wasteland, cliffs. From low plains to high mountains. Almost everywhere in Europe.*

> also known as 'White Man's Weed'
> can cover large areas
> perfect in hand-tied bouquets of meadow flowers

People still pluck the white ray florets from this 'oracle flower', in order to discover what the future holds. In Goethe's famous play 'Faust', Gretchen quizzes her destiny through the flower – 'He loves me – he loves me not ...'. Marguerite – an alternative name for the Oxeye Daisy – is French for 'pearl'. There were three beautifully embroidered marguerites on the robes worn by the wife of Henry VI, who regarded herself as a 'pearl among pearls'.

1 composite flower head overtopping stem, 2–7 cm across

stem mostly unbranched

sepal-like casing resembles roof tiles

sparse leaves on stem

yellow disc florets

up to 43 white ray florets

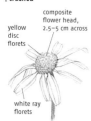

Scentless Camomile

Tripleurospermum perforatum (daisy family)

H 10–45 cm   June–Oct   annual or biennial

Habitat *Weedy patches on rocky scrubland, on wayside and roadside verges, central reservations of motorways, arable fields. Throughout Europe.*

> often forms large groups
> scentless, even when crushed

Scented Mayweed (also German Camomile) and Scentless Camomile often grow in the same spot and are easily confused. Yet it is usually easy to distinguish the more robust Scentless Camomile from the Scented Mayweed, as the former has no fragrance and densely packed, composite flower heads. Although Scentless Camomile has no medicinal power, it is attractive in hand-tied wild flower bouquets.

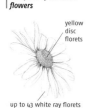

composite flower head, 2.5–5 cm across

yellow disc florets

solitary composite flower heads

leaves almost with thread-like sections

branched stem, often brownish-red

dense flower head, arched

white ray florets

Scented Mayweed

Matricaria recutita (daisy family)
H 15–40 cm   May–Aug   annual

In the 16th century, Scented Mayweed was regarded in northern Europe as one of the most important medicinal plants. It was used to treat many complaints, especially symptoms of hormonal changes in women. Today, the composite flower heads still count as effective medicines. Thanks to their natural substances, they act as a soothing agent for inflammations and cramps. People used to pick the plant in the wild for medicinal purposes. Nowadays, it is widely cultivated, especially in eastern Europe and Egypt.

Habitat *Cereal fields, pathways, rocky places, roadside verges. On nutrient-rich soil. Throughout Europe.*

> **strong, aromatic fragrance**
> **easy to recognise by hollow, composite flower heads**
> **often in abundant clusters**

Did you know?

If you extract the aromatic essential oil from the flower heads, you will be surprised to note its hue: an intense blue colour.

hollow composite flowers, conical

ray florets quickly deflexed

composite flower head, 1.5–2.5 cm in size

yellow disc florets

white ray florets

135

solitary flower heads

leaves with slender sections

branched stem

Feverfew
Tanacetum parthenium (daisy family)
H 30–60 cm   June–Aug   perennial   (❀)

Habitat Wasteland areas, wayside verges, fences, rocky scrub. Prefers warmer locations. Almost everywhere in Europe.

> aromatic fragrance when crushed, similar to camphor
> branching growth
> also an attractive ornamental plant

Feverfew is native to south-eastern Europe. After spreading from farmyard gardens, nowadays the plant has established itself nearly everywhere. The plant was previously used to treat women's hormonal conditions and was even misused to perform abortions (the Greek 'parthenos' means virgin). Today, the plant is commonly used to treat migraine. In powder form, the herbaceous plant is suitable as an insect repellent. Skin contact with the plant can cause allergies in humans.

Did you know?
Numerous cultivated varieties of Feverfew are grown in gardens. The composite flower head of dense varieties is more or less exclusively white and some varieties are without outer, ray florets.

base of flower head flat

white ray florets

yellow disc florets

136

compound leaves, 3–6 sections on each side

abundant composite flowers in loose clusters

composite flower head 1.5–2.5 cm across

Gallant Soldier

Galinsoga parviflora (daisy family)
H 10–60 cm   May–Oct   annual

The plant originally arrived in Europe from South America. All European plants are reputed to come from specimens that were planted in 1794 in the Jardin des Plantes in Paris. The plant was dispersed in eastern Europe in the early 19th century, about the time that the French army advanced across continental Europe.

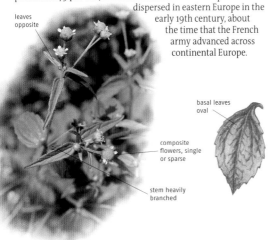

leaves opposite

basal leaves oval

composite flowers, single or sparse

stem heavily branched

Habitat *Weedy patches on arable fields, scrub areas, in gardens, vineyards. Grows almost everywhere in Europe up to altitudes of 700 m.*

> **one of the most important weeds worldwide**
> **acutely sensitive to frost, survives as seeds**

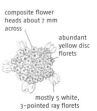

composite flower heads about 7 mm across

abundant yellow disc florets

mostly 5 white, 3-pointed ray florets

 137

---

leaves pinnately lobed

divided into multiple tips

Yarrow

Achillea millefolium (daisy family)
H 20–120 cm   June–Oct   perennial

Achilles, the Trojan hero in Greek mythology, is said to have harnessed the plant's medicinal power. It contains similar essential oils as the Scented Mayweed (p. 135) and helps wounds heal as well as acting as an antidote for digestive complaints. Sheep prefer eating the plant's foliage, while they avoid the flower heads.

upright stem

many composite tiny flower heads packed together

each flower head 4–10 mm in size

Habitat *Meadows, pastures, arable fields, wasteland, areas of lawn. On nutrient-rich soil from the plains to the high mountains. Throughout Europe.*

> **aromatic fragrance when crushed**
> **leaves mostly remaining green in winter**
> **tough stems, difficult to break off**

yellowish–white disc florets

4–6 white or pink ray florets

Silver Thistle
Carlina acaulis (daisy family)
H 2–60 cm   July–Sept   perennial

Habitat Rough meadows and pastures, stony slopes, arid grassland. Mountainous regions in central and south Europe, including the high mountains.

> requires plenty of sunshine in summer
> composite flower heads only open during dry weather

composite flower, 5–12 cm in size

very abundant disc florets

casing out of dry, silvery–gleaming bracts

138

The plant decorates many coats-of-arms as well as hiking club logos. The Silver Thistle is also used in dried flower bouquets and is cultivated for this purpose, since it is protected. Legend has it that, Charlemagne, the Holy Roman Emperor, had a vision of the Silver Thistle in a dream during an outbreak of the Plague. While the plant is not an effective antidote for this disease, its scientific name *Carlina* is nonetheless reputedly in honour of Charlemagne. Indeed, the plant is also known as 'Charlemagne Thistle'.

Did you know?
In damp conditions, the glossy outer leaves close up and encase the flower heads. Even dried plants behave in this way. Yet this plant is not a weatherglass, as it merely indicates current humidity conditions.

composite flowers mostly solitary

leaves pinnately lobed

leaf margin, spiny, toothed

Edelweiss
Leontopodium alpinum (daisy family)
H 5–20 cm   July–Aug   perennial

The scientific name means 'lion's paw', as the woolly-downy flower heads were compared to lion cub paws. The downy covering helps protect the plant in the high mountains from exposure to UV rays and excessive moisture loss. Edelweiss that is cultivated on the lower flatlands is less densely haired and therefore has a dull, dirty green appearance.

Habitat Mountain ledges, promontories, stony grassland at altitudes of 1,700 to 3,400 m. Mountains in central and south Europe.

> most well known plant in the high mountains
> do not pick!
> similar species from the Himalayas in stony rockeries

entire plant woolly-downy

leaves lanceolate

5–10 small composite flowers

star of 5–15 white downy bracts

139

Lily of the Valley
Convallaria majalis (lily family)
H 10–20 cm   May–June   perennial

Lily of the Valley is not only an important symbol within Christianity; it is also a valuable plant in medicine. The plant contains substances that, if used in the correct dosage, can prove an effective treatment for mild heart conditions that are common in old age. However, overdoses can prove fatal.

Habitat Deciduous forests, shrub, mountain meadows, rocky cliffs. Almost everywhere in Europe, in the south, only in the mountains up to altitudes of about 2,200 m.

> can form large groups
> strong fragrance, also used in perfumes
> also grows in gardens

flowers in clusters, facing one side

2 leaves above each another

leafless stem

red, spherical berries

flower 5–9 mm long, nodding

spherical, 6-pointed bellflower

Fragrant Solomon's Seal

Polygonatum odoratum (lily family)

H 15–45 cm   May–June   perennial   ☠

Habitat *Open forests, cliffs near woodlands, forest margins. Light to semi-shady locations throughout Europe.*

> often grows in groups
> fragrant flowers
> blue-black, poisonous berries

The conspicuous scars that the stems leave behind after withering on the rootstock resemble blobs of sealing wax. This is why the plant is named after the signet ring of King Solomon, who was a talisman for wisdom and magic in the east. A popular fable was that Fragrant Solomon's Seal could be used to open closed doors. The shape of the scars on the rootstock also explained the belief in the Middle Ages that the plant was an effective cure for corns.

parallel leaf nerves

blue-green leaf underside

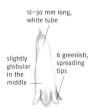

12–30 mm long, white tube

slightly globular in the middle

6 greenish, spreading tips

upperside of rhizome with scars

6 greenish, spreading tips

140

overhanging stems, sharp-edged

pendent flowers, solitary or up to 2

leaves arranged in 2 rows

Did you know?

The similar Solomon's Seal has 2–5 unscented flowers growing together and rounded stems. This species tends to grow in more damp forests.

Branched St Bernard's-lily

Anthericum ramosum (lily family)
H 30–80 cm   June–Aug   perennial

When flowerless, you can easily mistake the plants for grasses. Often, they also grow in among grasses and then are difficult to recognise. The flowers attract different insects that can easily reach the nectar dispensed at the top of the ovary.

Habitat *Forest margins, open woodlands, embankments, semi-dry lawns. On dry soil. Almost everywhere in Europe.*

> *requires warm locations*
> *often grows in larger groups*
> *also suitable as a garden flower*

raceme with over 30 flowers

grass-like leaf, up to 50 cm long

6 long stamens

6 white, 10–14 mm long petals

 141

White Asphodel

Asphodelus albus (lily family)
H 50–120 cm   April–June   perennial   (☙)

In Greek mythology, the White Asphodel creates wide and extensive meadows in the underworld, where last judgement is passed on the souls of the dead. People used to plant this herbaceous perennial on graves, so the intensely aromatic roots would nourish and give succour to the dead as their souls departed. For the living, too, the roots were once used as foodstuffs – either roasted or ground as flour – during times of shortage.

upright flower head, without foliage

Habitat *Meadows, overgrazed pastures, bright forests, roadside verges. Mediterranean, especially near coasts.*

> *root vegetable-like storage roots*
> *often growing in groups*
> *shunned by cattle*

6 petals, 1.5–2 cm long

St Bruno's Lily
Paradisea liliastrum (lily family)
H 20–50 cm   June–Aug   perennial

Habitat *Mountain meadows, pastures, light Chestnut groves. On dry soil at altitudes of 800 to 2,000 m. Alps and mountains of western Europe.*

> **large, striking blooms**
> **fragrant flowers**
> **protected in its natural wild habitats**

The plant's scientific name has nothing to do with the Garden of Eden. Instead, it is named after Giovanni Paradisi, an Italian horticulturalist from the late 18th century. Nevertheless, the German name for the plant is sometimes known as 'Paradise Lily'. The flower is not only striking in the wild, but also ideal for planting in gardens and cut flower sprays.

loose cluster with up to 20 flowers

leafless stem

grass-like leaves growing from the ground upwards

6 white, pointed petals

flower 6–8 cm across

142

Alpine Leek
Allium victoralis (lily family)
H 30–70 cm   July–Aug   perennial

Habitat *Mountain pastures, cliff corridors, mountain pastures, grassland above the tree line. Mountains in central and south Europe at altitudes of 1,000 to over 3,000 m.*

> **often forms groups**
> **when crushed, onion-like aroma**

Anyone who wears the bulbs of this ancient, magical healing plant as an amulet is supposed to be protected against wounds in combat and steal victory. This supposition was derived from the appearance of the plant's bulbs – their fibrous casing appears as if surrounded by a coat of chain mail. It is also said to protect against witches and evil spirits.

star-shaped flowers, up to 1 cm in size

flower head, spherical, up to 5 cm across

leaves 3–6 cm across, 10–20 cm long

leaf with parallel nerves

stamens longer than petals

bulb surrounded by fibrous casings

Wild Garlic

Allium ursinum (lily family)

H 20–50 cm   May–June   perennial

Wild Garlic, also known as Ramsons, has a similar effect to Garlic and is an antidote to loss of appetite, high blood pressure and chronic inflammation of the arteries. When finely chopped, the leaves can be used to flavour sour cream dressings or to make pesto sauce. The plant's natural substances only turn into strong-smelling onion oils when the leaves are crushed or wither. This is why you can smell Wild Garlic in the forest from a long distance during early spring, especially when the weather turns warm.

Habitat *Damp broadleaved forests with herbaceous undergrowth, riverside woodlands. Mostly in shady locations. Almost everywhere in Europe.*

> *also easy to cultivate in gardens*
> *can cover large areas*
> *similar smell as Garlic*

flower umbel with abundant petals

6 white, almost 1 cm long petals

star-shaped flower

143

leafless flower stem

thin leaf, up to 20 cm long

conspicuous leaf stalk

parallel leaf veins

Did you know?
You should only collect Wild Garlic if you know the plant well. Confusion with Lily of the Valley (right) or Meadow Saffron (left) repeatedly leads to cases of poisoning with a fatal outcome.

Snowdrop
Galanthus nivalis (amaryllis family)
H 8–20 cm   Feb–March   perennial   ☠

Habitat *Riverside woodlands, woodland ravines, damp forests. In semi-dry places on damp, nutrient-rich soil. Almost everywhere in Europe.*

> - **often naturalised, as a garden escape**
> - **spring plant with underground bulb**
> - **often already flowering in snow**

3 nodding, 12–30 mm long flowers

3 shorter flowers with green blotch

The flowers are frost-resistant. Insects also easily recognise the white flowers in the snow, as they reflect ultra-violet light intensely. For several years, a substance that can be isolated and extracted from snowdrops has been used in medicines to treat Alzheimer's disease. In cases of poisoning, however, symptoms of gastro-enteritis can emerge.

frosted blue-green, fleshy

grass-like leaves

2 basal leaves

each stem with 1 nodding flower

144

Spring Snowflake
Leucojum vernum (amaryllis family)
H 10–30 cm   Feb–March   perennial   ☠

Habitat *Damp riverside woodlands, woodland ravines, damp meadows near woodlands. On damp soil. Especially in central Europe, in the wild in northern Europe.*

> - **mostly growing in large groups**
> - **also known as 'Agnes Flower'**
> - **fragrance similar to violets**

bellflower, up to 2.5 cm long

6 almost identical long petals

green or yellow blotch beneath tip

This early-flowering bulbous plant is also very popular in gardens. However, if you want to plant the Spring Snowflake, you must not collect it from plants growing in the wild, as they are a protected species. The ovary is quite conspicuous and sits like a thick knot on the stalk beneath the flower petals. Symptoms of poisoning from this plant can be an irregular heartbeat.

nodding flower

mostly 1 flower per stem

leaves 10–25 cm long, 5–25 mm across

leaves shiny, fleshy

Pheasant's-eye Daffodil

Narcissus poeticus (amaryllis family)

H 20–60 cm   April–June   perennial   🕱

'*Narcissus*' is derived from the Greek 'narkaein' meaning anaesthetic or anaesthetising and probably refers to the flower's fragrance. The addition '*poeticus*', meaning poetical, was given because the famous Roman poet, Ovid, offered a precise description of the flower in antiquity. At the base of the long, extremely narrow tube, the flower secretes nectar, which only butterflies with a sufficiently long proboscis can reach. Bee-flies that also visit the flowers harvest nutritious pollen.

Habitat *Mountain meadows, open mountain woodlands with leafless trees in winter. Around the Mediterranean, central France.*

> this plant was used to propagate many garden varieties
> fragrance similar to cloves
> protected wild habitat

stem without green leaves

solitary flowers

central ring up to 3 mm long, with red-tinged centre

6–3 cm long flower tips

narrow, 2–3 cm long tube

145

leaves flat, 5–15 mm across

approximately as long as flower stem

Did you know?

Similar carotin-rich substances as occur in carrots are responsible for the colouring of the central ring. This part also has a different fragrance and is substantially more intense than the white flower parts, enabling insects to find their way more easily to the flower tube.

False Helleborine

Veratrum album (lily family)
H 50–150 cm   June–Aug   perennial

Habitat Mountain pastures and cattle grazing areas, moorland meadows, in wet woodland places. Mountains in central and south Europe, up to 2,000 m.

> cattle grazing on pastures avoid the plant
> conspicuous from a long distance
> without flowers, often confused for the Great Yellow Gentian (p. 233)

At the time of the ancient Greeks, the dried rootstock was already used as snuff, which was fairly dangerous. The belief was that sneezing clears the mind and sharpens the intellect or at least that mankind can be certain of what is true. The Latin *Veratrum* is therefore derived from 'verus' meaning true. The plant's deadly alkaloid substances can even penetrate unbroken skin.

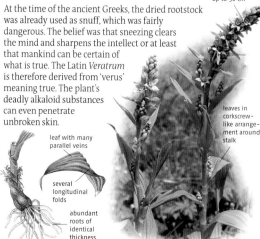

abundant flowers in clusters of up to 50 cm

leaves in corkscrew-like arrangement around stalk

leaf with many parallel veins

several longitudinal folds

abundant roots of identical thickness

star-shaped flower, 1–2 cm across

6 white, yellowish or greenish petals

146

Garden Star-of-Bethlehem

Ornithogalum umbellatum (lily family)
H 10–30 cm   April–May   perennial

Habitat Vineyards, parkland lawns, meadows, copses, tree-lined urban areas. Mostly in groups. Central and south Europe.

> flowers only open in sunshine
> contains glycosides, effective as heart stimulant
> also attractive as ornamental plant

The plant's scientific name means 'bird's milk' in translation. However, this probably refers to the protein, suggesting a comparison between the flower colour and the white of boiled eggs. Also, the plant contains a mucus-like juice, which looks rather similar to raw egg-white. Star of Bethlehem is also used in commercial homeopathic remedies.

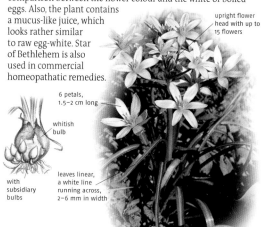

upright flower head with up to 15 flowers

6 petals, 1.5–2 cm long

outer surface with green stripe

star-shaped flower

whitish bulb

with subsidiary bulbs

inside milky white

leaves linear, a white line running across, 2–6 mm in width

Sea Squill

Urginea maritima (lily family)
H 50–150 cm   Aug–Oct   perennial   🐝

In antiquity, Sea Squill was already used as a rather dangerous medicinal plant. It contains substances, which have an intense effect on the heart. Additionally, the pungent-smelling bulbs were an effective source of mouse and rat poison and helped prevent insects from invading crops. According to an old Greek custom, hanging a bundle of Sea Squill above a door lintel is supposed to ward off evil spirits.

cluster with over 50 flowers

leaves ribbon-shaped, up to 1 m long

bulb up to 20 cm in size

Habitat Pastures, stony, dry coastal slopes, fallow land, wasteland areas, shrub, sandy beaches. Around the Mediterranean.

> autumn flowerer
> bulb protruding from the ground
> first shoots emerge after summer dry season

dark central vein

star-shaped flower

6 petals, 6–8 mm long

   147

Spring Crocus

Crocus vernus (iris family)
H 5–15 cm   Feb–May   perennial   (🐝)

The leaves have thickened tips that are designed to penetrate the snow cover. As soon as the sunshine disappears behind the clouds, the flowers close up. Flowers can be light violet or with white-violet strips. Every year, the plant produces a new bulb to replace the old one. Special fibrous, contractile roots ensure the bulbs reach the right depth.

Habitat Mountain meadows and pastures up to 2,800 m. On damp soil, also tolerates manure as fertiliser. Mountains in central and south Europe.

> often in groups
> flowers immediately after snow melts
> many other crocus varieties in Mediterranean

grass-like leaves

upright flowers, mostly solitary

white central stripe

6 petals

flower funnel-shaped

White Clover
Trifolium repens (pea family)
H 15–45 cm   May–Sept   perennial

Habitat *Pastures, parks, country paths, gardens, arable fields, wasteland. On nutrient-rich soil throughout Europe.*

> creeping plant
> salt-tolerant and resistant to footfall
> plants with 4 leaflets are very rare in the wild

Clover leaves are often seen on coat-of-arms and are the Irish national symbol. According to legend, St Patrick proclaimed the presence of the Holy Spirit upon catching sight of a clover leaf. Every year on St Patrick's Day 17 March, people in Ireland wear a clover leaf as a buttonhole. Prior to this day of national celebration, clover was seen as a symbol of the three Celtic priest grades of the Druids, Bards and Ovates.

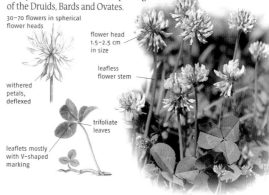

30–70 flowers in spherical flower heads

flower head 1.5–2.5 cm in size

leafless flower stem

withered petals, deflexed

trifoliate leaves

7–12 mm long

white or yellow to reddish-tinged pea flower

leaflets mostly with V-shaped marking

148

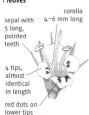

Gypsywort
Lycopus europaeus (dead-nettle family)
H 20–130 cm   July–Sept   perennial

Habitat *Banksides, ditches. On wet, temporarily flooded, nutrient-rich soil. Almost everywhere in Europe.*

> often standing between reeds
> requires wet conditions
> conspicuously shaped leaves

The red dots on the sepal tips act as beacons to insects and especially attract bee-flies as pollinators. When the extract of this herbaceous plant is used in the right preparations, it is an effective agent for treating thyroid problems and can help prevent mild conditions of an overactive thyroid.

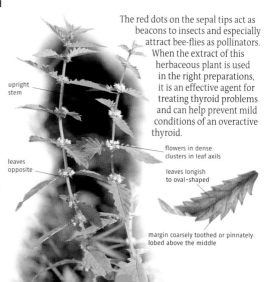

upright stem

corolla 4–6 mm long

sepal with 5 long, pointed teeth

leaves opposite

4 tips, almost identical in length

red dots on lower tips

flowers in dense clusters in leaf axils

leaves longish to oval-shaped

margin coarsely toothed or pinnately lobed above the middle

White Dead-nettle

Lamium album (mint family)
H 20–50 cm April–Oct. perennial

The scientific name is derived from the Greek 'lamos' meaning 'throat' and refers to the flower shape. This term also neatly summarises the plant's use, since tea made from White Dead-nettle leaves acts as a soothing agent for catarrh of nasal passages and inflammations in the mouth and throat. Traditional medicine also recommends the flower extracts as a soothing treatment for menopausal complaints.

Habitat *Weedy patches on country paths, hedgerows, forest margins, fences, ditches, walls, dung heaps, manure pits. Almost everywhere in Europe.*

> *attracted to nitrogen-rich soil*
> *often grows together with Spotted Dead-nettle (p. 75)*

leaves opposite

upper lip curved, hood-like, hairy exterior

corolla 2–3 cm long

sepal with 5 lanceolate teeth

149

4-edged stem

flowers in whorls of 6–16 in leaf axils

oval to heart-shaped blade

leaves stalked

toothed margin

Did you know?

When plucked, the tubes of the flower corollas – if not previously visited by insects – contain an abundance of sugary sweet nectar. No wonder that not only bumblebees, but also children love to empty out the sweet liquid from the flowers.

Eyebright
Euphrasia officinalis (figwort family)
H 2–45 cm   May–Oct.   annual

Habitat *Rough pastures and meadows, moorland meadows, mountain meadows. From low plains to altitudes of 2,300 m. Almost everywhere in Europe.*

> *attracted to poor soil*
> *very variable species*
> *in mass groups, detractor of meadow and pasture yields*

Herbals dating from the 16th century already recommended Eyebright, as the name suggests, as a medicinal plant to treat various eye complaints. The prettily marked petals were compared to lashes of an eyelid. In traditional medicine, the plant is still used to treat eye diseases. The plant's essences help prevent inflammation.

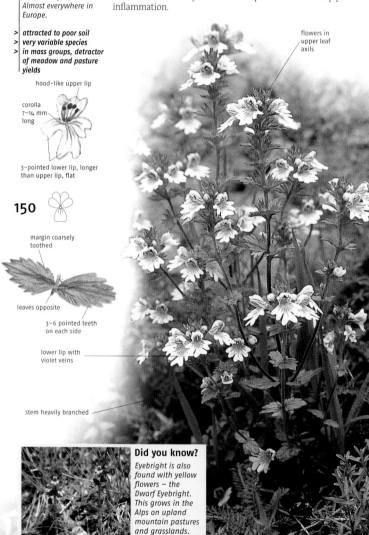

hood-like upper lip

corolla 7–14 mm long

3-pointed lower lip, longer than upper lip, flat

150

margin coarsely toothed

leaves opposite

3–6 pointed teeth on each side

lower lip with violet veins

stem heavily branched

flowers in upper leaf axils

Did you know?
Eyebright is also found with yellow flowers – the Dwarf Eyebright. This grows in the Alps on upland mountain pastures and grasslands.

Twinflower

Linnaea borealis (honeysuckle family)

H 5–15 cm   July–Aug.   Alpine, upland shrub

The delicate Twinflower was a favourite plant of Carl Linnaeus, the famous Swedish botanist. Linnaeus devised the system of plant classification by scientific name and his system is still used now. The Twinflower was therefore named after Linneaus – *Linnaea borealis*. In Sweden, Linnea or Linn remains a common girl's name today.

Habitat *Light coniferous forests, rocky mountain slopes and landslides. On acidic soil, mostly creeping over moss or between alpenroses. North Europe, Alps.*

> *slight vanilla fragrance*
> *thread-like stems, creeping up to 4 m*
> *leaves also green in winter*

nodding flowers, usually in pairs

crenate margin

leaves opposite

leaves 7–12 mm long

white or pink

flower 7–10 mm long

bell-shaped flower with 5 points

151

White Helleborine

Cephalanthera damasonium (orchid family)

H 30–60 cm   May–June   perennial

This orchid's flowers mostly remain half opened or completely closed and they only open a little further for a short time in hot temperatures. Although they do not provide any nectar, the upper wings of the flower possibly provide food for pollinators.

Habitat *Forests, not too dense. Shady, warmer locations. Central and south Europe.*

> *first blooms emerge at about 10 years*
> *similar with slender leaves*
> *the similar Narrow-leaved Helleborine has slender leaves*

loose flower head

leaves dark green, mostly slightly shiny

upright stem

almost 3 times as long as broad

half-closed flower

sparse leaves

no spur

bract-like petal longer than ovary

rounded petals

egg-white at front, with 3 upper wings

upward-arching lip

Perennial Honesty

Lunaria rediviva (cabbage family)
H 30–140 cm   May–July   perennial

Habitat Shady woodland ravines and mountain woodlands, forest slopes. On damp, nutrient-rich soil and stony rubble. Almost everywhere in Europe.

> occasionally also with white flowers
> requires sufficient humidity
> also known simply as 'Honesty'

The plant's scientific name *Lunaria* is derived from the Latin 'luna' meaning 'moon', since the watery, shimmering and translucent fruit capsules are reminiscent of silver moons. The seeds are dislodged when the fruits are shaken by the wind. The withered stems with parchment-like 'silver moons' are often left standing in the forest all winter long. The flowers have a similar fragrance to violets and attract moths and bees.

deflexed lid when ripe

5–8 cm long, flat fruit

flowers in short clusters

flower 1–2 cm in size, with 4 light violet petals

152

translucent fruit surface

flat seeds

heart-shaped leaves, sizeable

margin toothed

Did you know?

Honesty is native to the eastern Mediterranean and has almost circular, round fruits. It is not only a beautiful ornamental plant for the garden. The flowerless stems with the silvery, translucent fruit capsules are perfect for use in dried flower arrangements.

Cuckooflower

Cardamine pratensis (cabbage family)
H 10–60 cm   April–June   perennial

fruit
slender,
club-like

'Cuckooflower' is frequently covered with larvae from the Meadow Spittlebug. They are commonly found on the plant's stems. A light haze of pale flowers is characteristic of meadows colonised by cuckooflowers. The plant not only reproduces by dispersal of seeds, but also with the help of breeder plantlets forming on its basal leaves. These emerge when the leaves lie prostrate on damp soil or mosses.

Habitat Damp freshly mown meadows, moorland and wetlands, riverside woodlands, riverbanks, damp forests. On cool, nutrient-rich soil. Almost everywhere in Europe.

> sharp taste
> leaf rosettes often remaining green throughout winter
> can create magical violet meadows in springtime

flower 1–2 cm in size with 4 violet, purple or occasionally white petals

yellow anthers

Did you know?

The white froth produced by the Meadow Spittlebug or Froghopper is popularly called 'cuckoo spit': people once believed that a Cuckoo had spat on the plant! In fact, the froth is a protective covering for the immature insect.

153

basal leaves, pinnate with single terminal leaf

often with small plants on leaflets

flowers forming loose, terminal cluster

flower head umbel-like at top

stem leaves with slender sections

Fringed Gentian

Gentianella ciliata (gentian family)

H 7–30 cm   Aug.–Oct.   biennial, herbaceous perennial

Habitat *Rough grass-land, stony pastures, forest margins. On chalky soil in central Europe and in the mountains of southern Europe up to altitudes of about 2,500 m.*

> leaves only clasping stems
> fragrant flowers, similar to violets
> endangered and protected species

Flowers of all gentian species are only open during daytime and in fine weather. At night-time and also in rainy conditions, the flowers close up again. These movements of the flower petals are created by the corolla's expansion. The first flowers of the Fringed Gentian are therefore 2–3 cm in diameter, while later blooms grow to a diameter of up to 5 cm. The flowers are pollinated by bumblebees and butterflies.

4 flat-faced corolla tips

long fringes

trumpet-shaped, narrow flower tube

stem leaves opposite

slender, lanceolate, only 1 vein

flowers overtopping stems, 2.5–5 cm long

154

Germander Speedwell

Veronica chamaedrys (figwort family)

H 15–40 cm   May–July   perennial

Habitat *Hedgerows, copses and woodland margins, meadows, wayside verges, bright and dry oak forests. Throughout Europe.*

> characteristic stem hairs, in rows
> grows in sunshine or semi-shade
> suitable for wild grass-land areas

This plant is also known in Germany by the name of 'Männertreu' – literally 'man's fidelity'. This is an ironic reference to the way in which the flowers quickly wither away. If you pick the flowers, your pleasure will be short-lived, as the tiny violet flower corollas droop and wilt only minutes after their collection. Other popular English names include 'Bird's-eye Speedwell' or 'Angels' Eyes'.

margin coarsely serrated

leaves opposite

flower corolla 1–1.5 cm in size, bowl-shaped, with 4 unequal tips

darker veins

2 stamens

dense flower clusters in leaf axils

stalked flower heads

stems hairy on each side, especially in lower section

Slender Speedwell
Veronica filiformis (figwort family)
H 5–30 cm   March–June   perennial

Slender Speedwell is native to the Caucasus and was originally introduced in Europe as an ornamental plant, especially on grave sites, from where it escaped to grow wild. The plant has been established in northern Europe since about 1930. A very resilient plant that easily colonises wide areas, the Slender Speedwell is sometimes regarded as a nuisance. However, on lawns and in parks, it can create a pretty bluish haze of flowers.

Habitat *Meadows, pastures, garden lawns, parkland lawns. In warmer, preferably shady and humid locations. North and central Europe.*

> flower stems and stalks conspicuously slender
> prostrate growth
> resilient to grazing and footfall

Did you know?
Slender Speedwell spreads profusely and rapidly on decorative lawns when these are regularly mown: the lawnmower churns and grinds the plants into tiny pieces and disperses the parts that can grow again into new plants.

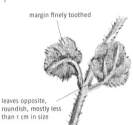

margin finely toothed

leaves opposite, roundish, mostly less than 1 cm in size

corolla 0.8–1.3 cm in size, salver to wheel-shaped, with 4 unequal tips

2 stamens

solitary flowers on very slender stalks, 1–4 cm long

155

Large Speedwell
Veronica teucrium (figwort family)
H 20–80 cm   May–July   perennial

Habitat *Edges of copses, rough grasslands, wayside verges, light oak and pine forests. Preferably on dry soil. Central and southern Europe.*

> *flowers mostly brilliant blue*
> *mostly growing as a conspicuous, solitary plant*
> *requires plenty of sun and warmth*

Large Speedwell is a magnificent plant to grow in sunny, wild flower gardens. During the Middle Ages, the related Heath Speedwell was highly prized as a medicinal plant. The Heath or Common Speedwell was commonly recommended for coughs or gastroenteritis. Nowadays, extracts are found effective in the treatment of sinus or ear infections.

corolla 1–1.5 cm in size, bowl-shaped, with Ð4 unequal tips

2 stamens

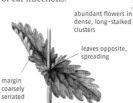

margin coarsely serrated

abundant flowers in dense, long-stalked clusters

leaves opposite, spreading

Devil's-bit Scabious
Succisa pratensis (teasel family)
H 15–80 cm   July–Sept.   perennial

Habitat *Moorland, rough mountain and wetland meadows, fens and marshes, up to approximately 1,500 m. Almost everywhere in Europe.*

> *thrives in poor soil*
> *requires sufficient dampness*
> *often many flowers in loose clusters*

corolla purple to bluish-violet, with 4 fairly unequal tips

sepal with 4–5 black, short bristles

The blackish, withering rootstock at the base looks as if it has been severed. Indeed popular belief held that the Devil had bitten off the roots – and thus, people were banished from reaping the benefits of this plant's healing powers. Herbalists traditionally used the plant to treat ulcers, lung conditions and as a cleansing agent for blood, among other things.

flowers in spherical clusters, 1.5–2.5 cm in size

long stamens

basal leaves oval to lanceolate

withered rootstock at base

abundant roots

Wild Teasel

Dipsacus fullonum (teasel family)
H 70–200 cm   July–Aug.   biennial

Raindrops regularly collect in pools in the leaf axils. These
moisture pools prevent insects from climbing up the stems.
The water is possibly an extra source of nitrogen for the plant,
especially if insects drown in it. Wild Teasel has a unique flower
head: the first part of the bloom that opens are the florets in the
centre. The flowers therefore gradually become visible in two
successive, ring-like sections.

Habitat *Weedy
patches on pathways,
reservoirs, riverbanks,
on waste ground. On
nutrient-rich soil. Fairly
common.*

> **withered plants visible
> throughout the winter**
> **often forming large
> groups**
> **attracted to loamy soil**

stem with
numerous
1–5 mm long
spines

oval to cylindrical flower
head, 3–8 cm tall

purple corolla, 4 tips,
approximately 1 cm long

spiny bracts

straight, pointed, flexible
petal-like bracts

157

midrib
toothed

leaves
opposite

fused together around
base, forming cup-like
pool

flowers in
centre of
bloom open
first

Did you know?

*Flowers of the similar Fuller's
Teasel have stiff, backwards-
curved sepal-like bracts. The
plant was cultivated into the 20th
century and nowadays grows as a
weed in southern and occasionally
in central Europe. The dried fruit
parts were utilised for combing
and roughening woollen fibre.*

Love-in-a-mist
Nigella damascena (buttercup family)
H 10–50 cm   May–June   annual

leaf with numerous fine tips

Habitat *On cultivated land, waste and fallow land around the Mediterranean. In central Europe, in gardens as an ornamental plant.*

> fruits decorative in dried flower arrangements
> crushed seeds with strawberry fragrance
> also known simply as 'Nigella'

Bees land on the flower petals and then crawl in a circle around the centre of the flower. In the process, they extract nectar from rather complex-shaped receptacles. The closely related Black-cumin (*Nigella sativa*) has no green foliage directly below the flower. The seeds contain oil, which is highly nutritious. They are also scattered as seasoning on top of Turkish pitta bread.

long stigmas   abundant stamens

petals 1.5–2 cm long, light blue

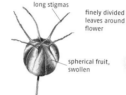

long stigmas

finely divided leaves around flower

spherical fruit, swollen

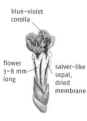

Common Sea-lavender
Limonium vulgare (thrift family)
H 20–50 cm   Aug–Sept   perennial

Habitat *Coastal grasslands and mudflats on North, Baltic and Atlantic coasts. On salt-rich soil.*

> all leaves basal
> can grow in groups or covering wide areas
> cultivars are used in dried flower arrangements

To adapt to its salty habitat, the Common Sea-lavender secretes a saline solution from special glands. If the solution dries on the leaves, a deposit of tiny crystals remains, only to be washed away again by the next rain shower. The colour of the flowers makes them reminiscent of Lilac.

flowers in tightly packed, dense one-sided spikes

blue-violet corolla

flower 3–8 mm long

salver-like sepal, dried membrane

leafless stem

tiny spine at top

smooth margin

leaf up to 20 cm long, evergreen, leathery

Flax

Linum usitatissimum (flax family)

H 30–60 cm   June–July   annual

Flax used to be the most important source of fibres to be woven into 'linen'. In the 16th century, Germany was among the leading industrialised countries on account of its linen production. Nowadays, cotton has replaced linen fibre in most cases, due to its more flexible structure. Flax is still cultivated, mainly for seeds and their oil. Linseed oil is also suitable for use in paint pigments, although it can also be used as healthy cooking oil.

Habitat *Arable fields, rocky places. Prefers nutrient-rich soil. Cultivated in central and south Europe, rarely growing wild.*

> *creates magical blue fields*
> *flowers already withered by midday*
> *also called 'Linen'*

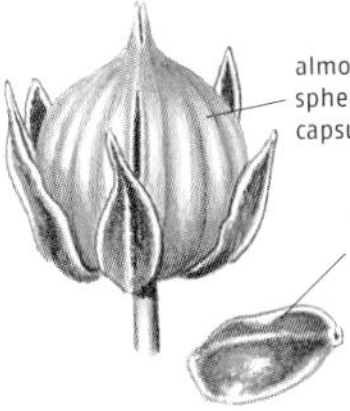

almost spherical fruit capsule

flat seed, brown, shiny

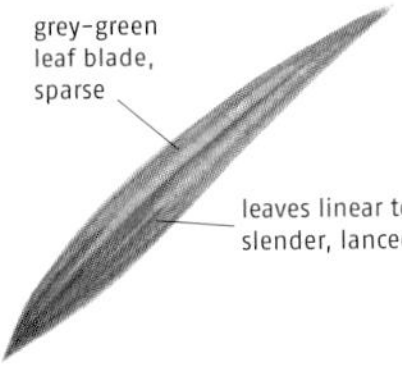

grey-green leaf blade, sparse

leaves linear to slender, lanceolate

blue anthers

flower 2–3 cm in size

upright buds

159

flowers in loose racemes

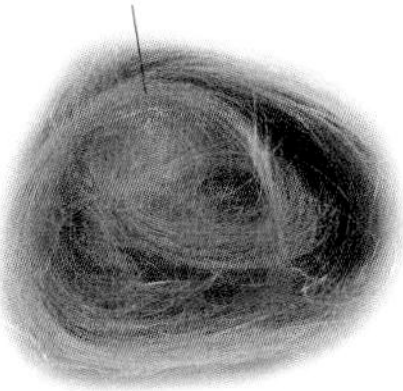

fibres extracted from stems

Did you know?

The similar Perennial Flax with nodding flower buds grows especially in the wild in southern Europe. It is also a delicate decorative garden plant. Each single flower opens at 6 am every morning over several days and closes again in the afternoons.

Meadow Crane's-bill
Geranium pratense (crane's-bill family)
H 20–60 cm   June–Aug   perennial

Habitat High-yielding meadows, ditch margins, roadside embankments. On nutrient-rich, mostly chalky soil. Almost everywhere in Europe.

> palmate, 7-part leaves
> often found in groups
> the similar Wood Crane's-bill flowers red-violet

The lower part of the fruit contains five seeds. The upper, elongated, seedless section ('bill') aids dispersal. Each different section grows taut when drying out and suddenly rolls up from below like the hand of a watch. At the same time, the seeds are catapulted and spun far and wide for distances of more than 2 m.

petals 1.5–2 cm long, rounded at front, blue-violet

stalks of unripe fruits pointed downwards

stalk and sepal with hairs

flowers protruding above leaf below

fruit with elongated 'bill'

nodding buds

160

Sea Holly
Eryngium maritimum (carrot family)
H 20–60 cm   June–Aug   biennial, herbaceous perennial

Habitat Sand dunes with sparse herbaceous growth and sandy ground along coastlines throughout Europe.

> resembling a Thistle, but actually belonging to the carrot family
> endangered, therefore a protected species

The flower stems were popular with beach tourists, who collected them for dry flower bouquets. The German name for the plant – literally 'man's fidelity' – is presumably connected to the plant's earlier usage as an aphrodisiac. Other, ironic explanations compare the straggling plants, which are blown about on the wind, with men's' fickleness.

flowers in dense umbels, up to 2 cm in size

5–8 greyish to bluish-tinged, thorny and toothed sepals

leaves stiff, rough, roundish to kidney-shaped

long, protruding stamens

flower about 5 mm long, steel-blue to violet

lobed margin, toothed with stiff spines

Alpine Sea Holly

Eryngium alpinum (carrot family)
H 30–80 cm   July–Aug   perennial

At night and in damp conditions, the conspicuous sepals close around the flower head. The flowers attract pollinators, while protecting the flower head from predators. However, the spines do not deter people, who like to collect them for dried flower bouquets, as the flower heads do not fade. In the wild, the plants are endangered and protected by law.

Habitat *Mountain meadows, stony grassland, groups of herbaceous plants. On chalky soil up to altitudes of 1,500 to 2,500 m in the Alps and northern Balkans.*

> **not related to true thistles**
> **conspicuous from afar**

Did you know?

The 'Culentro' spice is native to a closely related Sea Holly species from Central America. Its fresh, finely chopped leaves taste tangy and aromatic, a little like Coriander. The chopped herbs season food in the Caribbean and Vietnam.

5 slender petals

flower 2–3 mm in size, whitish–blue to blue

stem leaves palmately divided

abundant composite flowers

piercing, blue–violet sepals

spiny toothed margin

161

flower head spreading to a cylindrical shape

Trumpet Gentian

Gentiana clusii (gentian family)
H 5–10 cm   May–Aug   perennial

Habitat *Rough, stony grassland, rough mountain meadows in mountains of Europe at altitudes of 1,200 to 2,800 m. On chalky soil.*

> one of the most well-known Alpine flowers
> flowers of the similar Stemless Gentian have olive-green stripes inside

The flowers allow light to filter through them at the base and are divided into five chambers. Bumblebees crawl inside in search of light, extracting nectar from the chambers. The Trumpet Gentian and other blue gentian varieties are often depicted on decorative Schnapps labels. However this alcoholic drink is generally made from the Great Yellow Gentian (p. 233).

leaves forming a rosette

basal leaves 3–5 cm long, slightly leathery

solitary, terminal flowers, 5–6 cm long

5 broad corolla tips

dark blue corolla, narrow, bell-shaped

Willow Gentian

Gentiana asclepiadea (gentian family)
H 30–80 cm   July–Sept   perennial

Habitat *Moorland meadows, mountain woodlands, forest margins. On damp soil, also in shady locations. In mountains of central and southern Europe up to about 2,200 m.*

> mostly forming several flowering stems
> also known as 'Milkweed Gentian'
> once believed to ward off spells and witches

In non-flowering plants, the 'Willow Gentian' closely resembles White Swallow-wort (p. 124). In shady forests, the leaves grow horizontally in two rows, reaching upwards for the light to make full use of the sun's rays. In bright locations, the leaves spread outwards on all sides.

leaves opposite, long, pointed

1–3 flowers, almost resting in upper leaf axils

triangular tips

corolla 3–5 cm long, narrow, bell-shaped

leaf mostly with 5 parallel veins

Spring Gentian

Gentiana verna (gentian family)
H 5–20 cm   March–Aug   perennial

Pure blue flowers are a rarity in the plant kingdom, but gentians are an exception. As blue is the colour of fidelity, these flowers, especially the Spring Gentian, are regarded as a symbol of fidelity and trust. The flowers are sensitive to changes in temperature and the stress of exposure to rain or wind. They close up in bad weather conditions or temperatures below 10 °C.

Habitat Rough grassland, sheep's grazing pasture, fens. Mostly on chalky soil. Mountains in central and south Europe.

> often found in groups
> occasionally flowering for a second time in autumn
> another name is 'Lucy of Teesdale'

sparse grasslands, usually with abundant flowers

solitary flower

basal leaves up to 3 cm long, stiff

form a rosette

2-pointed attachments between tips

5 spreading tips

narrow tube

Lesser Periwinkle

Vinca minor (periwinkle family)
H 15–20 cm   April–May   perennial

This plant was introduced into gardens of northern Europe during the Middle Ages and became naturalised in many places. It reproduces almost exclusively by runners as seeds are rarely formed. Dispersal of the plants over wide distances is almost exclusively due to human activity. In woodlands, signs of earlier settlements are often still visible where the plant is established today.

Habitat Deciduous forests with species diversity, especially near old castles and settlements. On nutrient-rich ground. Central and south Europe.

> stems can grow up to 2 m during the year
> often covering large areas
> tolerates shady locations

solitary flowers, 2–3 cm in size

leaves opposite, up to 5 cm long

leaves leathery, evergreen

spreading growth

5 non-symmetrical, flat-faced petal tips

flower with up to 1 cm longer tube

Bittersweet
Solanum dulcamara (nightshade family)
H 30–200 cm   June–Aug   perennial   🐝

Habitat *Damp copses, ditch margins, riverbanks, Alder forests, spinneys. Mostly on wet to damp soil. Almost everywhere in Europe.*

> **often flowering and simultaneously producing fruits**
> **slightly twining growth**
> **very varied leaves, oval or pinnate**

The entire plant contains toxins that can lead to cramps and paralysis of the respiratory system. It is adviory therefore not to test out whether or not the fruits actually does taste bitter at first, then leaving a sweet aftertaste. At least this is suggested by the plant's name. Medication made with extracts of the stems helps cure chronic eczema.

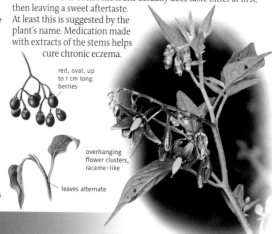

red, oval, up to 1 cm long berries

conspicuous stamens

overhanging flower clusters, raceme-like

flower with 5 spreading to backward-curving violet tips

leaves alternate

164 ✿

Apple of Sodom
Solanum sodomaeum (nightshade family)
H 50–300 cm   May–Sept   shrub   🐝

Habitat *Naturalised on wayside verges in the Mediterranean, rocky places and on sandy beaches.*

> **often flowering and simultaneously producing fruits**
> **originates from South Africa**
> **extremely spiny, sparse shrub**

'Sodom's apples' are treated as a symbol of falsehood and hypocrisy in literature. Their outer appearance suggests that they are edible. In the Bible, God destroyed the cities of Sodom and Gomorrah because of their sins.

midrib with up to 1.5 cm long spines

spiny sepal

flower 2.5–3 cm across, blue-violet

spherical berry, 2–3 cm in size, yellow when ripe

flat-faced corolla with 5 tips

stamens close together

leaves pinnately lobed

Mandrake Root

Mandragora officinarum (nightshade family)

H 10–20 cm   Feb–May

The Mandrake Root is one of those plants shrouded in superstition. According to popular myth, the plant's roots are supposed to fill a purse with sacks of money, spreading love and happiness. However the myth also held that people picked this plant's roots by hand at their peril. The correct way was to fasten a black dog's tail to the roots then slap the dog's back. The dog would leap up and bound off, unearthing the plant's roots, upon which, the Mandrake Root supposedly uttered a shriek causing the dog to drop dead.

Did you know?

Depending on their shape, people differentiated male from female mandrake roots. Anyone in possession of the valuable 'human roots' was sure to keep them carefully, even clothing and providing them with food and drink. If looked after properly, their power was reputed to be especially potent.

tinged greenish-white, violet-blue

flower about 2.5 cm in size

haired

165

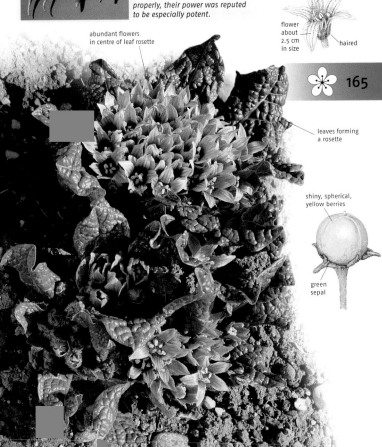

abundant flowers in centre of leaf rosette

leaves forming a rosette

shiny, spherical, yellow berries

green sepal

Jacob's-ladder
Polemonium caeruleum (phlox family)
H 30–80 cm   June–July   perennial

Habitat *Wild in damp meadows, floating in streams and rivers. Wild on waysides and in wall crevices. On damp soil. In north and central Europe.*

> **popular and robust ornamental plant in farm gardens**
> **flowers can also be white**
> **protected wild habitat**

'Jacobs-ladder' refers to the ladder-shaped, pinnate leaves with sky-blue, overhanging flowers. The plant's name alludes to Jacob, the biblical father, who had a vision of a ladder running between heaven and earth. This was a common garden plant, especially from the 16th to 19th centuries.

flower salver- to wheel-shaped

5 spreading tips

flowers 1.5–2 cm in size in a long, 10–30 cm raceme

leaf pinnate with 17–31 leaflets and single terminal leaf

upright stem

Phacelia
Phacelia tanacetifolia (waterleaf family)
H 30–70 cm   June–Oct   annual

Habitat *Native to California. Cultivated in Europe and naturalised in warmer waste areas in summer, on wayside verges, in vineyards.*

> **produces magical blue fields**
> **leaves resemble foliage of the Tansy (p. 251)**
> **pest-resistant in northern European**

Fields filled with Phacelia provide rich supplies of nectar for bees and are suitable as fast-growing green manure or as a source of silage for cattle fodder. For this reason, for a number of years, farmers often mix in Phacelia when preparing fallow fields. Phacelia is a persistent escape plant, although it usually cannot survive for longer periods in new habitats.

purple stamens, protruding a long way

5 rounded tips

corolla 6–9 mm long, blue-violet

flower heads rolled inwards, snail-like, before flowering

pinnately lobed or pinnatifid, with single terminal leaf

alternate leaves

coarse, hairy plant

Purple Gromwell

Lithospermum purpurocaeruleum (borage family)
H 30–60 cm   April–June   perennial 🐝

Each flower can produce four single-seeded, porcelain-like, white to light brown rock hard fruitlets. These remain surrounded by the sepal, only dropping from the dried plants during wintertime. In addition to the dispersal of seeds, the plant reproduces by creeping shoots, which form dense lawns.

without stalk

Habitat Sunny, open forests, woodland and copse margins on dry, level chalky soil. Central and south Europe.

> flower colour changing from red-violet to blue
> requires warmth
> also grows in shade, though non-flowering in this location

leaf lanceolate, short coarsely haired

corolla 1.4–2 cm long

lower flowers in leaf axils

corolla funnel-shaped with 5 tips

sepal with slender tips

Water Forget-me-not

Myosotis scorpioides (borage family)
H 10–100 cm   May–Sept   perennial

In lyrical poetry and folklore, Water Forget-me-not is known as a lovers' flower. It is reputed to have powers as an aphrodisiac and keep memories alive upon departure. The abundant, long-flowering blooms may have given rise to a comparison with love and friendship that is constantly undergoing renewal and replenishment.

flower clusters to one side, inrolled before flowering

Habitat Wetlands, ditches, riverbanks, riverside woodlands. On wet soil from plains to high mountains. Throughout Europe.

> requires damp conditions
> yellow ring inside flower attractive to insects
> flowers change from a reddish to blue colour

lanceolate leaf, growing apart or with short hairs

unstalked

corolla 6–8 mm in size

yellow ring

Alkanet
Anchusa officinalis (borage family)
H 30–80 cm   May–Aug   biennial, herbaceous perennial ☠

Habitat Weedy patches on wayside verges, rocky debris, wasteland. On sandy to gravely soil in sunny locations. Almost everywhere in Europe.

> flowers crimson immediately after opening
> requires lots of heat
> deep-growing roots

The coarsely haired leaves bear a genuine resemblance to ox tongues. People used to recommend the plant, as with Common Comfrey (p. 49 right), for treating bruises, aches and pains in bones and limbs, as well as by mouth, as a cough tincture. Yet the plant also contains toxins that can cause damage to the liver and may even cause cancer. Nowadays, you should avoid using the plant.

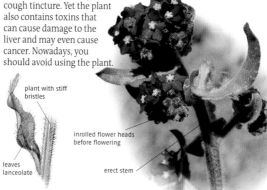

plant with stiff bristles

inrolled flower heads before flowering

erect stem

corolla dark blue-violet, about 1 cm across

leaves lanceolate

5 white, velvety haired scales

Lungwort
Pulmonaria officinalis (borage family)
H 10–30 cm   March–May   perennial

Habitat Forests with rich herbaceous undergrowth, shrub, forest margins. Preferably on damp soils from the low plains to high mountains. Almost everywhere in Europe.

> growing in shade or semi-shade
> flowers in alternate colours from red to blue
> suitable for wild flower gardens

The alternating hues of the flowers are reminiscent of the changing colours of a lung. Depending on how much oxygen a lung contains, this organ either appears red or blue. This feature, together with the mottled pattern on the foliage resembling the fibrous tissue of a lung, probably contributed to the plant's name. This plant was also once used to treat lung complaints such as tuberculosis.

leaves mostly light green to white-mottled

5 rounded tips

corolla up to 2.5 cm long, tubular to trumpet-shaped

plant with coarse hairs

inrolled flower heads

Borage
Borago officinalis (borage family)
H 20–70 cm   April–Sept   annual

The plant is grown in many gardens as a Cucumber plant to use as an extra garnish for salads and in cucumber salad. In antiquity, a commonly held belief was that the plant lightened the temperament, making men happy and strong. In the 16th century, Borage was regarded as one of the best natural substances to stimulate the heart. Nowadays, oil pressed from Borage seeds is used in herbalism and has proven an effective treatment for skin allergies and complaints such as neurodermitis.

Habitat *Cultivated land, fallow areas, wasteland, wayside verges, rocky areas. In sunny, warm locations. Around the Mediterranean.*

> *flowers over a long period*
> *occasionally a garden escape in central Europe*
> *aroma and taste resembles Cucumber*

flowers 1.5–2.5 cm in size, nodding

entire plant with coarse hairs

flat corolla, with 5 tips

stamens forming a cone

169

tongue-shaped leaves

Did you know?

Borage seeds have a nutritious attachment. Ants transport the seeds before they eat the attachment and thus ensure the plant's dispersal.

Vervain

Verbena officinalis (vervain family)
H 30–100 cm   July–Sept   annual, herbaceous perennial

Habitat *Rocky ground, pastures, wayside verges, walls, ditches. On moderately dry to damp soil. Almost everywhere in Europe.*

> *attracts bees*
> *nitrogen-loving plant*
> *flowers inconspicuous, striking for its sparse form*

In antiquity, Vervain was regarded as a lucky charm. People once believed that this plant had magical powers and could be used to fortify iron and prevent thunderstorms. However this effect on iron is less mystical than people presumed. If the herbaceous plant is added to an iron smelter, the plant's – and for that matter, any other plant's – natural carbon substances will harden the metal.

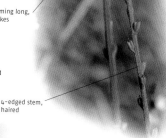

corolla 3–5 mm in size, pale purple

fused, with 5 tips

flowers forming long, slender spikes

leaf toothed to pinnately lobed

4-edged stem, haired

Sheep's-bit

Jasione montana (bellflower family)
H 10–45 cm   June–Aug   annual to biennial

Habitat *Sparse sandy to dry lawns, low in lime, dunes, rock ledges, sparse copses, reveres. On open ground. Almost everywhere in Europe.*

> *corolla tips of early flowers joined together*
> *very delicate appearance*
> *very suitable for wild flower gardens*

The roots of the Sheep's-bit can grow up to 1 m deep underground and therefore they can still absorb enough water even in sandy habitats. The plant grows in the mountains as well as on the plains.

flowers forming dense, spherical flower heads up to 1–2.5 cm in size

flower heads overtopping stems

corolla 0.5–1.5 cm long, light blue

5 slender tips

flower heads surrounded by several short, triangular sepal-like leaves

Black Rampion

Phyteuma nigrum (bell flower family)
H 20–50 cm   May–July   perennial

The corolla is rent open due to five slits running the length of the flower head. At the start, the corolla tips are still joined together with each other, thus pressing the anthers against the style and releasing the dark red pollen. Afterwards, the corolla tips also become separated at the tips and the stigmas unfold. The flowers attract bees and bee-flies.

curved flower buds

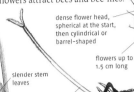

dense flower head, spherical at the start, then cylindrical or barrel-shaped

flowers up to 1.5 cm long

slender stem leaves

long style

slender corolla tips, later becoming completely separated

Habitat Deciduous mixed forests, mountain meadows. Especially in low mountain ranges and mountains with silicate rock. Central Europe.

> the darkest of the rampions
> elongated flower spike
> also flowers in shade

corolla tips fused at the top when flower opens

cleft open in the middle

Round–headed Rampion

Phyteuma orbiculare (bellflower family)
H 15–60 cm   June–Sept   perennial

The flower buds of rampions are distinctive with talon-like and inwards-curving flower heads, a unique quality that is especially easy to identify on the Round-headed Rampion. The shape of the flower heads also explains why the plant is sometimes called 'Round-headed Horned Rampion'.

flowers up to 1.7 cm long, curved in bud

spherical flower head

stem leaves oval to lanceolate, upper leaves sessile

Habitat Rough meadows, stony lawns on limestone, moorland meadows. From the low plains to altitudes of over 2,500 m. Central and south Europe.

> brilliant blue flower heads straight upward
> often growing in abundance in loose clusters
> requires plenty of light

corolla tip fused at point when flower opens

cleft open in the middle

Spreading Bellflower

Campanula patula (bellflower family)

H 30–60 cm   May–July   biennial

Habitat *Meadows, pastures, wayside verges, fallow areas. On nutrient-rich soil in sunny locations. Almost everywhere in Europe.*

> **one of the most common bellflowers**
> **heat-loving plant**
> **suitable for wild flower gardens**

At night and in dull weather, the flower heads droop downwards and so protect the pollen from rain and dewdrops. If the weather is fine, the flowers turn upwards, reorienting their position in the direction of the sunshine.

loose, spreading raceme

lanceolate, pointed

flowers up to 4 cm in size, light blue-violet

alternate leaves on stem

broad, trumpet-shaped corolla

5 slender, pointed tips

lanceolate sepal tip

Harebell

Campanula rotundifolia (bellflower family)

H 15–30 cm   June–Oct   perennial

Habitat *Rough lawns and meadows, heaths, open forests, woodland and wayside margins, rock and wall crevices. Everywhere in Europe, in the mountains in the south.*

> **often growing in groups**
> **thrives on poor soil**
> **long roots gaining foothold deep inside crevices**

The plant's basal leaves are rounded and mostly die off during the flowering period. The Harebell does not flower in shady locations. The basal leaves therefore remain intact and the short stems have a few stem leaves.

1–2 cm long, blue-violet, broad bell-shaped flowers in loose clusters

stalked basal leaves

roundish to kidney-shaped leaf blade

slender stem leaves, mostly over 2 cm long

sepal tips awl-shaped

corolla in 5 tips, up to about 1/3

Clustered Bellflower

Campanula glomerata (bellflower family)
H 30–60 cm   June–Sept   perennial

The colour pigment that is responsible for the beautiful blue colour of this plant's blooms is highly sensitive to acidic conditions. If you place a flower in an anthill or pour a drop of vinegar onto the petals, the flower immediately turns red.

Habitat Mountain meadows, light-filled forests, heathland areas. Up to altitudes of 2,800 m. On acidic soil.

> flowers always in dense clusters
> occasionally also white flowers
> attractive in wild flower gardens

1.5–2.5 cm long flowers in dense clusters

surrounded by leaves

leaves oval to lanceolate

corolla dark blue-violet, trumpet-shaped to slender bell-shaped

5 pointed tips

Common Cornsalad

Valerianella locusta (valerian family)
H 5–15 cm   April–May   annual

abundant flowers in dense clusters

The seeds germinate in autumn and the plant survives through the winter as a green leaf rosette. This plant is hardy and frost resistant and is a valuable aromatic winter salad with a high mineral and vitamin content. It was probably first cultivated as a green salad from the 18th century. In Switzerland, the plant is known as 'Nüsslisalat' or 'Nutlet Salad'. In Germany, people also refer to the salad as 'Rapunzel'.

Habitat Arable fields, fallow fields, vineyards, wasteland, wayside embankments, roadside verges. Everywhere in Europe.

> fruits attract birds
> often sown as salad plant
> taste fairly similar to nuts

corolla up to 3 mm long, pale purple or white

5 free tips

trumpet-shaped

branched, forking stem

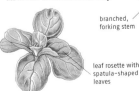

leaf rosette with spatula-shaped leaves

Pasqueflower

Pulsatilla vulgaris (buttercup family)
H 5–50 cm   April–May   perennial

Habitat *Rough grassland, occasionally chalky pine forests. On warm, dry, mostly chalky, low-nutrient soils in west and central Europe.*

> *flowers close up overnight*
> *roots reaching up to over 1 m deep*
> *suitable for rockeries*

The flowers gently waft to and fro on the breeze and are vaguely reminiscent of the shape of cowbells. The hairs on the fruitlets spread out in arid conditions ensuring that they are easily carried away by the wind. The related Small Pasqueflower has nodding, black-violet flowers and is the plant used to extract a key element for homeopathic medicines. The extract can be used to treat a range of conditions from sexual health complaints to the common cold.

6 violet petals, with ragged, white external hairs

abundant stamens

174

fruits reminiscent of a head of fuzzy hair

elongated flower stalks towards flower

fruitlet with elongated, feathery haired styles

solitary flowers, 3–6 cm long

stem leaves haired, with slender tips

basal leaves not fully grown in flowering season

Did you know?
The flower stalks and petals of the Spring Pasqueflower – a widespread Alpine plant growing at altitudes of about 3,600 m – are even more densely haired. The golden yellow furry coat is ideal for protecting the plants against frost.

Columbine

Aquilegia vulgaris (buttercup family)
H 40–80 cm   May–July   perennial   ☠

When bumblebees creep into the sack-like flower heads, they can extract nectar from the end of the spur. In contrast, other bees frequently bite the end of the spur from outside, stealing nectar from here, yet without pollinating the flowers. Bees can also collect the sweet syrup through these perforations.

Did you know?

Cultivated varieties display all the hues and colour variations from white to dark violet. In addition, the number of spurred flower petals is frequently greater and they can then slide into each other like cornucopia. Species from Asia and America are also found in gardens.

Habitat *Sparse deciduous forests, copses, hedgerows, shady meadows. Mostly on chalky soil. From low plains up to altitudes of 2,000 m. Almost everywhere in Europe.*

> occasionally with pink or white flowers
> heat-loving
> often in gardens as an ornamental plant

5 sack-like petals with hook-like, curved spur

5 petals, growing apart, up to 2.5 cm long

175

upright stems, branched

nodding, blue-violet flowers

upright 5-part fruit

leaf twice 3-part

mainly basal leaves

Liverleaf

Hepatica nobilis (buttercup family)
H 5–15 cm   March–April   perennial

Habitat Beech and oak forests with rich herbaceous undergrowth. Attracted to chalky soil. Almost everywhere in Europe.

> occasionally also with white flowers
> flowers close up at night time and during bad weather
> requires warm locations in summer

In the Middle Ages, Liverleaf was classified as an effective herbal treatment for liver complaints due to the leaf shape, which resembles a liver. Early settlers in North America also used the plant as a treatment for hepatitis, although there is no scientific evidence to support its efficiacy.

bare
3–part, cleft leaf blade
winter leaves often reddish
basal leaves
haired leaf stalk
flowers 1.5–3 in size, solitary

5–10 blue flower petals

abundant stamens

Alpine Snowbell

Soldanella alpina (primrose family)
H 5–15 cm   April–July   perennial

Habitat Mountain meadows and pastures in mountains of central and south Europe, above the tree line up to altitudes of about 2,000 m.

> grows on damp ground, moistened by snow
> overwinters with green leaves beneath snow mantle

The plants flower immediately after the snow melts. The flower stems often protrude upwards from beneath the snow mantle. The dark stems then bask in the sunshine and in their own heat, so they melt away a circle of sparkling white snow that surrounds them. This is how the plant quickly stimulates its metabolism once again and can form carbohydrates.

2–3 nodding flowers
stems without leaves
leaves roundish to kidney shaped, rough
smooth margin

trumpet-shaped
corolla 1–1.5 cm long
fringed to just over mid-way

European Michelmas-daisy

Aster amellus (daisy family)
H 20–40 cm   July–Sept   perennial

The leaves of the European Michelmas-daisy mainly point upwards, protecting them from moisture loss through evaporation. The hairs on the leaves also protect from moisture loss. Despite this, the species suffers if exposed to excessively dry or arid conditions, which cause the leaves and buds to die off.

leaves alternate

coarsely haired

composite flower 2–4 cm across

Habitat *Copse margins, wayside reveres, arid grassland, sparse pine forests. On chalky soils in arid locations. Central and south-eastern Europe.*

> *attracts flies and butterflies*
> *ornamental garden plant along with other asters*
> *requires poor-yielding soil*

ray florets about 3 mm across

several composite flower heads in loose clusters

yellow disc florets

☀ **177**

Sea Aster

Aster tripolium (daisy family)
H 15–60 cm   July–Sept   biennial

The Sea Aster also absorbs salt and ground water from its natural habitat. Although the salt acts as a toxin that can jeopardize the plant's metabolism, it stores it in its lower stem leaves. If a fatal concentration of salt is reached in these basal leaves, they turn yellow, wither and die off. As the plant sheds foliage, it also emits salt.

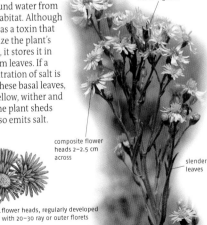

up to over 100 flower heads together

Habitat *Saline meadows along sea coasts, inland in salty areas. Coasts everywhere in Europe.*

> *thickish, fleshy leaves*
> *can cover large areas*
> *adapted to salty habitats*

ray florets 2–3 mm across, light blue or blue-violet

composite flower heads 2–2.5 cm across

slender leaves

yellow disc florets

composite flower heads often irregular

flower heads, regularly developed with 20–30 ray or outer florets

Glandular Globe-thistle

Echinops sphaerocephalus (daisy family)
H 60–180 cm   June–Aug   perennial

Habitat *Wayside verges, station sidings, wasteland. In dry, warm locations. Central and southern Europe.*

> **characteristic hedgehog-like flower heads**
> **flowers provide bees with ample nourishment**
> **fruits attract seed-eating birds**

The plant's native habitat is the Mediterranean. It has been cultivated in central Europe since the 16th century for ornamental purposes and was also a garden escape. As the flower heads come into bloom they are blue, later on turning a grey or whitish hue. The flowers attract bees. The pollen is also tinted blue, so the busy bees look as if they are wearing tiny blue breeches.

spherical flower heads, 3–6 cm in diameter

only 1 light-blue to whitish, deeply 5-lobed flower

composite flower, 1–2 cm long

flower with spiny sections

white downy underside

178

Perennial Cornflower

Centaurea montana (daisy family)
H 30–60 cm   May–Oct   perennial

leaf oval to lanceolate

tapers with stem

Habitat *Rocky cliff slopes, mountain and woodland ravines, mountain meadows. In central and southern European mountain ranges, up to altitudes of about 2,000 m.*

> **stems appear slightly winged**
> **requires dampness**
> **also cultivated in gardens and occasionally growing in the wild**

When you touch cornflowers of any variety, the anther tube gently draws downwards and a yellow parcel of pollen becomes visible. This process is easy to observe with the Perennial Cornflower by simply tapping the flower head with your finger. Pollen emerges within seconds and, a few minutes later, the anthers revert back to their original position.

flower cross-section before contact

the same flower after contact

composite flower, mostly single, 3.5–5 cm across

downy grey plant

composite flower, with disc florets only

outer petals blue, heavily enlarged

Cornflower

Centaurea cyanus (daisy family)
H 30–60 cm   June–Oct   annual

In the 19th century, Prussia's Emperor William I declared that the Cornflower was his favourite flower. This is why his entourage wore Cornflowers on their lapels. Cornflowers were dispersed all over the world when cereal crops were cultivated on a wide scale. However, from about the 1950s, Cornflowers were in rapid decline, due to the use of weedkillers and fertilisers as well as rapid ploughing stubble fields.

Habitat Arable fields with cereals, scrubland. On soil with low lime content. Originally presumed native to the Middle East, today all over Europe.

> requires heat
> flowers make a herbal tea with a pleasant colour
> often included in wild flower seed mixes

leaf slender–lanceolate, woolly underside

flowers of cultivated varieties also pink, white or double

composite flower, 2.5–3.5 cm across

composite flower, with disc florets only

oval capitulum

outer petals heavily enlarged

179

solitary, overtopping stems

Did you know?

Since 1967, this has been Estonia's national flower symbolising resistance to Communism. The Soviet authorities ordered all Cornflowers to be coloured red on the occasion of an Estonian singing festival in 1969, to make the cornflowers look like Socialist carnations!

Chicory

Cichorium intybus (daisy family)

H 30–150 cm   July–Oct   perennial

Habitat Wayside and roadside verges, debris and rubble, wasteland, station sidings. On exposed ground in bright locations. Almost everywhere in Europe.

> contains milky sap
> tolerates salty ground
> plant dispersed all over the world

The composite flower heads open at about 6 in the morning, closing again around midday, or a little later if the weather is dull or overcast. The blue pigment in the flowers is soluble in water and turns pale in the rain and when the flower heads close. Until shortly after the end of the Second World War, people highly valued a variant species of Chicory, which has a fleshy root. These plants not only provided a source of vegetables, but when roasted, they were used as a coffee substitute ('Chicory coffee').

Did you know?

Chicorée (left) and Radicchio (right) are various cultivars of Chicory and are tasty in salads.

only light blue, occasionally white ray florets

composite flower, 3–5 cm in size, grows sideways and overtopping stalks

180

large end section

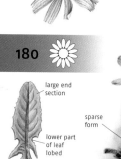

lower part of leaf lobed

sparse form

Grape-hyacinth

Muscari neglectum (hyacinth family)
H 15–30 cm   April–May   perennial

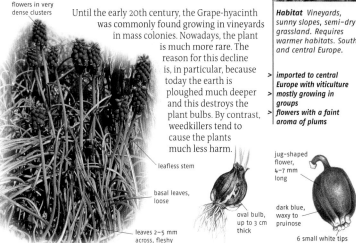

flowers in very
dense clusters

Until the early 20th century, the Grape-hyacinth was commonly found growing in vineyards in mass colonies. Nowadays, the plant is much more rare. The reason for this decline is, in particular, because today the earth is ploughed much deeper and this destroys the plant bulbs. By contrast, weedkillers tend to cause the plants much less harm.

leafless stem

basal leaves, loose

leaves 2–5 mm across, fleshy

oval bulb, up to 3 cm thick

Habitat Vineyards, sunny slopes, semi-dry grassland. Requires warmer habitats. South and central Europe.

> imported to central Europe with viticulture
> mostly growing in groups
> flowers with a faint aroma of plums

jug-shaped flower, 4–7 mm long

dark blue, waxy to pruinose

6 small white tips

181

Alpine Squill

Scilla bifolia (hyacinth family)
H 10–20 cm   March–April   perennial   ☠

The pretty Alpine Squill is an endangered species in many wild habitats, as people like to pick the flower. This causes severe damage to the plants, if the flower stems are picked and both the basal leaves are also torn up with them. On garden lawns, the similar Siberian Squill from Russia and central Asia mostly grows with nodding flowers.

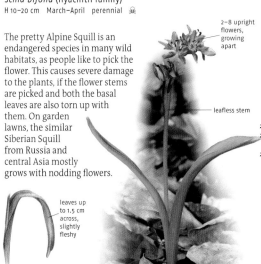

2–8 upright flowers, growing apart

leafless stem

leaves up to 1.5 cm across, slightly fleshy

Habitat Riverside woodlands and meadows, deciduous forests, orchard meadows near woodland. On damp soil in semi-shade. Central and southern Europe.

> mostly growing in groups
> occasionally also pink or white flowers
> 2 leaves emerging at the same time as flowers

6 star-shaped, spreading flower petals, 0.5–1 cm long

Bearded Iris
Iris germanica (iris family)
H 30–100 cm   May–June   perennial   (☠)

Habitat *Originates from eastern Mediterranean region. In central and all over southern Europe, found on walls, cliffs and slopes. Growing wild in wine-growing regions.*

> **fragrant flowers**
> **reproduction not by seeds, but division of rootstock**
> **attractive garden plant**

3 upwards-facing, broad elliptical flower petals

yellow 'beard'

3 deflexed flower petals

182

lance-shaped leaves, greyish-blue to green, pruinose

In Greek mythology, Iris was the goddess of the Rainbow, who acted as messenger to the Gods, bringing news from heaven to people on earth and to the underworld. The plant's name is an allusion to the magnificent colours that are displayed by all the different species. The yellow 'beard' on the lower flower petal is a trompe d'oeil – a clever simulation of a profusion of stamens.

up to 5 short-stalked flowers

outer flower petals up to 8 cm long

Did you know?
The dried rootstock smells similar to violets. People once gave this 'Violet root' to teething children to chew on and harden their gums. It was also used for colds and in perfumery.

Monk's-hood

Aconitum napellus (buttercup family)

H 50–150 cm   June–Aug   perennial   ☠

This is among the most poisonous plant species. It has been regarded as 'herbal arsenic' as 1-2 g is enough to prove fatal: death occurs under intensely painful fits due to cardiac arrest or paralysis of the respiratory organs. Emperor Claudius, the fourth Roman Emperor, was probably among the most famous victims to suffer death by poisoning by Monk's-hood – at his own wife's hand. The poison can also penetrate unbroken skin. Therefore, you must wear rubber gloves if you ever handle this plant!

basal leaves deeply 5–7-divided, palmate

Habitat *Riverside woodlands, damp pastures and edges of streams in low mountain ranges and mountains of central Europe up to altitudes of about 2,500 m.*

> **previously used as poison for arrows**
> **similar Variegated Monk's-hood has blue or white chequered flowers with protruding helmet**

helmet-shaped upper petal

flower dark blue-violet

183

flowers partially in long clusters

2 nectar petals, normally concealed in helmet

upright stem

Did you know?

Bumblebees visit the flowers to collect nectar. If you remove the helmet, you will notice two elongated, nectar-giving petals. The flower is reminiscent of a chariot with two harnessed animals, which is why the plant is also known as 'Venus's Chariot'.

Forking Larkspur
Consolida regalis (buttercup family)
H 20–40 cm   May–Aug   annual   🐝

Habitat *Arable fields with cereal crops, occasionally on country paths and rubble. Warm, nutrient-rich and alkaline loamy soil. Central and south Europe, southern Scandinavia.*

> plant appears very delicate
> heavily in decline due to intensive arable farming
> sometimes overwinters as leaf rosette

The spur conceals sweet nectar, which can only be reached by bumblebees and other insects with a proboscis of a minimum length of 15 mm. In the 16th and 17th centuries, people used Forking Larkspur to treat wounds, to induce birth and and as a soothing eye-bath. They also once used the flowers to dye wool a blue colour.

Did you know?
Ornamental plants growing in gardens up to over 1.5 m in height are usually cultivated varieties and crosses with other Larkspur species: Alpine Delphinium from the eastern Alps, the Siberian Larkspur from Siberia as well as various American varieties.

dark blue flower

spur 1.5–3 cm long

leaves divided into slender, pointed tips

straight or curved spur

184

flowers on long stalks

very loose flower clusters

Hairy Violet

Viola hirta (violet family)
H 5–10 cm   April–May   perennial

Many people love the delicate fragrance of violets. It is not surprising, therefore, that violets growing in the wild, which are not scented, are often referred to as rather dismissively as useless 'dog violets'. After flowering, the stalks bend downwards, so that the fruits lie on the ground.

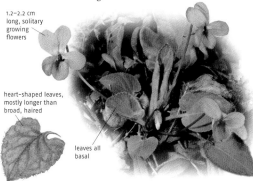

1.2–2.2 cm long, solitary growing flowers

heart-shaped leaves, mostly longer than broad, haired

leaves all basal

Habitat Margins of forests and copses, sparse pine forests, embankments, rough grassland. On chalky soil almost everywhere in Europe.

> **flowers without fragrance**
> **attracted to warm locations**
> **often forming large groups**

wing petals downwards-pointing at an angle

flowers light blue-violet

lower petal with line pattern

185

Sweet Violet

Viola odorata (violet family)
H 5–10 cm   March–April   perennial

The flowers contain a pleasant, fragrant oil that is supposed to have a soothing effect on the nerves. However, violet scent for soaps, perfume etc. has been also produced synthetically since the end of the 19th century. Violet extracts that can be obtained from the pharmacy generally contain the rootstock of the Bearded Iris (p. 182), which has a faint aroma of violets.

leaves heart-shaped to oval, about the same length as width

more or less glossy

stipules 1–4 times as long as wide

flowers 1–2 cm long, fragrant, growing individually

sometimes also with white flowers

leaves all basal

Habitat Streamside glades, forest margins, copses, wayside reveres, parks, gardens, cemeteries. Around the Mediterranean, western and central Europe.

> **requires a mild climate**
> **attracted to nutrient-rich soil**
> **found in central Europe, mostly within the vicinity of villages and hamlets**

flowers dark purple-violet

wing petals deflexed diagonally

Garden Lupin
Lupinus polyphyllus (pea family)
H 100–150 cm   June–Aug   perennial 🐝

Habitat *Seeded on embankments and woodland paths, partially growing wild and naturalised. On chalky soil. Almost everywhere in Europe.*

> *fragrant flowers*
> *native to around pacific North America*
> *seeds capable of germinating for over 50 years*

Some Garden Lupin varieties contain bitter constituents, which are highly poisonous, and some varieties have low bitters content (sweet lupins). The poisonous varieties are suitable for anchoring slopes and embankments and for improving soil quality. Tuberous growths that are typical of the pea family are attached to their roots and bacteria thrive in them. The bacteria process nitrogen from the atmosphere to enrich the soil with this nutrient. Sweet lupins are a very good source of wild fodder.

1.2–1.6 cm long
typical pea flower

curved, pointed keel

flowers in dense
upright clusters,
up to 60 cm long

digitate leaves
with 9–17 leaflets

leaflet with
sessile hairs

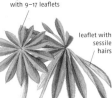

Did you know?
Many Lupin species for gardens bloom with colours ranging from white to red and yellow flowers or even two-tone colours. They form dense clusters and luxurious flower stems.

Lucerne

Medicago sativa (pea family)
H 30–80 cm   June–Sept   perennial

'Lucerne' means 'light' and refers to the light shiny seeds. The plant is originally native to the area around the Caspian Sea. Since ancient times, this plant has been widely cultivated, especially once wars were waged on horseback, as more fodder was then required. Today, the plant is still regarded as one of the most important sources of green fodder.

stalked flower head in leaf axils

bushy flower heads each with 5–25 flowers

Habitat Rough meadows, wayside verges, embankments. On warm ground. Frequently planted especially in hybrid varieties. Throughout Europe.

> also called 'Burgundy Trefoil' or 'Alfalfa'
> improves soil
> hybrids have 'contaminated' flower colours

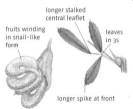

longer stalked central leaflet

fruits winding in snail-like form

leaves in 3s

longer spike at front

pea flower about 1 cm long, light or dark blue to violet hue

187

Tufted Vetch

Vicia cracca (pea family)
H 30–120 cm   June–Aug   perennial

The plant's tendrils complete circular and winding movements while searching for a place to anchor. Once they have found a contact point, they immediately react, clinging fast and entwining themselves around everything in a spiral shape. Tufted Vetch was once a much-feared weed out on the open fields, said to 'bring farmers to their knees.'

8–40 flowers in slender clusters

pinnate leaves with 12–20 leaflets

flowers growing to one side

end tendril mostly branched

Habitat Meadows, pastures, arable fields, wasteland, woodland margins, copses and riverbanks. Throughout Europe.

> clings to other plants with tendrils
> flowers can be blue to red-violet
> birds eat the seeds

typical pea flower about 1 cm in size

Bush Vetch

Vicia sepium (pea family)

H 30–60 cm   May–June   perennial

underside of stipules with brown nectar channel

Habitat *Meadows, wayside verges, wasteland, copses, woodland margins, woodland glades. Almost everywhere in Europe.*

> flowers often appear dirty
> attracted to rich nutrient supply
> ants crawl around on the plant

1.2–1.5 cm long, red-violet to dirty dark blue pea flower

Ants march around the Bush Vetch in droves. The mystery about their behaviour is soon revealed when you examine the shiny dark grooves that are hidden beneath the stipules (tiny outgrowths) at the base of each leaf and close to the stem: these outgrowths siphon off some of the sweet nectar that is a welcome food store for the ants. In return for their bounty, the tiny visitors keep the foliage free of parasites such as plant-eating caterpillars.

branched tendril

pinnate leaves

3–6 flowers apart or nodding in each of leaf axils

Arabian pea

Bituminaria bituminosa (pea family)

H 20–100 cm   April–Aug   perennial

Habitat *Wayside verges, fallow areas, weedy patches, olive groves. Especially on dry, sunny locations. Mediterranean region.*

> usually with a penetrating odour of tar
> occasionally also with white flowers
> requires heat

corolla murky violet

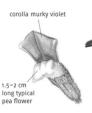

1.5–2 cm long typical pea flower

flower head with 7–30 flowers

long stalked

leaflet entire

If you have ever experienced the tar or asphalt-like smell of this plant, you will have no difficulty in immediately recognising this species again. In herbalism, the leaves used to be regarded as a stimulant for improving stamina and are also supposed to alleviate women's complaints. Nowadays, however, the plant is no longer in use.

leaves in 3s, clover-like

Viper's Bugloss

Echium vulgare (borage family)

H 25–100 cm   May–Sept   biennial

The flowers are red when in bud and then turn pink. They only appear an intense shade of blue when fully opened. Changes to the acid content of the flower cells are responsible for the transition. The fully opened, yet still pink-coloured flowers provide insects, especially bees, with the most nectar. The long protruding stamens make this flower resemble a snake's head. The plant has hispid or stiff bristly hairs as an effective natural protection against predators who attempt to eat it. Moreover, the plant also contains toxins.

Habitat *Weedy patches on pathways, station sidings, cliffs, rocky areas, wasteland, in quarries. Everywhere in Europe.*

> **flower head unfurls further apart during flowering**
> **often growing in groups**

conical flower head, up to 50 cm long

stamens protruding far out

deep trumpet-shape

corolla 1.5–2 cm long

189

plant with bristly hairs on cushions, up to 3 mm long

leaves alternate, lanceolate

bristly leaf rosette during 1st year

Did you know?

An astounding number of 25 different bugloss species are found growing on the Canary Islands. 24 of them occuring nowhere else in the world. They have quite different forms, ranging from annuals to herbaceous shrubs and species with flower spikes that stand up to 3 m tall.

Monk's Pepper
Vitex agnus-castus (vervain family)
H 100–600 cm   June–Nov   shrub

fruits the size of peppercorns

Habitat *Along coasts and riverside verges. Prefers sunny, warm locations with nutrient-rich soil. Around the Mediterranean.*

> *occasionally also with white flowers*
> *also a container plant in central Europe*
> *strong aromatic fragrance when crushed*

2-lipped corolla, 6–9 mm long

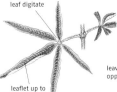

leaf digitate

leaflet up to 10 cm long

In antiquity, the plant's soothing effect on women's complaints was already known and the plant was dedicated to Hera, goddess of fertility, who in mythology was supposedly born beneath a Monk's Pepper shrub. Monks brought the plant to central Europe and used it to season their food with freshly ground fruitlets, thus suppressing their libido and maintaining their vow of celibacy. The plant is therefore also popularly known as 'Chaste Tree'.

Did you know?
Substances contained within the fruits affect the production of sex hormones. Herbal medicines containing extracts of the plant's fruits help, among other things, to prevent premenstrual tension.

terminal flower clusters, more in spikes

leaves opposite

Bugle
Ajuga reptans (mint family)
H 7–30 cm   May–Aug   perennial

labiate flowers, 1–1.5 cm long

leaves between flowers with smooth margin

dense flower stem, upright

Bugle used to be commonly known as 'Carpenter's Herb' and was regarded as a medicinal plant suitable for stemming blood flow. Nowadays, Bugle is ideal as an ornamental plant in gardens and as a creeping, ground-loving plant.

Habitat *On meadows, lawns, in copses, woodlands with herbaceous undergrowth, reveres. From plains to high mountains, almost everywhere in Europe.*

> *forms runners that lie prostrate or creep along the ground*
> *foliage remains green in winter*
> *attracted to nutrient-rich, preferably damp soil*

leaves opposite, sparsely haired

smooth margin or inconspicuously toothed

minute upper lip

3-part lower lip

191

Geneva Bugle
Ajuga genevensis (mint family)
H 7–30 cm   April–June   perennial

The fruitlets bear an appendage that is high in fat content and makes a tasty treat for ants. This is why ants like to transport the fruitlets away from the plant, thus ensuring its dispersal. The Geneva Bugle – sometimes also known as Blue Bugle – was first recorded growing in the region around Geneva.

Habitat *Rough grassland, embankments, wayside reveres, dry woodland. Mostly in sunny, warm locations on chalky ground. Central and south Europe.*

> *no runners, in contrast to the Bugle*
> *with ragged hairs*
> *also attractive as a garden plant*

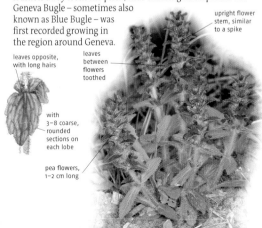

upright flower stem, similar to a spike

leaves opposite, with long hairs

leaves between flowers toothed

with 3–8 coarse, rounded sections on each lobe

pea flowers, 1–2 cm long

tiny upper lip

3-part lower lip

Ground-ivy
Glechoma hederacea (dead-nettle family)
H 10–40 cm   April–June   perennial

Habitat *Meadows, pastures, grassland areas, riverside glades, woodland margins, hedgerows, embankments. On nutrient-rich soil. Throughout Europe.*

> **stems creeping, extensive ground coverage**
> **leaves remain green throughout winter**
> **often early coloniser of newly cleared habitats**

upper lip flat

3-part lower lip

Ground-ivy was used as a medicinal and magical plant by the Germanic tribes. Herbalism still recommends the aromatic plant as a treatment for diarrhoea, coughs and skin ailments. The herbaceous plant tastes spicy, bitter and, after a brief period, slightly irritates the back of the throat. It can be mixed in salads and with quark cheese or prepared as a vegetable similar to Spinach. However, large quantities of the freshly picked plant are said to have a fatal effect on horses.

4-edged stem

upright flowering stem sections

leaves opposite, kidney to heart-shaped

pea flowers, up to 2 cm long

margin rounded, roughly toothed

2–3 flowers in axils of leaves

Did you know?

Ground-ivy was also once used as a substitute for Hops as bitters when brewing beer, until the introduction of strict laws in Germany from 1516 that were designed to keep beer free of any kind of additives.

Selfheal

Prunella vulgaris (mint family)
H 5–30 cm   June–Sept   perennial

leaves oval, elongated

dense flower clusters overtopping stem

Sepals surrounding the ripe fruitlets only open in damp weather. If raindrops then fall on them, the sepals and calyx are pressed downwards and when they bounce back, as if recoiling from a catapult, the tiny fruitlets shoot outwards and spin far and wide. The fruitlets are damp and sticky and cling everywhere e.g. to the soles of shoes.

Habitat Meadows, pastures, along rivers, woodland paths, parks, garden lawns. On fresh or damp soils in light locations. Everywhere in Europe.

> *attracted to nutrient-rich soil*
> *dry fruit stems visible from afar*
> *the similar Large Selfheal has flowers of up to 2.5 cm in size*

leaves opposite

withered sepal remnants after flowering

4 fruitlets

hood-shaped upper lip

typical pea flower, 0.7–1.5 cm long

Skullcap

Scutellaria galericulata (mint family)
H 10–40 cm   June–Sept   perennial

The sepal closes up as soon as the flower corolla withers away. It then looks like a helmet with the visor pulled down because of the helmet formation that remains on top. The helmet now functions like a catapult. If raindrops fall on it, the flower is depressed, scattering tiny fruitlets out of the sepal as it recoils.

Habitat Riverbanks, ditches, wetlands, fens. On wet, also temporarily flooded, nutrient-rich soil. Throughout Europe.

> *attracts bees*
> *often growing hidden among other plants*
> *also flowers in partial shade*

leaves longer than flowers

upper lip with helmet

double-lipped sepal

closed sepal

leaves opposite

2 flowers each in axils of upper leaves

sparsely toothed, broad to lanceolate

curved upper lip

1–1.5 cm long, violet-blue typical pea flower

long, upwards bending tube

Sage
Salvia officinalis (mint family)
H 20–70 cm   May–July   shrub

Habitat Semi-dry grasslands, rocky grassland areas, stony slopes and cliffs in warmer locations. South Europe, growing wild in central Europe.

> lower stems mostly woody
> plant with an intensely aromatic fragrance when crushed
> many cultivated varieties

The plant's reputation in antiquity was as a guarantor of a long life. This is why the name is derived from the Latin 'salvus' or 'healthy'. However the healing power is not quite so potent, although Sage extracts are still used as a gargle to sooth soar throats or as a herbal tea as a cure for heavy perspiration. Sage leaves are a popular ingredient in butter or oily sauces in Mediterranean cuisine.

upper lip almost perpendicular

violet typical pea flower, 1.8–2.5 cm long

leaves oval to broad, lanceolate

wrinkled, densely haired underside

loose flower clusters overtopping stems

leaves opposite

Clary
Salvia sclarea (mint family)
H 30–120 cm   May–Aug   biennial

Habitat Wayside verges, rocky cliffs, open woodlands, also cultivated as a medicinal, herbal and ornamental plant. Native to the Mediterranean.

> resin-like aroma
> upper section of stems sticky
> also attractive in gardens

long flower clusters

In the 19th century, vintners especially used the tender young leaves of Clary to intensify white wines by creating a hint of Muscat wine. Today, it is no longer allowed to enhance the aroma in this way, although there are liqueurs and Wormwood spirits (absinthe or vermouth) as well as soaps and cosmetics that include Clary extracts.

upper lip broad, crescent-shaped

2–3 cm long, light blue or pink labiate flower

pink to purple-tinged leaves in flower head

crinkled leaves

margin irregularly crenate

Meadow Clary
Salvia pratensis (mint family)
H 30–60 cm   May–Aug   perennial

The two stamens look like small railway tracks resting side by side and suspended in mid air. If a bee creeps inside the flower, it depresses the shorter end of the formation so that the longer end and the anthers enclose around and cover the insect's back. The insect is then dusted with a coat of pollen. If flowers are more developed, the style adopts the position of the downwards-depressed anther, so the pollen from the insects clings on.

Habitat Rough grassland, semi-dry grassland, poor-yielding meadows, pathways, embankments, reservoirs. In warmer locations. All over Europe.

> occasionally also with white flowers
> only 1–3 opposite leaf pairs on stem
> plant has aromatic fragrance when crushed

broad upper lip, crescent-shaped

dark or violet-blue labiate flower, 1.5–2.5 cm long

195

4–8-petals in whorls forming loose flower heads

crinkled leaves

margin rounded, toothed

stamens concealed in upper lip

longitudinal section through flower

limb

4-edged stem

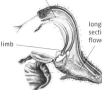

Did you know?

In 1984 a special stamp was issued in Germany depicting a bee hovering above a Sage flower. The illustrator cannot have been aware of the flower structure: the anthers are only lowered when the bee is inside the flower.

Garden Lavender

Lavandula angustifolia (mint family)

H 20–100 cm   June–Aug   shrub

Habitat *Dry shrubberies, rocky areas, from the plains to mountain uplands. Especially around the Mediterranean.*

> **characteristic, intense fragrance**
> **also fairly hardy plant in central Europe**
> **many different varieties for gardens and cultivation**

The name 'Lavender' is derived from the Latin verb 'lavare' meaning 'to wash'. Yet Lavender is not an effective cleaning agent, but produces an intense aromatic scent that creates the illusion of cleanliness. Place a Lavender sachet amongst fresh laundry in order to keep away moths. Lavender is an important essential oil for the perfume industry and is especially cultivated on a wide scale in France.

blue-violet labiate flower, about 1 cm long

slender leaves, up to 4 cm long, downy at the start, later bare

long, dense flower heads at the top

lower whorls slightly apart

calyx covered in short hairs

196

French Lavender

Lavandula stoechas (mint family)

H 30–100 cm   March–June   shrub

Habitat *Dry and bright shrubberies, pine forests. On silicate rock. Around the Mediterranean.*

> **colourful leaf tuft attracts insects**
> **leaves with Camphor fragrance**
> **suitable for balcony or terrace**

French Lavender's scientific name is inspired by a group of islands near Marseille, which the Greeks called 'stoechas'. Nowadays, on these islands known as 'Îles des Hyères', the plant is reputed to grow in such abundance that sailors navigate merely by following the fragrant aroma of flowers.

conspicuous tuft at end

leaves 1–4 cm long, hoary

leaf curved downwards

black-violet labiate flower, 6–8 mm long

spike-like flower head up to 3 cm long

Rosemary
Rosmarinus officinalis (mint family)
H 50–200 cm Jan–Dec shrub

Rosemary used to be regarded as an aide-memoire and as a symbol of love. Before bridal bouquets were made out of garlands of Myrtle sprigs, Rosemary was used. A Rosemary wreath plays a symbolic role in Shakespeare's 'Hamlet' as a symbol of trust. The plant used to symbolize remembrance of the dead and the hope for resurrection at funeral services. At the same time, its fragrance would also conceal the odour of death.

Did you know?
'Queen of Hungary's Water' or 'Eau de la Reine d'Hongrie' contains essential oil in alcohol that is distilled from Rosemary. The recipe dates from the 14th century and was named after the Queen of Hungary. This was one of the earliest perfumes of its kind. 'Eau de Cologne' still contains Rosemary oil today.

Habitat *Dry shrubberies and grassland, sparse grassy areas and open woodland. Mediterranean, cultivated in central Europe as a shrub for medicinal and for herbal seasoning.*

> **leaves appear like pine needles**
> **characteristic fragrant aroma**
> **popular as herb for seasoning food**

leaf up to 4 cm long, slender linear

downwards-curving margin

underside white and downy

2 stamens, protruding far out

lower lip with darker mottled pattern

197

labiate flowers about 1 cm long, mostly pale blue

small flower heads in amongst foliage

Ivy-leaved Toadflax

Cymbalaria muralis (figwort family)

H 10–40 cm   June–Sept   perennial   (🌱)

Habitat *Vertical walls, cliffs. On slightly damper, mostly chalky stony soil and in crevices. Almost everywhere in Europe.*

> **flowers turned towards light**
> **originally ornamental plant native to Mediterranean**
> **especially prolific growth near towns and villages**

For a plant that grows upright against walls and along cliffs, it is crucial that the seeds do not simply scatter down to the ground. Toadflax is therefore its own gardener: while the fruits ripen, their stalks become extremely elongated and curve away from the light. This is how the fruits slide inbetween crevices in walls or along cliffs, where the seeds find a suitable place for germination.

long leaf stalk

prostrate or pendent plant

roundish blade, 5–7-lobed, bare

2-lipped flower about 1 cm in size

upwards-arched, yellow lining

often tinged red-violet

198

fruits curving to undergrowth

solitary flowers on long stalks

Did you know?

The scientific name for Toadflax 'cymbalaria' is derived from Latin 'cymbalon'. This means 'cymbel' or 'sound pool' and alludes to the shape of the leaves that look a little like this musical instrument.

Alpine Toadflax

Linaria alpina (figwort family)

H 8–15 cm   June–Aug   perennial

This plant was reputed to have magical powers, especially around Austria. It was used as a charm to ward off influences from witchcraft and the devil and to frighten off sprites and hobgoblins. In some areas, Alpine Toadflax is almost exclusively found with uniform, violet-coloured flowers.

fleshy leaves, 1–3 mm across

grows in flat cushions

blue-green plant

Habitat Damp stony rubble, scree, gravel banks. In central and southern European mountain ranges, especially at altitudes from 1,200 to above 3,800 m.

> **conspicuous from a long distance**
> **requires exposed locations**
> **stems creeping above or in rubble**

upwards-arching, orangey yellow lining

flower 1.5–2.5 cm long, double lipped

long spur

Heart-leaved Globe Daisy

Globularia cordifolia (plantain family)

H 3–10 cm   May–July

The minute solitary flowers are only conspicuous because there are so many of them grouped closely together, giving the plant its name. Globe daisies contain a bitter, poisonous substance that can lead to vomiting, diarrhoea, light-headedness and collapse of the circulatory system.

flowering stems upright

flowers form spherical heads, 1–1.5 cm across

cleft in heart shape at front

leathery leaves, gradually tapering to the stem

Habitat Dry, chalky scrubland, cliff edges and ranges, stony grassland. In mountain ranges of central and southern Europe from the valleys to altitudes of about 2,800 m.

> **evergreen leaves**
> **can form flat carpets above stones**
> **helps anchor rocky cliffside rubble**

slender upper lip, with 2 points

flower 6–8 mm long

3-pointed lower lip

Common Butterwort
Pinguicula vulgaris (bladderwort family)
H 5–15 cm   May–June   perennial

Habitat *Fens, outlets of natural springs, lawns with water sprinklers. In bright locations. North Europe, in central Europe in mountain ranges above 1,600 m.*

> *carnivorous plant*
> *the similar 'Alpine Butterwort' has white flowers*
> *disappears if exposed to fertiliser or removal of moisture*

Butterworts trap small insects that act as an additional source of nitrogen in nutrient-poor locations. In order to do so, they isolate sticky mucus from the leaf's upperside, where tiny flies, beetles and spiders are caught fast. Larger insects can also become caught when the leaf margins curl inwards. Afterwards, the plant emits enzymes and digests the prey. The digestive substances are soluble and can be absorbed by the foliage.

often with insects stuck fast

5–8 yellow-green leaves forming a basal rosette

flower white at central ring, with short hairs

2–lipped flower, with long spur

solitary flowers on leafless stems

flower 1–2.5 cm long

Did you know?
The leaves were once occasionally used to thicken milk for cheese production. The enzymes that they contain cause the milk to curdle and produce rennet, or as with Lady's Bedstraw (p. 214) cause milk to curdle. This is a protected plant today.

Field Scabious
Knautia arvensis (teasel family)
H 30–80 cm   July–Aug   perennial

Field Scabious can also be confused for Small Scabious (see below) which has black sepal bristles. This plant, along with other scabious species, has been used in the past to treat stomach ulcers, and its juice applied to the skin to remove pimples.

Habitat Meadows, semi-dry grassland, wayside verges, woodland margins, arable fields. On nutrient-rich soil in warmer locations. Almost everywhere in Europe.

> *fragrant flowers*
> *flower heads attract many insects*
> *occasionally also with white flowers*

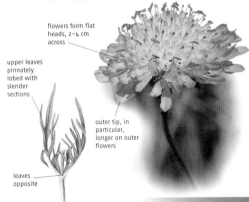

flowers form flat heads, 2–4 cm across

upper leaves pinnately lobed with slender sections

outer tip, in particular, longer on outer flowers

leaves opposite

calyx with short, light bristles

corolla blue to red-violet, up to 1.8 cm long

4 tips of different lengths

201

Small Scabious
Scabiosa columbaria (teasel family)
H 25–60 cm   July–Nov   perennial

'Scabious' is derived from the Latin 'scabies' meaning 'scratches, scabies, scab'. In the 16th and 17th century, the plant was already used against these and other skin ailments. Nowadays, scabious varieties are no longer used for medicinal purposes, although they are attractive as decorative plants in wild flower gardens.

Habitat Sunny rough grassland and meadows, woodland reveres, sparse pine forests. On dry, mostly chalky soils. Especially in central and south Europe.

> *intolerant of fertiliser*
> *roots up to 1.5 m deep*
> *fruits can fly in strong wind*

flowers form flat heads, 1.5–3.5 cm across

black bristles on calyx

outer tips of outer flowers clearly elongated

fruit-bearing flower head

corolla blue-purple to violet, up to 1.8 cm long

5 tips of unequal lengths

Greater Celandine

Chelidonium majus (poppy family)
H 30–70 cm   April–Oct   perennial

Habitat *Weedy areas on waysides, woodland margins, hedgerows, walls, in overgrown, wild gardens, prefers semi-shade or shade. Almost everywhere in Europe.*

> **often forming large groups**
> **mostly near towns or villages**
> **wilts if location too sunny**

The plant's noticeably milky juice led to the common belief in mediaeval times that it could act as an antidote for 'yellow diseases'. Therefore, the plant was recommended to treat cases of jaundice and other complaints of the liver and gall bladder. Greater Celandine is one of the few plants for which this type of classification – according to the plant's colour and appearance – is actually true. Today, extracts are still used to treat complaints of the liver and gall bladder.

abundant stamens

4 broad oval petals, about 1 cm long

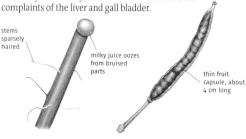

stems sparsely haired

milky juice oozes from bruised parts

thin fruit capsule, about 4 cm long

sparsely flowered clusters

compound or pinnate leaves

Did you know?

In herbal remedies, Greater Celandine extracts were used to treat warts. To do so, the orangey-yellow juice needs to be evenly sprinkled on the wart, taking care to avoid the skin.

Yellow Horned Poppy

Glaucium flavum (poppy family)
H 30–90 cm   April–Sept   biennial, herbaceous perennial

The Yellow Horned Poppy is distinguished from other genuine poppy varieties (pp. 19 and 20) not merely by the conspicuous long, horn-shaped capsule. Other poppy petals are crinkled when in bud, thus giving a crinkled appearance, but the petals of the Horned Poppy are rolled up. They then unroll as soon as both the bristly sepals have withered and fallen away.

Habitat *Exposed locations, wasteland, roadside verges, rubble, especially near coasts. Mediterranean, solitary as far as central Europe.*

solitary flower, 6–9 cm in size

rough fruit capsule, up to 20 cm long

plant pruinose, blue-green

> **contains yellow milky juice**
> **fairly salt tolerant**
> **sepals fall away when flowers open**

linear ovary

leaves slightly fleshy, pinnately lobed

abundant stamens

Winter-cress

Barbarea vulgaris (cabbage family)
H 30–90 cm   May–July   biennial

The scientific name of Winter-cress is derived from Saint Barbara, a bringer of aid in times of crisis. Perhaps another popular belief was that the plant's leaves can also be harvested on St Barbara's day (4 December). This unusual harvest time was important, because in winter the leaves could provide an important source of Vitamin C and therefore offer an essential dietary supplement.

Habitat *Weedy patches on country pathways, stream and riverside meadows, edges of arable fields, spinneys, earth banks, gravel quarries. Almost everywhere in Europe.*

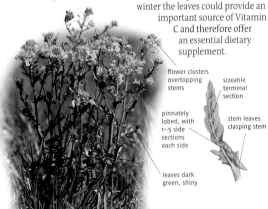

> **leaves also remain green in winter**
> **acidic to tangy taste, slightly like Cress**

flower clusters overtopping stems

sizeable terminal section

pinnately lobed, with 1–5 side sections each side

stem leaves clasping stem

flower 4–9 mm in size

4 reverse, oval petals

4 light green, sparse sepals

leaves dark green, shiny

Woad

Isatis tinctoria (cabbage family)

H 40–120 cm   May–July   biennial, herbaceous   (☉)

Habitat *Weedy patches on country pathways, in stone quarries, on station sidings and wasteland. Almost everywhere in Europe.*

> *often grows in groups*
> *originally native to Asia*
> *requires warmth and light*

In ancient times, the Romans and Greeks used the plant's leaves to extract blue pigment for indigo. In mediaeval times, Woad was the most important plant for obtaining colour pigment. Fresh leaves do not produce any dyeing agents. Only after fermentation and the addition of urine could a colour bath be prepared for dipping the fabrics. Once the fabric was removed from the bath, it was dyed greenish-yellow and gradually turned blue when exposed to the air.

Did you know?

*From late mediaeval times onwards, Woad was in competition with the tropical True Indigo shrub (*Indigofera tinctoria*). In spite of official rulings, the Indigo shrub won out in the 17th century. In 1897, the first synthetic production of indigo was a success.*

4 petals

flower 4–8 mm in size

4 elliptical sepals

204

extensive, leafless inflorescences

leaves lanceolate

clasping stem, with pointed tips

upright stem

entire plant blue-green

with winged margin

pendant fruits, up to 25 mm long

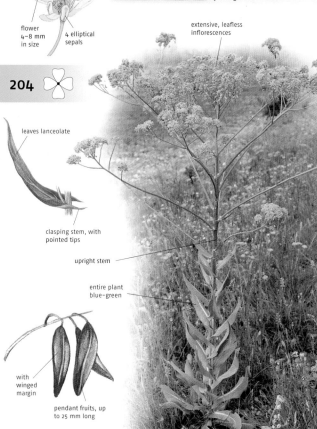

Yellow Whitlowgrass
Draba aizoides (cabbage family)
H 3–10 cm   April–Aug   perennial

This very slow-growing species can only survive in habitats where little competition exists with other flowering plants. Only cohabitation with a particular species of cliff moss is relatively common. In favourable instances, the plant cushions can live for up to 10 years. However these plants are under severe threat along popular hill climbing routes.

Habitat *Cliffs, rocky grassland. In crevices or in more or rocky debris with low limestone content. In mountains of central and southern Europe.*

> requires sufficient light
> in the German Jura mountains, a relic from the last ice age
> evergreen leaf rosette

short, dense clusters with 5–25 flowers

elliptical fruit, 5–10 mm long

4 petals, 4–6 mm long

4 broad oval sepals

evergreen leaves in rosettes

fringed leaf margin

Buckler-mustard
Biscutella laevigata (cabbage family)
H 15–30 cm   May–July   perennial

Buckler-mustard fruits are highly distinctive and easy to identify, unlike other plants in the cabbage family. Each half of the spectacle-shaped fruits contains one seed. In blustery and very windy conditions, the seeds loosen and are carried away on the breeze.

Habitat *Stony grassland, rubble, promontories, bogs and moorland. Mostly on chalky soils up to over 2,500 m. Central and southern Europe.*

> often protruding above surrounding plants
> especially conspicuous by fruits
> light-loving

flowers in loose clusters

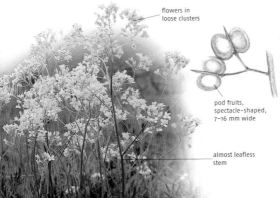

pod fruits, spectacle-shaped, 7–16 mm wide

almost leafless stem

4 light yellow, 4–7 mm long petals

rounded or notched at front

Charlock
Sinapis arvensis (cabbage family)
H 30–60 cm   June–Oct   annual

Habitat Weedy patches on arable fields, fallow areas, rocky places, wasteland, along waysides, roadside embankments. Almost everywhere in Europe.

> often growing in groups
> typical mustard aroma when bruised
> seeds with long germination period

The pungent-smelling, sharp and tangy mustard oils protect bruised plants from fungus invasion and herbivorous predators. 'Cabbage white' butterfly caterpillars prefer plants containing these substances. The mustard oils can even be detected in grown moths and protect them from predators. Charlock was already a common weed during the Bronze Age, as proven by finds in pile dwellings.

flower 1–2 cm in size

4 petals

4 green, slender sepals

flower clusters overtopping stems

sparse fruits pods, when ripe 2.5–4 cm long, 2–3 mm thick

margin irregularly notched, toothed

leaves stalked

Did you know?
The similar White Mustard (Sinapis alba) *is a cultivar from the eastern Mediter-ranean. Nowadays, this plant is often grown on open fields for use as a fertiliser, herbal season-ing, oil or fodder plant. Its fruit pods have hispid, or stiff hairs and the pods are flattened at the front.*

Wallflower

Erysimum cheiri (cabbage family)
H 20–50 cm   April–June   biennial, shrub-like 🐝

The Wallflower was an ornamental plant in ancient gardens. In those days and well into the mediaeval period, the plant was thought to belong to the violet family due to its fragrance – the flower shape had no bearing on this inaccurate classification. Multi-coloured and double-flowered varieties have been common since the end of the 16th century. The plant contains substances that act as a heart stimulant.

Habitat *Rocky, warm locations, walls, stony grassland. Wild originally in eastern Mediterranean.*

> also tolerates dryness
> widely dispersed as ornamental plant
> flowers with pleasant and strong fragrance

flowers 1.2–2.2 cm in size

fairly dense flower clusters

3–7 cm long fruit pod

flowers in different yellow or orange hues

leaves longish to lanceolate

margin entire

petals roundish to reversed oval-shaped

207

Roseroot

Rhodiola rosea (stonecrop family)
H 10–30 cm   June–Aug   perennial

The Vikings are reputed to have replenished their physical prowess and stamina by taking Roseroot. The plant has been commonly used in Russia and Scandinavia for many centuries. It is only in recent years that the plant has become popular in Europe as a medicinal herb that enhances the immune system and intensifies the powers of concentration and intellectual capacity.

Habitat *Cliff crevices, stony mountain grass-lands. On poor, silicate soils. North Europe, in mountains of central and southern Europe.*

> dried roots with fragrance of roses when crushed
> flowers occasionally also reddish
> male and female plants

leaves fleshy, bluish-green

very dense, umbel-like flower head

margin smooth or slightly toothed

leaves in spiral arrangement around stem

flower head 4–6 mm in size

at the most, 4 short sepals

at the most, 4 petals

Alternate-leaved Golden-saxifrage

Chrysosplenium alternifolium (saxifrage family)
H 15–20 cm   March–May   perennial

Habitat *Riverside and woodland ravines, stream banks. On wet, chalky soils. Especially in north and central Europe up to altitudes of 2,500 m.*

> requires humid locations
> mostly growing in groups
> leaf shape influences the plant's name

The fruit capsules open out into flat cups or bowls and raindrops that fall into them wash the seeds out of the capsules. With a little luck, the rainwater also carries the seeds even further away. In the Middle Ages, people believed that the spleen-like shape of the leaves could help cure conditions affecting the spleen. However Saxifrage does not contain any substances that could prove beneficial.

Did you know?

The more delicate Opposite-leaved Golden-saxifrage has opposite leaves. It colonises similar locations, though mostly in cooler areas. The plants are quite inconspicuous with only pale yellowish bracts.

flower 3–5 mm in size

4 yellowish sepals

open fruit capsule, bowl-like

kidney-shaped leaves

abundant seeds

leaves alternate

crenate leaf margin

8–20 flowers

several yellowish-green to gold-green leaves around flowers

Common Lady's-mantle

Alchemilla vulgaris (rose family)

H 3–30 cm   May–Sept   perennial

Small incisions on the leaf margins can actively emit moisture. This moisture, along with raindrops, does not flow on the leaf's water-repellent upperside, but floats as tiny, silver and gleaming droplets on the leaf's surface. In mediaeval times, alchemists therefore grew to regard this plant as a magical herbaceous plant that was ideal for use by goldsmiths.

Habitat Meadows, pastures, copses, woodland pathways, ditches. On nutrient-rich soil. Almost everywhere in Europe from low plains to high mountains.

> very varied species
> foliage more conspicuous than flowers
> Garden Lady's Mantle is more heavily haired and more common in gardens

margin leaves round to kidney-shaped

often with droplets on

with semi-circular to triangular-shaped lobes

abundant, tufted flower clusters

matt, haired leaves

flower 4–6 mm in size

4 outer and 4 inner sepals

209

Silver Lady's-mantle

Alchemilla conjucta (rose family)

H 5–30 cm   June–Aug   perennial

In herbalism, all species of lady's-mantle are regarded as an important source of medication for treating women's complaints. This has probably been promoted not merely because of the plant's natural substances, but also by the shape of the leaves. They are reminiscent of the large, folded cloak that the Virgin Mary was commonly depicted wearing in many early images of the saint.

Habitat Rough mountain grassland, pastures, cliffs, cliffside rubble, mostly on chalk-limestone. In mountains of central and northern Europe.

> name probably derives from plant's silvery hairs
> the similar Alpine Lady's-mantle grows on silicate ground

digitate leaf with 7–9 leaflets

dark green upperside

margin and underside silvery hairs, sessile

tufted flower head

yellowish-green inner sepals

petal 3–4 mm in size

external sepals small or missing

Tormentil

Potentilla erecta (rose family)
H 10–30 cm   May–Aug   perennial

If you cut into the rootstock of Tormentil, after only a short time, it turns a red colour as though it were bleeding. Tannins are responsible for this process and they make the plant an effective medicinal herb. This plant cannot only be used to stem bleeding, but in mediaeval times, it was even regarded as an effective cure for the Plague, even if this was completely ineffective. Today, herbal tea or a tincture made from the plant is still used to treat diarrhoea as well as sore throats and mouth infections. Tormentil Schnapps is also a popular digestif.

flowers about 1 cm in size

4 petals, slightly notched at front

green sepal

210

colours blood-red where cut

dark green, glossy leaves

bulbous to cylindrical rootstock, blackish brown

mostly 3-part leaf

2 large stipules

sessile or with short stalk

Did you know?

The scientific name, 'Potentilla' means strength and refers to the healing power of this and several other species of the plant.

Common Evening-primrose
Oenothera biennis (willowherb family)
H 50–200 cm   June–Aug   biennial

The flowers have an intense fragrance and open in the evening. During the final phase, the sepal folds back and the flower unfurls, with petals that were initially creased spreading out. This phase lasts all of about three minutes. Everything happens so quickly that the process is easily visible to the naked eye and a persistent, delicate and light rustling sound is also audible. By the next day, the flowers have already wilted – during the morning on hot days, or otherwise by the afternoon.

Habitat Weedy patches on wasteland, rubble, station sidings, embankments. Preferably on dry soils. Almost everywhere in Europe.

> each flower cluster continues flowering over a long period
> originally native to North America
> attractive in wild flower gardens

Did you know?
The roots are fleshy during the first year and when harvested in this state, they were once a popular vegetable. They are prepared like Black Salsify and are best mixed with other vegetables, as they have a slightly bitter taste if eaten alone.

sepals with membrane, quickly falling away

4-part stigma

4 reversed, oval petals

211

dense flower cluster, heavily elongated during flowering period

flowers in axils of leaves

leaves forming a rosette in first year

longish to oval, pointed

reddish taproot

corolla 2–5 cm long

fruit capsules often remain throughout winter

Cypress Spurge
Euphorbia cyparissias (spurge family)
H 15–30 cm   April–Aug   perennial

Habitat Rough pastures and grassland on chalky stone, waysides, wayside reveres, embankments, wasteland. Throughout Europe.

> plant with white milky juice
> mostly growing in groups
> preferably on dry soils

Groups of the Cypress Spurge quite often include plants that could be mistaken for another species. These specimens are yellowish green, with slender and unbranched, tall growth. They are non-flowering and the undersides of the leaves have tiny orangey pustules (see detail). These plants have been attacked by a rust fungus, which can affect the plant in such an adverse way that it completely changes appearance.

fungus-infected stem with deviant form

2 diamond-shaped to triangular greenish-yellow leaves

4 half moon-shaped, yellow glands

terminal flower cluster with 10–20 stalks

flower stem often branched

leaves alternate

212

leaf 1–3 cm long, 2–3 mm across

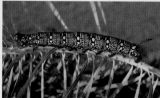

Did you know?
Spurge varieties are the favourite source of food for the conspicuous caterpillars of the Spurge Hawkmoth. In many places, the Cypress Spurge is the caterpillars' sole source of nutrients.

Spiny Spurge

Euphorbia verrucosa (spurge family)
H 30–50 cm   May–June   perennial

The milky juice from the Spiny Spurge is wholly unsuitable for humans and can even be poisonous. If the juice comes into contact with the skin, it can cause inflammation and, internally, causes blood in the stool and can even prove fatal.

Habitat Arid, rough meadows and pastures, sunny embankments. Central and southern Europe.

> white milky juice
> requires warmth
> mostly growing in larger groups

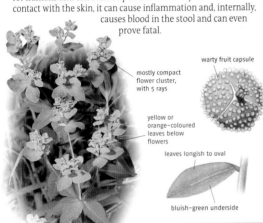

mostly compact flower cluster, with 5 rays

warty fruit capsule

yellow or orange-coloured leaves below flowers

leaves longish to oval

bluish-green underside

4 oval, yellow glands

2 broadly oval or reversed oval leaves

 213

Crosswort

Cruciata laevipes (bedstraw family)
H 15–50 cm   April–June   perennial

The plant's name refers to the cross-shaped leaf arrangement that makes it easy to identify the plant, even if it is not in flower. The species is occasionally available as a decorative garden perennial. The plant was once regarded as a medicinal herb to treat rheumatism. Nowadays, however, this is no longer a common practice in herbalism.

Habitat Weedy patches along hedgerows, woodland margins, fences, ditches, in riverside woodlands. In sunshine in semi-shade. Almost everywhere in Europe.

> flowers with honey-like fragrance
> mostly grows in groups
> easy to cultivate as a garden plant

yellowish-green plant

flower clusters in leaf axils

long soft hairs

oval to broad, lanceolate

whorls of 4 leaves

petals 2 mm across

wheel-shaped corolla with 4 points

Lady's Bedstraw
Galium verum (bedstraw family)
H 30–60 cm   June–Sept   perennial

Lady's Bedstraw is well adapted to its mostly dry habitats. The
leaves appear almost needle-like because of their inwards-
curving margins and so they hardly lose any moisture through
evaporation. According to a Christian legend, Lady's Bedstraw was
used to line the manger where Baby Jesus lay. If placed as 'straw'
in shoes, the plant was also reputed to ease childbirth and ward
off magical spells.

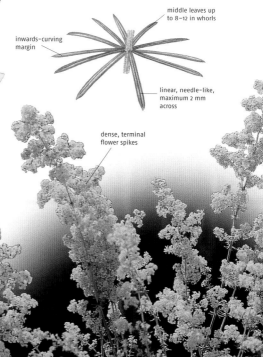

middle leaves up
to 8–12 in whorls

inwards-curving
margin

linear, needle-like,
maximum 2 mm
across

flower 2–4 mm
across

golden
yellow corolla
with 4 tips

dense, terminal
flower spikes

214

Did you know?

*Lady's Bedstraw can
be effective in cheese
production, as it has
the same effect as
rennet. Both help
milk curdle – 'gala'
is the Greek for milk.
In ancient times, milk
was therefore poured
through a sieve woven
from Lady's Bedstraw.*

Rue

Ruta graveolens (rue family)
H 30–50 cm   June–Aug   shrub

fruit capsule
dotted with
oil glands

Rue used to be added to wine in order to enrich the aroma. It was also part of fragrant posies that people carried with them to suppress unpleasant odours or protect against infection with diseases such as the Plague. Essential oils from the Rue were, however, also misused to aid abortions that frequently ended in fatalities. Inflammations can be caused that are similar to abrasive burns, if the plant comes into contact with the skin and simultaneous exposure to intensive sunshine.

Habitat Scrubland, cliffs, walls, vineyards, copses, often planted in gardens. Southern Europe, rarely growing wild in central Europe.

> requires dry, warm locations
> tangy aromatic fragrance
> use very sparingly as herbal seasoning!

Did you know?

Rue, Dittany (p. 73) as well as Fennel (p. 232) and other members of the carrot family containing fragrant substances make good fodder for swallowtail butterfly caterpillars.

flower
1.2–1.8 cm
in size

petals greenish-yellow, spoon-shaped, finely toothed

215

heavily branched terminal flower cluster

flowers and fruits often emerge simultaneously

alternate

leaves blue-green, fleshy

pinnate with pinnately lobed sections

sparse plant

Yellow Water-lily

Nuphar lutea (water-lily family)

H 50–250 cm   June–Aug   perennial

Habitat Still and slow flowing water up to depths of 6 m. Almost everywhere in Europe from the low plains to lower mountain regions.

> flowers protruding slightly above water's surface
> fruits ripen under water
> roots on waterbed

A popular myth holds that nymphs and water spirits protect the Yellow Water-lily. Therefore a common belief was that the floating flowers should not be plucked from the water's surface, as otherwise the spirits would drag the culprit into the water.

solitary flowers

broad oval leaves, 10–30 cm long, floating on water's surface

flowers 3–5 cm in size

abundant stamens

Yellow Anemone

Anemone ranunculoides (buttercup family)

H 10–20 cm   April–May   perennial

Habitat Damp deciduous and riverside woodlands, hedgerows. Often grows in larger groups. Almost everywhere in Europe.

> requires nutrient-rich soil
> flowers mostly in pairs
> closely resembles the Wood Anemone (p. 130)

The juice that flows fresh from the plant is an irritant to skin and mucus membranes, but dried plants no longer have this effect. The rootstock contains a rich store of nutrients so that the plant can rapidly develop in spring. Flowers are in bloom before the foliage emerges on nearby trees to provide shade.

mostly 2 flowers on 1 stem

whorl with 3 leaves

leaves 3-part to base

flower 1.8–2.5 cm in size

abundant stamens

Marsh Marigold

Caltha palustris (buttercup family)
H 15–30 cm   April–June   perennial

leaves roundish

Sometimes the Marsh Marigold stands in water literally up to its neck. However the plant is well adapted to these conditions, since its hollow stems contain pockets of air. If the flowers fill up with rain water, this can even be an advantage for the plant, as pollen can float on to the stigma. Thus, self-pollination occurs even if no insects are flying about.

base heart or kidney-shaped

Habitat *Meadowland fens, springs, along streams and ditches, in riverside woodlands. On wet, nutrient-rich soils. Throughout Europe.*

> *on the decline due to flood protection measures*
> *can bloom a second time later in the year*
> *stems can be pressed together*

fruitlets open in star shape

flowers 2–4 cm in size

Did you know?

The petals contain a substance that is related to carotin pigment. People once used this to give butter its rich yellow colour. Along with other members of the buttercup family, the Marsh Marigold is often used in children's games to see whether someone likes butter.

abundant stamens

217

sparse plant

glossy leaves

several flat-faced, shining flowers

Meadow Buttercup
Ranunculus acris (buttercup family)
H 30–100 cm   May–Sept   perennial

Habitat *Meadows and pastures of all types, from the low plains to mountain uplands. On slightly damp, nutrient-rich soil. Throughout Europe.*

> **most common buttercup**
> **often grows in vast quantities in meadows**
> **can cause skin inflammation and blisters**

flower 2–3 cm in size, golden yellow

abundant stamens

Grazing cattle avoid the bitter-tasting plant that is poisonous, if it is consumed when the leaves and flowers are fresh. The dried plant is, however, harmless, even if eaten in large quantities. This is one of the reasons why areas where mass colonies are growing are mostly not used as pasture, but more often as meadows, to produce hay. In areas where the plant does grow, farmers often keep cattle in their sheds while haymaking is in progress.

heavily branched, loose flower clusters

upright stems

leaves 5–7-divided

basal leaves stalked

Celery-leaved Buttercup
Ranunculus sceleratus (buttercup family)
H 20–60 cm   June–Oct   annual

Habitat *Pond edges, marshes, partially in water, in drained lakes and dykes. Throughout Europe.*

> **often form larger groups**
> **attracted to rich nutrient supply**
> **requires muddy ground**

light yellow flowers, 0.5–1 cm in size

This is the most poisonous buttercup found in Britain and northern Europe. If the plant comes into contact with the skin, it causes irritation and inflammation of mucus membranes. If eaten, it has an anaesthetising effect, causing dizziness, faintness and even proving fatal. Beggars used to rub their skin with the plant's juice in order to gain sympathy.

upper leaves sessile

stems with abundant flowers

leaves fairly fleshy

lower leaves on long talks, often floating

fruitlets form a cylindrical to oval flower head

Goldilocks Buttercup

Ranunculus auricomus (buttercup family)
H 15–45 cm   April–May   perennial   ☠

The Goldilocks Buttercup produces
seeds even without pollination.
This is why groups of plants often
grow close together as clones, with
the fruitlets being dispersed by ants.
As the plant develops in springtime,
this variety requires a great deal of
light, thus it cannot develop among
coniferous tree plantations.

Habitat *Mixed
deciduous forests
with herbaceous
undergrowth, riverside
woodlands, meadows.
Almost everywhere in
Europe.*

> very variable species
> flowers often look
> bedraggled
> only on meadows where
> woodland once stood

stem leaves with
slender sections

upright stem

petals often incomplete

basal leaves with
roundish outline,
3–5-part

sepals close to petals

flower 1–2.5 cm in size

golden yellow
petals, shiny

✿ **219**

Common Purslane

Portulaca oleracea (blinks family)
H 10–30 cm   June–Sept   annual

Common Purslane is sensitive to frost and
requires an optimal temperature of over 25°C to
germinate. In addition to the wild plant, there is
also a cultivated subspecies with the plant parts being
slightly larger. The young, tender shoots of this plant can
already be gathered only 3–4 weeks after germination to
use in salads or garnish soups. The leaves are rich in vitamins and
taste slightly bitter, but refreshing.

fruit capsule
opens with
a lid

Habitat *Weedy patches
in gardens, vineyards,
crevices in cobblestones,
wayside verges, in
arable fields. South and
central Europe.*

> flowers only bloom for a
> single morning
> transported to central
> Europe by the Romans
> requires warm locations

leaves1 0–30 mm long, fleshy   inconspicuous
flowers

leaves in clusters
at end of stems

flower about 8 mm in size

golden yellow petals

Perforate St John's-wort
Hypericum perforatum (St John's-wort family)
H 30–60 cm July–Aug perennial

Habitat *Rough pastures, grassland, heaths, wasteland, margins of copses and woodlands, embankments, station sidings and gravelled areas, rocky scrubland. Throughout Europe.*

> *flowers produce a red juice when crushed*
> *also known as 'Klamath Weed'*
> *begins flowering on St John's day (24th June)*

Superstition has it that the translucent dots on the leaves are the work of the Devil who is said to have perforated the leaves with a needle in a fiery rage against the plant's power. Herbalists in mediaeval times used the plant's red juices to help heal blood disorders. They also believed that the dotted leaves would cure all types of wounds caused by severe bruising or stabbing. Nowadays, the plant is especially appreciated as an anti-depressant, however, its use should be carefully monitored.

asymmetrical, one side toothed

50–100 stamens

unstalked leaves, 1–2 cm long

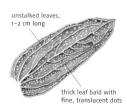

thick leaf bald with fine, translucent dots

petals up to 13 mm long

heavily branched with abundant flowers

very hard, stiff stem

220

leaves opposite

Did you know?
St John's-wort was commonly regarded as one of the best herbal remedies to ward off evil and demonic influences. In the witch hunts of the Middle Ages, the 'witches' were made to drink the plant's juice. People believed that the witches would then tell the truth when tortured.

Common Rock-rose
Helianthemum nummularium (primrose family)
H 10–20 cm   June–Oct   shrub

upright flowers when open

The flowers only open in sunshine and during the morning; in the afternoon, they close again and the petals drop off. However the plants are ideally suited to rockeries, as over a longer period, new flowers are constantly emerging. Nurseries offer special cultivars with a range of flower colours from white to brilliant red.

pendent buds

flowers in clusters

stems creeping or climbing

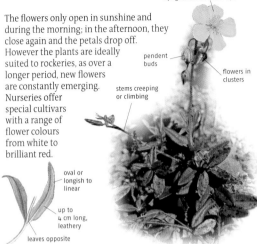

oval or longish to linear

up to 4 cm long, leathery

leaves opposite

Habitat *Sunny semi-dry and dry grassland, embankments, verges and reveres, dry Pine forests. On heavily chalky soil. Almost everywhere in Europe.*

> **characteristic crinkled petals**
> **stamens move upwards when touched**
> **leaves green in winter**

petals 8–18 mm long, golden yellow

abundant stamens

wrinkled

Squirting Cucumber
Ecballium elaterium (white bryony family)
H 20–100 cm   April–Sept   perennial

4–5 cm long berries

The pressure that builds up in a ripe fruit can reach up to about 6 bar – in other words, the same as required for a car tyre! Then, the slightest touch can cause the shooting mechanism to release and fruit to catapult out from the stalk. The seeds and mucus can then shoot out from their casing and travel distances of up to more than 12 m. They also reach speeds of up to about 10 m/sec.

triangular outline

fleshy leaves, about 10 cm across

coarse-haired plant

Habitat *Fallow areas, wayside verges, rocky areas. In nutrient-rich, sunny locations. Around the Mediterranean.*

> **extremely bitter, explosive fruits**
> **interesting, yet not to be toyed with!**
> **severe irritant, deadly poisonous**

flower about 2 cm long, yellowish

corolla fused with 5 tips

fruit stalk with hook-like curve

Creeping Jenny
Lysimachia nummularia (primrose family)
H 10–50 cm   May–July   perennial

Habitat *Damp meadows and pastures, gardens, riverbanks, ditches, riverside woodlands, wayside verges. On nutrient-rich soil. Almost everywhere in Europe.*

> **leaves also green in winter**
> **suitable for ground coverage in gardens**
> **requires damp conditions**

This plant can even be cultivated under water in an aquarium. In mediaeval times, the plant was recommended as a cure for hundreds of illnesses and was therefore also known as 'Centimorbia'. The Latin family name, *nummularia*, meaning 'coin' refers to the shape of the leaves that are reminiscent of coins.

up to 3 cm in size, roundish outline

leaves opposite

flower 1–2.5 cm in size

corolla golden yellow, almost 5-points to base

flowers in leaf axils

creeping stems

222

Dotted Loosestrife
Lysimachia punctata (primrose family)
H 50–100 cm   June–Aug   perennial

Habitat *Wayside verges, riverbanks, copses, wasteland. On damp, nutrient-rich and highly alkaline soil. Central and south-eastern Europe.*

> **frequent ornamental garden plant**
> **the similar Garden Yellow Loosestrife forms a flower spike at end of stems**

Dotted Loosestrife is an uncommon plant, the flowers of which contain essential oils. The flowers attract their pollinators with fatty oils that are excreted from glandular hairs. Some wild bees extract the oil with tiny pads on their legs, which absorb the liquid and transport the oil mixed with pollen into their nest. Here, they use it as a food source for their larvae.

upright stem

corolla 2–3 cm in size, golden yellow

filaments with tiny glandular hairs

flowers in leaf axils

leaves in whorls of 3–6

5 oval points

Oxlip

Primula elatior (primrose family)

H 10–30 cm   March–May   perennial

Some Oxlip plants have flowers with long styles and stamens that are embedded deep within the flower tube. Other plants have short styles and stamens nestling higher up in the flower tube. Both types are equally as common and usually occur in the same location. Seeds mostly emerge whenever the pollen from one plant type escapes and finds its way to the other plant.

wrinkled

leaf up to 25 cm long

Habitat Woodlands with herbaceous undergrowth, woodland ravines, mountain meadows. On damp soil. Central and southern Europe.

> grows and also flowers in shady spots
> also known as 'Great Cowslip'
> flowers with mild fragrance

stamens

style

sepal clinging to corolla tube

corolla 1.2–2 cm in diameter, light yellow

ridged calyx

flowers in one-sided umbels

leaves forming a rosette

stems without leaves

❀ **223**

Did you know?

The similar Native Primrose is included among brightly coloured cultivars, often also with developed stems, as well as crosses with other varieties that are some of the most popular spring plants for gardens and balconies.

Cowslip

Primula veris (primrose family)

H 10–30 cm   April–June   perennial

umbel, mostly nodding to one side

Habitat Rough grassland on limestone, lowland meadows, woodlands, verges, open woodland. Central and southern Europe.

> - endangered and protected species (in Northern Ireland), and should not be picked!
> - flowers with a sweet fragrance
> - indicator of poor soil

In some other European languages the Cowslip is called 'key flower', alluding to the flower umbel's resemblance to a bunch of keys. Legend has it that St Peter, the guardian of the gates of Heaven, allowed his keys to drop down to earth and that this was the spot where the 'keys of Heaven' sprang shoots. The flowers have a soothing effect if used as a tincture for coughs. Cowslip extracts are still used today in herbal remedies.

corolla funnel-shaped at front, golden yellow

angular calyx, not directly flat to corolla tube

leaves forming a rosette

leaf up to 12 cm long, wrinkled

Auricula

Primula auricula (primrose family)

H 5–25 cm   April–June   perennial

Habitat Stony mountain grasslands, cliff crevices, fens or marshland. Mountains in central and southern Europe at altitudes of 1,500 to over 3,000 m.

> - fragrant flowers
> - requires damp ground
> - leaves evergreen

Auricula often grows at altitudes that make people dizzy. A popular myth is that the plant could cure mountain goats and their hunters of altitude sickness. Garden auriculas emerged from crosses between Alpine auriculas and the purple-red flowering Stinking Primrose that is native to the Alps and Pyrenees.

fleshy leaf

surface mostly with floury coating

leaves form a rosette

margin rough, notched

umbel nodding to one side

flower 1.2–2 cm in diameter

short calyx

corolla brilliant yellow

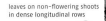

Biting Stonecrop
Sedum acre (stonecrop family)
H 3–15 cm   June–Aug   perennial

leaves on non-flowering shoots
in dense longitudinal rows

thick fleshy,
rounded

When fresh, the plant has a burning hot and
peppery taste, which disappears as soon as the
plant is dried. However this plant is not suitable
for use as herbal seasoning because it contains
substances that irritate the mucus membranes and can
cause vomiting and diarrhoea. Folk medicine was once accustomed
to use the juice of the plant to
treat warts and wounds.

leaves 3–6 mm
long, semi-oval

forms loose lawns

flowers in
clusters

Habitat *Colonising
plant on warm, dry,
sunny cliffs, walls,
station rubble, gravel
roofs, crevices in
cobblestones, gravel
quarries. Throughout
Europe.*

> **stores water**
> **can continue to grow in
>   plant frame**
> **requires plenty of
>   sunshine**

flower 5–9 mm in size,
brilliant yellow

petals lanceolate, pointed tips

Yellow Saxifrage
Saxifraga aizoides (saxifrage family)
H 5–20 cm   June–Oct   perennial

The flowers of this member of the
saxifrage family attract more than
85 types of flies and insects,
including bumblebees, wasps,
honeybees, butterflies and
beetles. The plant often
creates extensive lawns that
represent a major source
of nutrients for insects.

not all stems
have flowers

Habitat *Cliffs with
trickling water, rubble,
gravel banks, damp
slopes. At altitudes of
600 to over 3,000 m.
Northern Europe, Alps,
Pyrenees.*

> **can cover wide areas**
> **leaves evergreen**
> **occasionally also orange
>   or dark red flowers**

flowers in clusters
overtopping stems

grows in lawn-like areas

margin
with hairs

leaf fleshy,
1–2.5 cm long

sepals visible
between petals

flower
7–15 mm
in size

petals rounded at front

Agrimony
Agrimonia eupatoria (rose family)
H 30–100 cm   June–Sept   perennial

Habitat *Hedgerows, embankments, rough grassland. Prefers sunny locations. From plains to lower mountainous regions. Almost everywhere in Europe.*

> *fruits often cling to stockings and trousers*
> *stems very tough*
> *also known as 'Church Steeples'*

The fruits cling like burrs with their tiny hooks to animals' coats and are transported over wide areas. The plant contains tannins and can therefore be used to treat mild cases of diarrhoea, soar throats, mouth ulcers and slight skin inflammations. The plant was also once thought to be an effective treatment for haemorrhoids.

petals 4–6 mm long, golden yellow

10–20 stamens

fruit spherical, furrowed

numerous tiny hooks at the front

pinnate, with single terminal leaf

5–9 pinnate leaf pairs

Did you know?

In mediaeval times, Agrimony was regarded as one of the most important herbal remedies for treating wounds. It was also included in the French herbal remedy known as 'Eau d'Arquebusade', used to treat gunshot wounds.

smaller pinnate pairs often inbetween

haired

long, loose flower clusters

upright stem

Wood Avens

Geum urbanum (rose family)
H 30–120 cm May–Oct perennial

The dried roots of the Wood Avens are aromatic. The smell is similar to cloves and the roots actually contain the same essential oil as the tropical spice, yet in a dosage that is only about a hundredth as strong. The plant was once used as a substitute for cloves and to treat inflamed gums. Extracts of the roots are suitable as an additive for toothpaste or liqueurs.

flowers mostly upright, 1–1.8 cm in size

Habitat Woodlands, fences, walls, woodland paths, wasteland. Also found in shady locations. Almost everywhere in Europe.

> *often grows around villages or towns*
> *attracted to rich nutrient supply*
> *fruitlets with burr-like hooks*

3-part stem leaves

with hooks

fruitlets grouped together

sepals visible from above

abundant stamens

petals roundish

Gold Drop Potentilla

Potentilla aurea (rose family)
H 5–20 cm June–Sept perennial

This plant can be used to treat mild cases of diarrhoea and throat inflammations. The plant survives through the winter beneath the snow mantel with green leaves and can even develop new foliage before the snow melts. In the mountain uplands, the plant therefore uses the short interval without snow to its advantage.

Habitat Stony, dry grassland, rough pastures, at altitudes of 1,300 to 3,000 m. Mountains in central and southern Europe.

> *leaves reminiscent of the fingers of a hand*
> *requires acidic ground*
> *especially attracts flies as pollinators*

flowers 1.5–2.5 cm in size

leaves palmate, with 5 partial leaflets

margin with silvery, shiny hairs

orange patch on each petal

abundant stamens

Spring Cinquefoil
Potentilla tabernaemontani (rose family)
H 5–20 cm   March–June   perennial

Habitat *Dry grassland, rocky slopes, rock faces, vineyard walls, roadside embankments. In sunny locations. Northern and central Europe.*

> **requires heat**
> **especially conspicuous as early flowerer**
> **also overhanging edges of walls**

The flowers are fully open in bright sunshine and especially attract wild bees. Spring Cinquefoil occasionally flowers a second time during late summer or autumn. Ants transport the seeds that are capable of germinating for a period of more than 30 years.

partial leaflet, 1–3 cm long

margin on each side with 2–5 teeth

loose flower heads

lower leaves mostly 5-part, palmate, haired

flower 1–2 cm in size

petals indented at front

abundant stamens

stems prostrate or climbing

Silverweed
Potentilla anserina (rose family)
H 15–80 cm   May–Aug   perennial

Habitat *Wayside and roadside verges, river-banks, arable fields, pastures, in villages and on wasteland. Almost everywhere in Europe.*

> **geese avoid the plant**
> **plant can soothe symptoms of diarrhoea**

Silverweed was a frequent sight on village greens and pastures where geese grazed. Many people even believed the plant grew out of goose droppings, whereas the rich source of nitrates in these areas merely promoted growth. The tender leaves were used by the poor as cheap in-soles for wooden shoes and clogs.

partly always haired on upperside and underside

creeping stems

mostly solitary flowers

leaves pinnate with single terminal leaf

flower 1.5–3 cm in size

petals longer than sepal

Procumbent Yellow-sorrel

Oxalis corniculata (wood-sorrel family)
H 10–50 cm   June–Sept   annual   perennial

The seeds of the ripe fruits are released from the capsules and scattered across wide distances – a record flight path of up to 1.6 m has is even on record. This is an amazing result for a small plant!

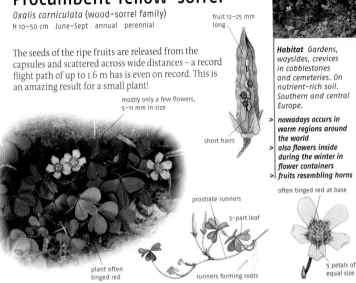

fruit 12–25 mm long

mostly only a few flowers, 5–11 mm in size

short hairs

prostrate runners

3-part leaf

plant often tinged red

runners forming roots

often tinged red at base

5 petals of equal size

Habitat Gardens, waysides, crevices in cobblestones and cemeteries. On nutrient-rich soil. Southern and central Europe.

> nowadays occurs in warm regions around the world
> also flowers inside during the winter in flower containers
> fruits resembling horns

Bermuda-buttercup

Oxalis pes-caprae (wood-sorrel family)
H 20–30 cm   Oct–May   perennial

The species was probably first introduced to the Mediterranean as an ornamental garden plant. However it quickly became established. While the plant mostly spreads in Europe by bulbs and roots, in the Mediterranean, it has now become a nuisance weed, as no animals feed on the plant.

Habitat Country paths, edges of arable fields, hedgerows, orange groves, edges of ditches. Naturalised around the Mediterranean.

> native to South Africa
> often covers wider areas
> occasionally also flowers with more than 5 petals

heart-shaped leaflet

juicy, green

leafless stalk

trifoliate leaf

basal leaves

up to 12 flowers in umbels

5 bright yellow petals

flower 2–2.5 cm across

flared, trumpet shape

Small Caltrops

Tribulus terrestris (caltrop family)

H 10–60 cm   May–Sept   annual

Habitat *Fallow land, wayside verges, wasteland, cultivated ground. Often on sandy, exposed ground in sunny, dry locations. In the Mediterranean.*

> mostly on built-up ground or near small-holdings
> prostate
> resistant to footfall

The fruits are a nuisance for animals and anyone who is walking barefoot. They lie on the ground so that their spines catch on people's feet and can be transported over wide distances. For some time, extracts of the plant have been available as a performance stimulant to sportsmen. There is some doubt about the plant's suitability for this purpose and the plant may even prove toxic.

stems creeping across ground

solitary flower

flower up to 5 mm in size

fruits 2–3 cm across

10 stamens

consisting of thorny partial fruits

pinnate leaves

Rock Samphire

Crithmum maritimum (carrot family)

H 10–60 cm   July–Oct   perennial

Habitat *Coastal beaches, rocky coastlines, also near to sea spray. Coastlines from the Mediterranean to south England.*

> tolerates salty ground
> aromatic, spicy, like Fennel when crushed
> leaves with waxy coating

Fresh Samphire leaves can be used to prepare a vegetable that tastes similar to Fennel. If preserved in brine, the leaves are also meant to taste pleasant. The plant has also earned a place in the literary canon: one of Shakespeare's characters in 'King Lear' collected Rock Samphire.

profusion of umbels

furrowed ovary

greenish, yellow inrolled petals

pinnate leaves

bluish-green plant, sparse, fleshy to leathery

Wild Parsnip
Pastinaca sativa (carrot family)
H 30–100 cm   July–Sept   biennial

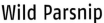

Wild Parsnip probably originates from western Asia and was collected by the indigenous population. The plant has been cultivated since the days of antiquity and arrived in central Europe as a result of naturalisation. Wild Parsnip roots were among the essential basic foodstuffs, until the potato's popularity soared in the 18th century. In many locations, the plant now grows wild and its extensive distribution may be explained by the earlier cultivation.

Habitat *Meadow fringes, wayside verges, embankments, sparse weedy patches on station sidings, in stone quarries. Almost everywhere in Europe.*

> one of the few members of the carrot family in central Europe
> roots of wild plants tasteless

plant more or less grey, heavily haired

flowers in umbels, 4–8 cm across

flower about 2 mm in size

furrowed ovary

231

upright stem

pinnate leaves with single terminal leaflet

side leaves in 3–7 pinnate pairs

margin irregular, serrated

Did you know?
When harvested during the first winter, cultivated Wild Parsnip roots taste sweet and aromatic. They have a herbal flavour resembling vegetable stock of carrot and parsley and are ideal served as a vegetable. They contain Vitamins A, B and C as well as minerals.

Giant Fennel

Ferula communis (carrot family)

H 100–300 cm   April–July   biennial

large flower head comprised of many umbels

Habitat *Shrubberies, exposed, dry pasture areas, roadside verges, often near villages or towns. Around the Mediterranean.*

> **conspicuous due to size**
> **dead stems often remain standing for a long time**
> **grows alone or in groups**

Giant Fennel stems were used in antiquity as walking sticks, though also as whips to torture slaves. *Ferula* is possibly a derivation of the Latin verb 'ferire' or 'to beat'. The fibrous core of the stems also supplied tinder for making fire. Prometheus, who stole fire from the gods in Greek mythology, is reputed to have brought fire to earth that was concealed inside one of these stems.

shiny centre due to nectar

5 inrolled, yellow petals

leaves finely divided

large, conspicuous leaf node

232

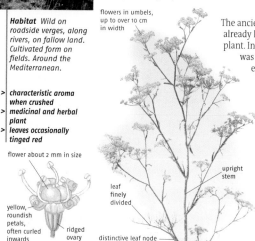

Fennel

Foeniculum vulgare (carrot family)

H 50–250 cm   July–Sept   biennial

Habitat *Wild on roadside verges, along rivers, on fallow land. Cultivated form on fields. Around the Mediterranean.*

> **characteristic aroma when crushed**
> **medicinal and herbal plant**
> **leaves occasionally tinged red**

flowers in umbels, up to over 10 cm in width

The ancient Egyptians probably already knew Fennel as a cultivated plant. In mediaeval times, Fennel was especially used to treat eye diseases. Nowadays, various varieties of Fennel are distinguished. Fruits of the Bronze Fennel are used to treat coughs and stomach upsets, whereas sweeter varieties of the plant are suitable for seasoning pastries and liqueurs. Fennel can also be enjoyed as a bulbous root vegetable.

flower about 2 mm in size

yellow, roundish petals, often curled inwards

ridged ovary

leaf finely divided

upright stem

distinctive leaf node

Great Yellow Gentian

Gentiana lutea (gentian family)

H 45–140 cm   June–Aug   perennial

The plant contains bitter substances that protect it against predatory animals. If the plant is taken as medication, it stimulates production of saliva and the digestive juices. Amarogentin is one of the bitters contained in the Great Yellow Gentian. This substance still tastes bitter, even if diluted to a concentrate of 1:58, 000, 000. After distillation, the bitters largely remain in the mash, so schnapps made from the gentian has a keen aroma and a bitter taste that is intensified by the alcohol.

Habitat Rough grassland, pastures, fens, scrubland, bright pine forests. Up to altitudes of 2,500 m. Mountains in central and southern Europe.

> first flowers only appear after 10 years
> a single plant can form up to 10,000 seeds
> roots up to 1 m long

flowers in upper leaf axils

flower broad, trumpet-shaped or star-shaped

long ovary

with 5–6 lanceolate tips, almost to base

233

rootstock almost the thickness of an arm

bare plant

unbranched stem, upright

roots up to 1 m long

bluish-green

5–7 parallel leaf veins

leaves opposite

Did you know?

Confusion of this species (left) with the poisonous Helleborine (right and p. 146) is a frequent occurrence and can prove fatal. However non-flowering plants can equally be distinguished by the leaf arrangement (this is alternate for the Helleborine).

Spotted Gentian

Gentiana punctata (gentian family)
H 20–60 cm   June–Sept   perennial

Habitat *Grassland above the tree line, scree deposits. Mountains in central and southern Europe up to altitudes of over 3,000 m.*

> shunned by cattle
> flowers appear dirty from a distance
> many plants usually next to each other

The botanical name for the plant, *Gentiana*, is said to date from the time of the Illyrian King Gentius, who recognised gentians' healing power. Spotted Gentian contains fewer bitters than the Great Yellow Gentian. However as it forms a fairly robust and, therefore, high-yielding root, people also tended to use the plant to produce Gentian Schnapps.

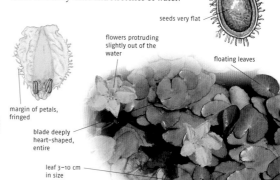

flowers unstalked, in upper leaf axils

stems unbranched

leaves opposite

shiny, green

up to about the middle with 5, sometimes up to 8 tips

bell-shaped corolla, 2.5–4 cm long

light yellow with dark dots

mostly 5 curving central veins

Fringed Water-lily

Nymphoides peltata (bogbean family)
H 80–150 cm   May–June   perennial

Habitat *In stagnant or slow flowing, nutrient-rich water up to depths of 1.5 m. Central and southern Europe.*

> leaves resemble water-lilies
> requires heat in summer
> mostly among other floating plants

The fringes on the petals ensure that the flowers appear especially attractive to insects as pollinators. The seeds can float and are therefore dispersed by the water's currents. They also cling to waders and the birds transport the seeds to nearby lakes and stretches of water.

seeds very flat

flowers protruding slightly out of the water

floating leaves

margin of petals, fringed

5 flat-faced tips

blade deeply heart-shaped, entire

golden yellow corolla, about 3 cm in size

leaf 3–10 cm in size

Henbane

Hyoscyamus niger (nightshade family)
H 20–80 cm   June–Oct   annual to biennial   ☠

Henbane is one of the oldest known
poisonous plants. In mediaeval times it
was used to make witches' ointments, as
it could produce hallucinatory effects.
In cases of poisoning, however, the
plant sends its victims into a deep sleep,
causing chronic and fatal respiratory
paralysis. In 'Hamlet', Shakespeare
stages the King's death with Henbane.
In medicine, a mixture of Henbane
and Opium Poppy (p. 19) was used in
conjunction with other plants as an
anaesthetic.

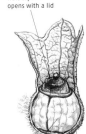

fruit capsule
opens with a lid

contains numerous seeds

Habitat Scrubland,
wasteland, occasionally
as weed on arable
fields. Mostly on
nitrogen-rich ground.
Almost everywhere in
Europe.

> requires plenty of sun
and warmth
> only flowers in light
conditions (sunlight
lasting up to 10 hours)

corolla 2–3 cm long,
wide bell-shaped

5 slightly unequal tips

Did you know?

*Henbane seeds were
once also occasionally
added to beer in
order to intensify its
inebriating effect.
This was a dangerous
custom. It is quite
possible that 'Pils', the
name of the German
beer, was derived from
this early practice.*

leaf spear or
oval-shaped

margin toothed with rough lobes

235

greyish-yellow,
mostly dark
violet veins

solitary flowers in leaf axils

mostly oriented
to one side

plant with
ragged hairs

Dense-flowered Mullein
Verbascum densiflorum (figwort family)
H 50–250 cm   July–Sept   biennial

Habitat *Wasteland, rocky areas, wayside verges, spinneys, riverbanks. In sunny, slightly warmer locations. Central and southern Europe.*

> **can form many thousands of seeds per plant**
> **attractive ornamental garden plant**
> **flowers over a long period**

This species provides an excellent demonstration of how plants also show reactions. If you vigorously shake one of the stems covered in abundant flowers on a warm day and then wait for a few minutes, a large quantity of flower corollas is frequently released suddenly and all at once. Instead of the flowers being shaken off by the movement, the plant lets them go. Tinctures containing plant extracts are suitable as cough mixtures and as an expectorant, which makes it easier to cough up mucus.

corolla 30–35 mm in size

2 longer and 3 shorter filaments

236

upright, longer, dense flower head

crenate margin

blade lanceolate or elongated, lanceolate

stem leaves visibly clasping stem, decurrent

plant covered in yellowish white downy hairs

Did you know?
The dried fruit stems of mullein plants used to be coated in resin or wax and used as torches to light the way. The flower head is impressive and dried fruit stems were coated with resin or wax for use as torches.

Dark Mullein
Verbascum nigrum (figwort family)
H 50–120 cm   June–Sept   biennial

The violet hairs on the stamens are a stark contrast to the yellow of the flower corolla. Therefore the flowers especially attract insects. The lower flowers of the Mullein open first, as is the case with most plants that have elongated flower spikes. Bees are therefore regular visitors to these flower heads and buzz up and down the stems collecting nectar.

violet filaments, with woolly hairs

Habitat *Weedy patches in spinneys, rocky areas, on wayside verges, embankments. Almost everywhere in Europe.*

> only with a leaf rosette during first year
> striking colour combination of flowers
> seeds can germinate over long time periods

long, spike-like flower head

upperside dark green

dark yellow corolla, 1.5–2.5 cm in size

5 tips

stems often tinged brown-violet

upper leaves sessile

underside dense, downy

basal leaves up to 25 cm long, stalked

red centre

237

Wall Lettuce
Mycelis muralis (daisy family)
H 60–80 cm   July–Aug   perennial

fruits with hair tuft

It is easy to mistake the composite flower head with the five ray florets for a single petal. However the flowers are comprised of five individual petals, with each ray floret containing its own nectar. United in a single composite flower head, the flowers are more conspicuous to insects. At the same time, however, an insect can also pollinate several flowers in a single visit.

Habitat *Woodlands with herbaceous undergrowth, woodland pathways, damp cliffs and walls, prefers urban locations. Almost everywhere in Europe.*

> grows in shade or partial shade
> produces white milky juice when bruised
> composite flower, only open during daytime

large terminal section

flower head in loose, sparse spike

bare plant

lighter underside

leaves pinnately lobed

composite flower 1–1.5 cm in size

5 yellow, 5-pointed ray flowers

Spring Pheasant's-eye
Adonis vernalis (buttercup family)
H 10–40 cm   April–May   perennial 🕱

Habitat Dry grassland, dry meadow grassland, arid, sunny hillsides with shrubbery. Warm locations in summer months. Central, southern and eastern Europe.

> in England, in decline and protected species
> frequently occurring in eastern Europe
> elongated stems after flowering

The flowers only open in sunshine and, just like a sunflower, they follow the sun's rays. Pheasant's-eye is recommended in herbal remedies as a palliative for mild heart conditions and neuralgia. However this plant is toxic and under no circumstances should it be used without professional consultation. Symptoms of poisoning include a weak pulse resulting in cardiac arrest.

fruitlets form a spherical cluster

solitary flower

flowers 4–6 cm in size

profusion of stamens

leaves very finely divided

12–20 shining petals

238

Winter Aconite
Eranthis hyemalis (buttercup family)
H 5–15 cm   Feb–April   perennial 🕱

Habitat Woodlands, copses, vineyards, orchards, park areas. In southern Europe, wild in central Europe.

> already flowering in snow
> popular early-flowerer in gardens
> reminiscent of a buttercup

The flowering season lasts for up to one week. During that time, the petals develop and grow by opening and shutting to about twice their length. The fruitlets open until they form little spades and the seeds are dispersed on raindrops that carry them for distances of over 40 cm.

solitary flowers, 2–2.5 cm in size

funnel-shaped leaves inside petals filled with nectar

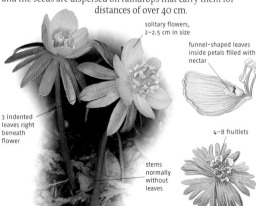

abundant stamens

3 indented leaves right beneath flower

4–8 fruitlets

stems normally without leaves

6–10 petals

Globeflower

Trollius europaeus (buttercup family)

H 30–60 cm   May–June   perennial   ☠

According to one legend, hobgoblins and sprites were supposed to have carried Globeflowers as torches. The plant's name is presumably derived from the spherical shape of the flowers. Globeflower meadows were once very common in hills and mountain uplands. Nowadays, however, the plant has disappeared in many places, as many wetland meadows have dried out.

mostly 1, occasionally 2–3 flowers at end of stems

flowers 2–3 cm across

upright stems

spherical flower

10–15 petals

leaves divided as far as leaf node

sections further indented

Habitat Damp to wet-land meadows, lowland fens, alongside streams. Especially in high mountains to altitudes of over 2,000 m. Almost everywhere in Europe.

> protected species in England
> occasionally flowers again in autumn
> mostly grows in loose groups next to one another

239

Did you know?

Only small insects reach the flower as pollinators. Three species of flies drink not only the nectar but also lay their eggs in the ovary, where their larvae then feed. However enough seeds are usually left over to ensure the plant's reproduction.

Alpine Pasqueflower

Pulsatilla alpina ssp. *apiifolia* (buttercup family)
H 10–40 cm   May–Aug   perennial   (🌸)

Habitat Stony mountain grasslands, locations with dwarf shrubs. On acidic soil. Mountains in central and southern Europe from about 1,500 to over 3,000 m.

> many flowers often in loose clusters
> conspicuous due to large flower size

The fruits of the Alpine Pasqueflower protrude high above nearby plants and are conspicuous by their feathery hairs and often heavily tousled appearance. The plant is also known as Parsley-leaved Pasqueflower. In dry conditions, the hairs spread out so that the wind easily catches hold of the fruitlets and blows them away. The plant used to be regarded by mountain farmers as an effective treatment for blood in the urine of cattle.

solitary flowers, 3–6 cm in size

6–9 bright yellow petals

abundant stamens

240 ❋

stems with 3 deeply divided leaves

fruitlets with elongated, thread-like, haired styles

other, similar basal leaves

Did you know?

The White Alpine Pasqueflower also grows in mountain uplands and is mainly distinguished by its white flowers. These do not contain any colour pigment but reflect the light, explaining their white appearance.

Lesser Celandine
Ranunculus ficaria (buttercup family)
H 5–20 cm   March–May   perennial

The plant reproduces more or less only through small breeder tuberous roots, which sit in the leaf axils instead of side shoots, and are easily washed away by the rain. Fresh, very young leaves were once used to help prevent scurvy. However, the plants are poisonous once they develop.

Habitat *Riverside woodlands, deciduous forests with herbaceous undergrowth, orchards, damp meadows, parks. On damp soil. Everywhere in Europe.*

> attracted to nutrient-rich soil
> only visible in springtime, after flowering quickly finishes

flowers, 2–3 cm in size protruding above leaves

tiny breeder tuberous roots often in lower leaf axils

leaves roundish to heart-shaped

flat, spreading growth

8–12 shiny petals

3 green sepals

Wild Mignonette
Reseda lutea (mignonette family)
H 20–60 cm   May–Sept   annual to biennial

stands upright

fruit 8–12 mm long

The scientific name for all mignonette varieties is *Reseda*. This name is derived from the Latin 'resedare' meaning to calm or heal. One species, Weld, was previously used as a sedative. Wild Mignonette contains yellow, yellowish-green or brown pigments. It was used as a pigment for textiles and artists' paints, though was never as important as the similar Weld.

Habitat *Sparse weedy patches on country pathways, on rocky ground, station sidings and harbour sites, wasteland. Central and southern Europe.*

> flower clusters heavily extended
> requires warmth
> also known as 'Yellow Mignonette'

light yellow flowers in clusters of up to 30 cm long

upright stem

leaves with long, narrow sections

upper petals 3-part, 2–5 mm long

6 sepals

abundant stamens

Reflexed Stonecrop

Sedum rupestre (stonecrop family)
H 10–35 cm   June–Aug   perennial

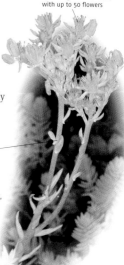

spreading flower cluster, with up to 50 flowers

Habitat *Pioneer plant on cliffsides, dunes walls, stony debris and rock deposits. On warm, dry sandy and stony ground. Almost everywhere in Europe.*

> well suited to dry conditions due to fleshy leaves
> many growing as garden escapes
> also conspicuous without flowers

Reflexed Stonecrop used to be a common garden plant. The fresh tangy and crispy leaves and tender shoots can be used to garnish and season salads, sauces and raw vegetables. Another name for the plant, 'Trip Madam' is possibly derived from the French 'trique' meaning innards or intestine and could refer to the juicy shoots.

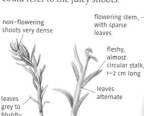

non-flowering shoots very dense

flowering stem, with sparse leaves

flower 1.2–2 cm in size

fleshy, almost circular stalk, 1–2 cm long

leaves grey to bluish-green

leaves alternate

mostly 6–7 petals

Creeping Avens

Geum reptans (rose family)
H 5–25 cm   June–Aug   perennial

fruitlet with appearance of a feathery wig

Habitat *Open, damp rocky cliffsides, glacier moranes. Mountains in central and southern Europe, mostly at altitudes of between 2,500 and 3,500 m.*

> helps anchor rubble
> the similar Alpine Avens has no runners and grows on mountain meadows

The flowering plant is conspicuous in its natural habitats and also when bearing fruits. The feathery fruitlets are on tall, protruding stalks so that they can easily be blown away on the wind. The plant, also known as 'Drooping Avens', covers the surrounding area with its long runners and can form large colonies.

solitary flowers, 3–5 cm in size

long runners

pinnate leaves

6–8 petals

numerous stamens

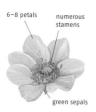

green sepals

indented pinnate leaf

Hottentot-fig

Carpobrotus edulis (iceplant family)

H 5–20 cm   March–July   perenial

In South Africa, it is popular to make jam out of the fruits or mix them in curries. The fruit flesh is like a sweet and sour gelée. The fleshy leaves are also edible either when cooked or preserved in vinegar. African herbalists clean wounds with the juice of crushed leaves and use the plant to treat eczema and insect bites.

Habitat *Embankments and dunes near coasts. Native to South Africa, established in Mediterranean.*

> anchor plant for sand dunes and sand banks.
> flowers only open in sunshine
> requires very little water

Did you know?

The red-flowering Sour Fig often grows in the same locations and looks similar to the Hottentot-fig. Both species grow very rapidly and in some places have become nuisance plants.

profusion of slender petals

many stamens

grows up to 2 m in flat, outspreading mats covering the ground

leaves fleshy

triangular, even

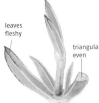

fused together at leaf node in pairs

243

solitary flowers, 6–10 cm in size

leaves turn red colour in sunshine

Arnica

Arnica montana (daisy family)

H 20–50 cm   June–July   perennial   (☠)

rootstock with abundant roots

Habitat *Damp meadows, grassland, pastures, heaths and moors. Intolerant of chalky soils. Central Europe, almost only in mountains.*

> intolerant of fertiliser
> strong aroma when crushed
> well-known medicinal plant

Extracts of Arnica petals can alleviate inflammations and act as a soothing agent for chronic pain. The tinctures can help soothe bruises, crushing and rheumatism in the muscles and limbs as well as insect bites. However allergies can develop if the substance is applied too liberally and too frequently. If taken by mouth, Arnica can lead to poisoning with symptoms of vomiting, palpitations and ultimately collapse.

composite flower head 4–8 cm across

abundant yellow disc flowers

golden yellow ray flowers 3–6 mm across

244

usually 1–3 composite flowers

upright stem, haired

almost all leaves in basal rosette

leaves entire

opposite

Did you know?

Arnica is sometimes also known as 'Medicinal Leopard's Bane'. This popular name was probably coined in reference to the plant's healing power.

Common Ragwort

Senecio jacobaea (daisy family)

H 30–100 cm   July–Sept   biennial, perennial ☠

pinnately divided leaves

sections widened towards end

many composite flowers, 1.2–1.5 mm in size

Fruits of the Common Ragwort are covered in a profusion of white hairs. This very common plant is known by a variety of other names such as 'Ragweed' or 'Tansy Ragwort' (in America). The first flowers appear around St Jacob's Day (25th July).

Habitat *Pastures, meadows, semi-dry grassland, embankments, woodland margins. Almost everywhere in Europe.*

> **one of many similar ragwort or groundsel varieties**
> **contains substances that may cause cancer**

abundant disc flowers

fruits with white hair tufts

12–15 ray flowers, about 1.5 mm across

upright angular or ridged stem

245

Groundsel

Senecio vulgaris (daisy family)

H 10–30 cm   Feb–Nov   annual ☠

Thanks to their tufts of hair, the fruits can reach higher air pockets and fly over great distances. Scientists found evidence of this species among the first settlers of the newly created volcanic island of Surtsey. The fruits must therefore have travelled over distances of at least 40 km.

Habitat *Exposed weedy patches on arable fields, in gardens, on wasteland, scrubland, spinneys. Throughout Europe.*

> **flowers almost the entire year**
> **can become a nuisance in gardens**
> **entire plant often with a reddish tinge in sunny locations**

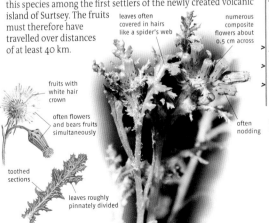

leaves often covered in hairs like a spider's web

numerous composite flowers about 0.5 cm across

fruits with white hair crown

often flowers and bears fruits simultaneously

often nodding

composite flower head about twice as long as wide

toothed sections

leaves roughly pinnately divided

mostly only disc flowers

cylindrical, bare capitulum

Colt's-foot
Tussilago farfara (daisy family)
H 7–30 cm   March–April   perennial

rounded, black teeth at front covering entire leaf margin

Habitat *Pathways, roadside verges, rocky deposits, gravel quarries, riverbanks. On mostly exposed, chalky soil. Throughout Europe.*

> **flowers before leaves appear**
> **acts as anchor plant**
> **often grows in groups**

Extracts of the plant are tried and tested medicine for coughs and hoarse throats, although they can damage the liver and lead to cancer. You are therefore advised not to collect the wild flowers, but rely on specially propagated plants or tested prescriptions and pay close attention to the instructions for use. Cigarettes made from Colt's-foot leaves were once used to help people give up smoking.

stem whitish, downy

single composite flower head

leaves heart-shaped to roundish

stem with oval scales

downy covering releases on leaf upperside

initially white and downy on both sides

composite flower head with up to 300 slender ray flowers

disc flowers in centre

Pineapple Weed
Matricaria discoidea (daisy family)
H 5–30 cm   June–Aug   annual

composite flower head, 5–8 mm across

at end of stalks

Habitat *Grassland areas and well trodden path-ways, especially near residential sites. Often growing in larger groups on exposed ground. Throughout Europe.*

> **originates from north-east Asia**
> **fragrance similar to Scented Mayweed (p. 135), yet without the same medicinal effect**

This robust species was regarded as something of a novelty in botanical gardens, as it has no ray florets, in contrast to the other camomile species (p. 134 and p. 135). The fruits develop slippery mucus in wet conditions and disperse by sticking to moving objects. The plant was able to escape from gardens and spread all over Europe from about 1850 onwards.

branched stem

with broad linear sections, 0.5–1 mm across

composite flower head, only with yellow-green disc florets

bare capitulum

bare leaf

Jerusalem Artichoke

Helianthus tuberosus (daisy family)
H 100–250 cm   Oct–Nov   perennial

The Jerusalem Artichoke was first cultivated in Europe in about 1619. The roots of the plant were important as a basic foodstuff after the end of the Thirty Years War. However the potato was later found to give higher yields and replaced cultivation of the Jerusalem Artichoke, which is nowadays mainly planted only as fodder for cattle and game.

Habitat Often wild and established along riverbanks by nutrient-rich stretches of water, regularly cultivated. In areas with a mild climate, especially in central Europe.

> originates from North America
> reminiscent of a small-flowered Sunflower
> bulbs only develop in late autumn

basal and middle leaves opposite

rough

bulbs of wild plants mostly slender, longish, 1–4 cm long

12–20 ray florets

yellow disc florets

247

composite flower head, 4–14 cm in size

bulbs comprised of spherical parts, can grow to the size of a fist in cultivated varieties

composite flower heads at end of stems

Did you know?

The bulbs of cultivated plants are suitable as a potato substitute for diabetics. They contain inulin, which does not require insulin for processing. When the body breaks down inulin, fructose is produced, which diabetics can tolerate.

Goldenrod

Solidago virgaurea (daisy family)
H 10–100 cm   July–Oct   perennial

Habitat *Open wood-lands with herbaceous undergrowth, spinneys, heaths, rough pastures. Throughout Europe.*

> tolerates dry conditions
> grows as dwarf variety in mountain uplands
> attracts many insects

Goldenrod is named after the long, rod-like stems and flower colour. In herbalism, this plant is regarded as one of the tried and tested diuretics. It is used effectively to treat inflammations of the urinary tracts and helps flush out the urinary passages, removing stones and renal gravel, or preventing them.

composite flower head 1–2 cm across

6–12 golden yellow ray flowers

yellow disc flowers

sepals arranged in roof tile formation

248

slender flower head with composite flowers facing all directions

slender leaf

usually abundant fruits

fruits with tufts

winged stalk

Did you know?

Along with the Fox Groundsel, herbalists used Goldenrod as a vulnerary, at the latest, from the 16th century onwards. Depending on the recipe, the patient had to drink a decoction or cleanse his injuries. Occasionally, the plants' leaves were also placed on the wound.

Canadian Goldenrod
Solidago canadensis (daisy family)
H 50–250 cm   Aug–Oct   perennial

countless composite flowers, 3–5 mm across forming pyramid-shaped racemes

Canadian Goldenrod originates from North America and became common in Europe from the 19th century onwards. It reproduces both by numerous seeds as well as below ground with the aid of runners from the tough rootstock. As it develops in mass colonies, the plant suppresses native flora and conservationists often try to reduce the numbers.

Habitat Weedy patches on rubble, station embankments, urban wasteland, also riverside glades or along riverbanks. Almost everywhere in Europe.

> can form giant, dense colonies
> attracts many insects
> also as an ornamental plant in many gardens

sparse disc florets

sharply toothed margin

leaf lanceolate

10–17 short ray florets

flowering branches, spreading or overhanging

stems with tuft-like hairs

249

Golden Thistle
Scolymus hispanicus (daisy family)
H 20–80 cm   June–Sept   biennial

There are many references in the Bible to 'thorny plants' or 'thistles'. Scientists believe that the thorns, which 'choked' the seeds in the Parable of the Sower, were actually the thorns of Golden Thistles. While Golden Thistle tends to grow on waste ground and in deserted areas, the related Spotted Golden Thistle is a nuisance plant on arable fields around the Mediterranean.

Habitat Sunny wayside verges, scrubland and fallow areas. Mostly in locations with signs of cultivated land. Southern Europe.

> tolerates dry conditions
> roots edible as vegetable

leaves very rigid, lobed, thorny

slightly decurrent on stem

surrounded by spiny leaves

abundant golden yellow ray florets

composite flower heads at end of stem and in leaf axils

composite flower head, 1–2 cm across

Wormwood
Artemisia absinthium (daisy family)
H 60–120 cm   July–Sept   perennial, shrub

Habitat *Weedy patches on rubble, by motorways, in rubbish tips, by reservoirs, on sheep grazing pastures, cliffs. Mainly in central and southern Europe.*

> **strong aroma when crushed**
> **requires plenty of sunshine and heat**
> **entire plant covered in hoary down**

As a medicinal plant, Wormwood stimulates the appetite and soothes a bloated feeling and prevents flatulence. However, extracts can prove fatal if taken in too great quantities. Absinthe used to be famous as a cause of brain damage and radical distortions of the personality and was therefore forbidden. Nowadays, you can safely drink Wormwood wines and Schnapps.

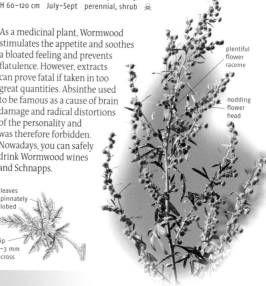

plentiful flower raceme

nodding flower head

only disc flowers

composite flower head 2–4 mm across

leaves pinnately lobed

tip 1–3 mm across

Mugwort
Artemisia vulgaris (daisy family)
H 60–250 cm   July–Nov   perennial

Habitat *Weedy patches along wayside verges, on rocky and waste ground, along riverbanks and by lakes. Throughout Europe.*

> **faint, peculiar fragrance when crushed**
> **pollen dispersed on wind**
> **in antiquity, a well-known herbal remedy for women's complaints**

composite flower heads in all directions, more or less upright

Mugwort is prized as herbal seasoning for game and goose, yet it is feared as a cause of hay fever. A popular superstition suggests that a Mugwort leaf placed in a shoe before hiking helps prevent the onset of fatigue. It has also been used to treat stomach complaints. The plant grows in Siberia and Alaska and for the Inuit Eskimos it counts among the few native medicinal herbs.

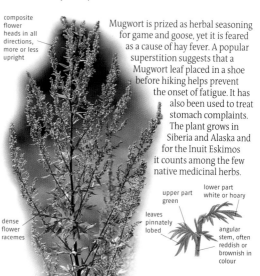

yellowish or brownish disc florets

white, downy sepals

oval capitulum 3–4 mm long

dense flower racemes

upper part green

lower part white or hoary

leaves pinnately lobed

angular stem, often reddish or brownish in colour

Tansy

Tanacetum vulgare (daisy family)
H 60–120 cm   July–Sept   perennial

Tansy has similar foliage to some ferns and is used as de-worming material for beef livestock. In the 16th and 17th centuries, the plant was also used to de-worm humans and as an antidote for gout, fever and plague epidemics.

Habitat *Weedy patches on embankments, pathways, riverbanks, on rocky ground, wasteland, fire spots. Almost everywhere in Europe.*

> *often grows in clusters*
> *tangy aroma when crushed*
> *suitable for dried flower arrangements*

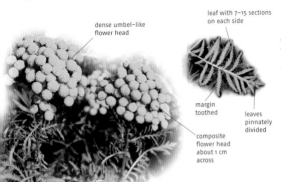

leaf with 7–15 sections on each side

dense umbel-like flower head

margin toothed

leaves pinnately divided

composite flower head about 1 cm across

dense flower head, with abundant golden yellow disc flowers

Yellow Everlasting Flower

Helichrysum arenarium (daisy family)
H 10–30 cm   July–Aug   perennial

When used for medicinal purposes, extracts from the flowers act as a diuretic, alleviating cramps and complaints of the gall bladder. In herbal teas, the flowers enrich the colour of the infusion.

dense, umbel-like flower head with 3–40 composite flower heads

capitulum, semi-spherical

Habitat *Sandy grassland, dunes, dry Pine forests. In warm locations in summer time. Almost everywhere in Europe.*

> *aromatic fragrance, like curry*
> *suitable for dried flower bouquets*

sepals spread out in dry conditions

stems hoary

leaves alternate, with downy hairs

composite flower, 6–7 mm across

sepals with dry, lemon yellow attachment

Crown Daisy

Chrysanthemum coronarium (daisy family)
H 30–80 cm   March–Sept   annual

Habitat *Cultivated ground, wasteland and fallow areas, roadside verges. Also as an ornamental plant. Around the Mediterranean.*

> often in large, conspicuous groups
> flower heads uniform colour or white and yellow
> intense fragrance when crushed

Two-tone varieties of the Crown Daisy often grow in gardens as an ornamental plant. In east Asian cuisine, the leaves and stems of the Crown Daisy are cooked as vegetables. The ancient Greeks also knew of this use and regarded the plant as a magical herb that could give protection from evil spirits and witches. They also referred to the plant as Dios ofrya meaning 'Zeus's brows'.

composite flower head, 3–6 cm across, at end of stems

ray flowers often two-tone

yellow disc flowers

stem heavily branched

pointed sections

leaves with double pinnate lobes

Downy Elecampane

Inula hirta (daisy family)
H 15–45 cm   June–July   perennial

Habitat *Open oak and pine forests, dry grassland, copses. In warm locations in summer. Mainly in central and eastern Europe.*

> requires warm locations in summer
> tolerates dry conditions
> leaves feel rough

In 1804, scientists first isolated the substance inulin from the related Elecampene. Inulin is a carbohydrate which plants of the daisy family use as a storage substance instead of starch. Nowadays, many foodstuffs contain inulin that is suitable for diabetics as the body does not require insulin to process it. Instead, the breakdown of inulin produces fructose, which is beneficial for diabetics.

unstalked

leaf oval or lanceolate, firm

upright stem

composite flower head, 3–5 cm across

stems and leaves with rough hairs

numerous golden yellow ray flowers, 1–2 mm across

golden yellow disc florets

solitary flower head overtopping stem

Safflower

Carthamus tinctorius (daisy family)

H 15–120 cm   July–Sept   perennial

The Egyptians were already cultivating the Safflower 4,000 years ago in order to extract the plant's colour pigment. The flowers contain red and yellow colour pigments and red was especially coveted as it was used to dye cotton and silk and also used in cosmetics and confectionery. Nowadays, thistle and Safflower oil is pressed from the seeds and is supposed to prevent blocked arteries.

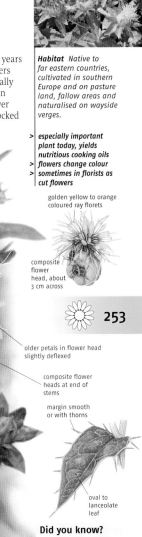

Habitat *Native to far eastern countries, cultivated in southern Europe and on pasture land, fallow areas and naturalised on wayside verges.*

> **especially important plant today, yields nutritious cooking oils**
> **flowers change colour**
> **sometimes in florists as cut flowers**

golden yellow to orange coloured ray florets

composite flower head, about 3 cm across

253

reddish tinge when flowers wither

older petals in flower head slightly deflexed

composite flower heads at end of stems

margin smooth or with thorns

oval to lanceolate leaf

Did you know?

If Saffron is offered at a very reasonable market price, it is probably not sold as genuine Saffron threads. Instead of the highly valuable stigmas of the Saffron crocus bulb, Safflower florets are frequently on sale, as they can still colour food a rich yellow tone.

Blessed Thistle

Cnicus benedictus (daisy family)

H 10–60 cm   April–July   annual

In the 16th century, the Blessed Thistle was regarded as one of the most effective antidotes for the Black Death. Yet the plant contains no substances that could help prevent this disease. Instead, it proves an effective medication for alleviating digestive and gall bladder complaints. It can also be made into a herbal liqueur. Liqueur that is sold as 'Benedictine' contains many herb varieties, including Melissa and Thyme, though not necessarily extracts from the Blessed Thistle.

composite flower head surrounded by upper leaves

cobweb-like hairs

only yellow disc florets in composite flower head

red-brown sepals, spiny

254

composite flower head, 3–4 cm across

lobed margin, with spiny teeth

with cobweb-like hairs

upper leaves clasping stem

solitary composite flower head

Did you know?

The oldest references to medicinal herbal gardens in monasteries date back to the 6th century and the monastic order founded by Benedictine monks. Their name shares the same origin as that of the plant: in Latin, 'benedictus' means 'blessed, with healing power'.

Cabbage Thistle
Cirsium oleraceum (daisy family)
H 50–150 cm   June–Sept   perennial

Farmers used to prefer giving cattle Cabbage Thistle as fodder. People also used the young shoots and tender leaves in salads or as a cabbage-like vegetable. The base of the flower heads can even be used as a substitute for artichokes, although they are not nearly as tasty or nutritious.

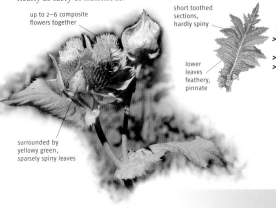

up to 2–6 composite flowers together

short toothed sections, hardly spiny

lower leaves feathery, pinnate

surrounded by yellowy green, sparsely spiny leaves

Habitat Wetland meadows, riverside woodlands, banks of streams, springs, spinneys. On wet, nutrient-rich soil. North, central and west Europe.

> butterflies prefer hovering around the flowers
> attracted to wet ground
> a Thistle with hardly any thorns

composite flower head, 2.5–4 cm long

pale yellow disc florets

Spiniest Thistle
Cirsium spinosissimum (daisy family)
H 20–70 cm   July–Sept   perennial

margin lobed, with spiny sections

leaves stiff

The translation of the scientific name means something like 'very spiny Thistle'. It is therefore hardly surprising that cattle shun this Thistle. Only small animals feed on the young flower heads. The bleached bracts are said to have been used in mediaeval times for brocade and embroidery as well as ornaments.

2–10 composite flowers together

entire plant very thorny

composite flowers, surrounded by pale, spiny bracts

Habitat Pastures, near cattle sheds, banks of streams, areas with rubble and rough ground. In the Apennines and higher uplands of the Alps to altitudes of 3,000 m.

> conspicuous from afar due to pale bracts
> requires damp ground
> left standing on cattle grazing pastures

composite flower heads about 2 cm across

about 100 light yellow petals

Carline Thistle

Carlina vulgaris (daisy family)
H 15–60 cm   July–Sept   biennial

solitary composite flower at end of twigs

Habitat *Rough grassland and pastures, semi-dry grassland, wayside verges, open forests. Mostly on chalky soil. Throughout Europe.*

> **tolerates dry conditions**
> **sometimes called 'Weather Thistle'**
> **composite flowers close in damp conditions**

At first sight, it is difficult to distinguish flower heads in bloom from those bearing fruit. Similar to the Silver Thistle, the yellow, dried bracts that draw attention to the flower heads remain on the Carline Thistle long into the winter.

composite flower head, 3–5 cm in size

profusion of yellow disc flowers

leaves with spiny teeth

inside of bracts slender, with dry membrane, straw-coloured or golden yellow

stems with cobweb-like hairs, no spines

squarrose plant

256

Nipplewort

Lapsana communis (daisy family)
H 30–100 cm   June–Sept   annual, perennial

several longish fruits enclosed within single flower head

Habitat *Weedy areas along hedgerows, fences, roadside verges, in woodlands, gardens, on rocky ground, arable fields. Almost everywhere in Europe.*

> **attracted to nutrient-rich soil**
> **prefers partial shade or shady conditions**
> **white, milky sap**

The composite flower heads of the Nipplewort only open in good weather during the morning from about 6 am to 11 am. In poor weather, the flowers are self-pollinating, with the outer flowers bending over the inner ones and thus allowing the anthers to come into contact with the stigmas.

many composite flowers, 1–1.5 cm across

heavily branched stem

large terminal leaflet

lower leaves with up to 4 small pinnate pairs

composite flowers with 8–18 light yellow ray florets

Dandelion

Taraxacum officinale (daisy family)

H 5–40 cm April–July perennial

Dandelion is a medicinal plant and effective for treating complaints of the gall bladder and as a diuretic. Children love blowing the fruits of the 'Dandelion clocks'. The fruits emerge even if no pollen clings to the stigmas. Due to this 'immaculate conception' it seems appropriate that the plant is depicted on many Christian images of the Virgin Mary.

Habitat *Well fertilised meadows, pastures, weedy patches along waysides, arable fields, parkland lawns. On nutrient-rich soil. Throughout Europe.*

> **when bruised, emits white, milky sap**
> **creates yellow meadows in springtime**
> **very well-known plant**

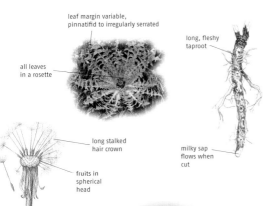

leaf margin variable, pinnatifid to irregularly serrated

long, fleshy taproot

all leaves in a rosette

golden yellow composite flowers

long stalked hair crown

milky sap flows when cut

abundant ray florets of varying lengths

fruits in spherical head

257

composite flowers, 2.5–4 cm across

leafless stems

Did you know?

If you separate the hollow stems and place them in water, these quickly roll up in a spiral form. The cells on the inner wall of the tube are responsible for this, as they extend heavily.

Prickly Lettuce
Lactuca serriola (daisy family)
H 60–120 cm   July–Sept   annual to biennial

Especially in very sunny locations, the leaves stand upright and point in a northerly and southerly direction like the needle of a compass. This is how they avoid too much exposure to the midday sun, preventing overheating and moisture loss. The leaf arrangement is less pronounced in the shade. The roots can grow downward for up to 2 m, thus absorbing moisture in seemingly dry locations.

flower heads
initially overhanging

flower head
1–1.5 cm
across

15–25 light
yellow ray
florets

stems stiff,
upright

258

vertical leaves
or diagonal
and arranged
in rows

lobed leaves with
sections far apart

light yellow
ray florets

white
hairs

underside of main veins
and margin spiny

Did you know?
The origins of lettuce go back to the Prickly Lettuce. Nowadays, this wild species is regarded as the standard plant for propagating different cultivated varieties. In China, the stems of a Prickly Lettuce cultivar are commonly eaten like green Asparagus.

Goat's-beard

Tragopogon pratensis (daisy family)
H 20–70 cm   May–July   biennial, perennial

fruit up to 4 cm across, with parachute

ray florets often conceal bracts

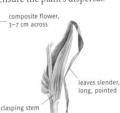

When closed up, the fruit of the Goat's-beard is reminiscent of a goat's beard – hence the scientific name *Tragopogon* ('tragos' is Greek for 'beard'). In dry conditions, the fruit opens and the fine and densely woven parachutes of the fruitlets are released and unfold. They are well adapted to flight and ensure the plant's dispersal.

composite flower, 3–7 cm across

leaves slender, long, pointed

clasping stem

***Habitat** Often in large colonies on meadows, semi-dry grassland, along waysides, stations. In warm locations in summer. Almost everywhere in Europe.*

> **flowers only opened during the morning and in good weather**
> **white milky sap**
> **slightly reminiscent of a large Dandelion (p. 257)**

composite flower with ray flowers of different lengths

8 green bracts

259

Smooth Sow-thistle

Sonchus oleraceus (daisy family)
H 30–100 cm   June–Oct   annual

The plant is not spiny like a thistle. It contains many nutrients and farmers value Smooth Sow-thistle as grazing fodder. The tender young stems, leaves and roots were once cooked and served as vegetables or as a soup ingredient – the Latin term *'oleraceus'* means to use as a vegetable.

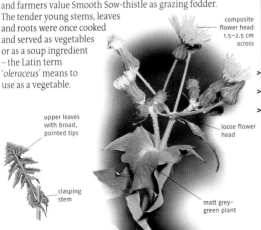

composite flower head 1.5–2.5 cm across

upper leaves with broad, pointed tips

loose flower head

clasping stem

matt grey-green plant

***Habitat** Sparse weedy patches along country paths, walls, on scrubland, arable fields, gardens, wasteland. On nutrient-rich soil. Everywhere in Europe.*

> **attracted to nitrogen in soil**
> **very resilient in natural habitat**
> **plant with milky juice**

composite flower head with yellow to whitish ray florets

often reddish on the outside

Autumn Hawkbit

Leontodon autumnalis (daisy family)

H 15–45 cm   July–Sept   perennial

Habitat *Pastures, ornamental lawns, waysides, well-trodden locations, roadside verges. On nutrient-rich, dense, mostly exposed ground. Throughout Europe.*

> **tolerant of salty ground**
> **flowers much later than Dandelion**
> **contains milky sap**

composite flower head with numerous golden yellow ray florets

When people refer to the 'Dandelion' (p. 257), they often mean the Autumn Hawkbit. The scientific name refers to the conspicuous leaf form. (In Greek, 'leon' means 'lion' and 'odontos' means tooth).

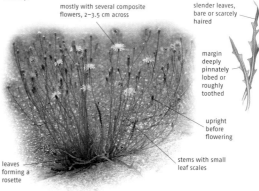

mostly with several composite flowers, 2–3.5 cm across

slender leaves, bare or scarcely haired

margin deeply pinnately lobed or roughly toothed

upright before flowering

stems with small leaf scales

leaves forming a rosette

leaf upper side with 3–7 mm long hairs

Mouse-ear Hawkweed

Hieracium pilosella (daisy family)

H 5–30 cm   May–Oct   perennial

Habitat *Rough meadows, dry forests, series of cliffs. On dry, mostly slightly sandy ground with poor nutrients. Almost everywhere in Europe.*

> **often forming extensive groups due to runners**
> **can become a nuisance on parkland lawns**
> **characteristic haired leaves**

composite flower head 2–3 cm across

light yellow ray florets, often with red stripes on the outside

The plant's name is a reference to the leaf shape and downy covering on the foliage. In dry conditions, the leaves curl inwards and the leaf surface shrinks. The leaf's underside also reflects light, which is why the foliage does not heat up so rapidly. Both factors counteract the loss of moisture through evaporation and the plant reserves the moisture for survival.

leaves often curled inwards

stems without leaves

with 1 composite flower head

leaves form a rosette

downy grey hairs below

leaves flat on ground

Rough Hawk's-beard
Crepis biennis (daisy family)
H 50–120 cm   May–Aug   biennial

The Rough Hawk's-beard does not tolerate planting in pastures and disappears as soon as freshly mown meadows are turned into pasture. The flowers attract bees and are self-pollinating or form seeds without pollination. Reproduction is therefore guaranteed. The fruits are a favourite food of seed-eating birds; canaries especially enjoy them.

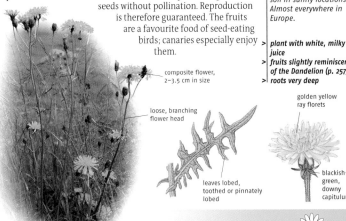

composite flower, 2–3.5 cm in size

loose, branching flower head

leaves lobed, toothed or pinnately lobed

golden yellow ray florets

blackish-green, downy capitulum

Habitat Mown meadows, country paths. On nutrient-rich soil in sunny locations. Almost everywhere in Europe.

> plant with white, milky juice
> fruits slightly reminiscent of the Dandelion (p. 257)
> roots very deep

 261

Winter Daffodil
Sternbergia lutea (lily family)
H 10–30 cm   Sept–Oct   perennial   (☠)

The foliage of this bulb plant appears slightly before or at the same time as the flowers. Another name is 'Lily of the Field'. The plant is named after Count Kaspar von Sternberg, a botanist from what used to be known as Bohemia (modern Czech Republic) and a correspondent of the German poet, and botanical researcher, Johann Wolfgang von Goethe.

solitary flowers on leafless stem

leaves linear, 7–11 mm across

Habitat Exposed shrubland, stony, cliffside areas, pastures. Also an ornamental plant. Mediterranean.

> reminiscent of a crocus
> mostly with abundant flowers
> ornamental plant in central Europe, only slightly hardy

6 tips

golden yellow flower, 3–4 cm long

Centuryplant

Agave americana (centuryplant family)

H 300–600 cm   June–Aug   perennial   (☠)

Habitat *Cliffsides, especially along coasts, rocky areas. Established in Mediterranean. Also cultivated, especially along walls.*

> originates from America
> forms a striking leaf rosette
> withered fruits often visible for a long time

Nowadays, the Centuryplant looks like a normal, Mediterranean flower, yet it only arrived here after the discovery of America. This was a popular plant that was used to decorate gardens in southern Europe in the early 17th century. As a garden escape, the plant gradually found a new habitat. The wax coating on the leaves, the fibres that store water and roots growing deep below ground all aid the plant's survival in arid and hot locations.

6 petal tips

stamens protruding far out

long flower tube

leaf margin with spines

gigantic, upright flower head

up to over 1,000 flowers per plant

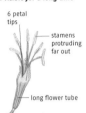

262

leaves form a rosette

leaves thick, fleshy, up to a length of over 1 m

Did you know?

Even in favourable conditions, the Centuryplant only flowers after many years and then it only does so once. While the magnificent flower head is growing, the leaves shrink and ultimately wither and dry out. As soon as the seeds are ripe, the plant dies.

Daffodil

Narcissus pseudonarcissus (lily family)
H 20–40 cm   March–May   perennial   🐝

Daffodils are commonly used to decorate crucifixes and altars at Easter time. In Greek mythology, however, the handsome youth, Narcissus, is said to have ignored the adoring nymphs and fallen in love with his own image. This is why the gods punished him, for as he was about to embrace the mirror image of his own face, which he saw reflected in a lake, he fell into the water and drowned. The gods then transformed the youth into a Daffodil. The flower and its wreath-like garland is said to represent the image of Narcissus.

Did you know?

The flower is often uniform yellow, although cultivars nowadays have many different hues. At the base of the flower, there is an ample store of nectar to attract pollinators. Bumblebees can still access the flower tube, although in some varieties, this may extend up to 7 cm.

Habitat *Mountain meadows, deciduous woodlands, naturalised on woodland meadows. Low mountainous regions, especially in west Europe.*

> *also known as 'Lent Lily' or 'Lent Rose'*
> *wild habitats under threat*
> *numerous cultivated varieties*

dark yellow trumpet, up to 4 cm long

1.5–2 cm across, wavy rim

6 light yellow flower tips, up to 4 cm long

263

long leaves

leafless stem

mostly solitary, nodding flowers

flat leaf

underside ridged or keeled

Yellow Star-of-Bethlehem

Gagea lutea (lily family)
H 10–30 cm   April–May   perennial

Habitat *Riverside woodlands and forest margins, orchard meadows near woodland, hedgerows. On chalky and nutrient-rich ground. Almost everywhere in Europe.*

> **requires soil with sufficient moisture**
> **mostly grows in shade of trees**
> **scentless flowers**

The sweet syrupy nectar is freely accessible to small flies and beetles that extract the sugary drink from the base of the petals. After flowering, the stems lie loosely on the ground. The seeds that drop out of the ripe capsules have a nutritious attachment and are dispersed by ants.

exterior of flowers greenish-yellow

basal leaf protrudes above flower head

umbel with 1–10 flowers

1 basal, flat leaf

bulb about 1.5 cm long

many roots

6 lemony yellow petals, about 1.5 cm long

rounded tip

264

Wild Tulip

Tulipa sylvestris (lily family)
H 20–45 cm   April–May   perennial

Habitat *Vineyards, woodland meadows, copses, arboretum. Southern Europe, introduced to central Europe in the 16th century as ornamental plant and partially naturalised.*

> **fragrant flowers**
> **requires plenty of sunshine**
> **other Wild Tulip varieties grow in the Mediterranean**

Wild Tulip flowers only open during daytime and in fine weather. At night, they close up again. The outer and inner sides of the petals growing at different speeds cause the movement. This is how the blooms grow bigger and, at the same time, the flower stems lengthen. When the flowers are fully grown, the movements stop.

1 flower at end of stem

upright stem

2–4 slightly fleshy leaves, up to 2 cm across

6 pointed petals, up to 7 cm long

yellow, often greenish exterior

stigma narrower than ovary

6 stamens

filaments with dense hairs at base

Yellow Iris

Iris pseudacorus (iris family)

H 50–100 cm   May–June   perennial

The Yellow Iris flower has one petal, one stamen and one style, which join forces to create a single formation. However pollinators treat the three parts of the bloom as separate flowers that they visit one after the other. On coats-of-arms, the rigid, sharp-edged Iris leaf is depicted like a sword, brandished for combat, and is seen as a symbol of knights' chivalry.

Habitat Banks of ponds, disturbed streams, ditches. Woodland and meadow marshes. Almost everywhere in Europe.

> requires wet ground
> also known as 'Yellow Fleur-de-Lis'
> a poisonous plant that causes vomiting and diarrhoea

3 upright, short petals

petal–like style

3 petals, facing downwards

up to more than 3 cm across

stem slightly compressed

265

flower clusters with 4–12 flowers

leaves linear, 1–3 cm across

Did you know?

A stylised image of this flower adorns coats of arms and gateway aas a 'fleur-de-lis insingia or so-called 'Bourbon Lily.' However, this Spanish and French emblem is also said to date back to the Frankish King Govis I, said to have taken the plant across the river Rhine.

Birthwort

Aristolochia clematitis (birthwort family)
H 30–70 cm May–June perennial

Habitat *Vineyards, margins of cultivated land and copses, damp woodlands. On nutrient-rich soil. Central and southern Europe.*

> **rarely forms fruits**
> **heat-loving**
> **becoming less and less common**

Birthwort thrives in warm locations, as does the Grape Vine. This is why Birthwort is especially found in central Europe where old vineyards are abandoned. In mediaeval times, the plant was prized for its healing properties as a vulnerary and to induce birth. Nowadays, however, it is recognised that the plant contains substances that may cause hereditary conditions and even tumours. If the plant is used for herbal remedies, it should only be taken in small doses.

leaves deep, heart-shaped

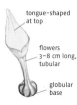

tongue-shaped at top

flowers 3–8 cm long, tubular

globular base

main leaf veins start at base

spherical to pear-shaped fruit, pendent

upright stem

2–8 flowers in leaf axils

Did you know?

The flower is actually a trap: the inside of the tube is covered in downwards-pointed hairs. Small flies may crawl inside, yet they cannot escape. The exit is only free again once the hairs wither after pollination and the flower nods to the ground.

Alpine Wolfsbane
Aconitum lycoctonum (buttercup family)
H 50–150 cm   June–Aug   perennial   🐝

It is difficult for pollinators of Alpine Wolfsbane varieties to reach the nectar. Access to the flower is tricky and only bumblebees can pollinate the flowers, as other bees often bite into the helmet at the upper end of the flower. The plant was once used to set poisonous bait for wolves and foxes.

Habitat *Woodland ravines and lowland forests, damp locations with perennial undergrowth. Alps, mountains in central and southern Europe up to 2,300 m.*

> *requires sufficient moisture*
> *deadly poisonous*

flowers 1.5 to 2 cm high

flowers in clusters

longitudinal flower section

2 nectar petals in helmet

helmet about 3 times as tall as wide, with downy hairs

pale yellow flower

🌸 **267**

Yellow Corydalis
Pseudofumaria lutea (fumitory family)
H 15–30 cm   May–Oct   perennial   (🐝)

Whenever an insect visits the flowers, it depresses both inner petals on the wing-like formations. This causes the anthers and stigma to catapult back upwards. The insect touches them with its back whenever it drinks nectar. Rather than closing up again, the open flowers indicate that they are waiting for insects to visit.

Habitat *Limestone cliffs, wall crevices with drainage water or in gentle shade. Originates from southern Alps, otherwise a garden escape.*

> *ants transport seeds into wall crevices*
> *attractive ornamental plant, but poisonous*
> *rapidly wilts after picking*

leaf loosely pinnate

mostly with many stems and leaves

dense, more or less one-sided clusters

bare

1.2–2 cm long, pendent flowers

labiate-shaped corolla at front

short spur

Alpine Yellow-violet
Viola biflora (violet family)
H 8–15 cm   May–Aug   perennial

Habitat *Mountain woodlands, flooded meadows, shady cliff faces, stony rubble. In the mountains of central and southern Europe from lowland valleys to over 3,000 m.*

> **survives with very little light**
> **requires moist ground and high air humidity**
> **mostly with 2 flowers**

The spur of the Alpine Yellow-violet is so short that even flies and bee-flies reach the nectar with their short proboscis. Ants transport the seeds or else they are eaten by foraging deer and other animals and excreted while still intact.

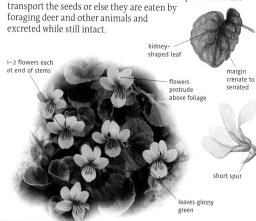

kidney-shaped leaf

margin crenate to serrated

1–2 flowers each at end of stems

flowers protrude above foliage

side petals pointing upwards

yellow flowers, 1–1.5 cm in size

lower petal with pattern

short spur

leaves glossy green

268

Mountain Pansy
Viola lutea (violet family)
H 10–20 cm   June–Aug   perennial

Habitat *Rough, sparse mountain meadows and pastures. Just above the tree line. Central and west Europe.*

> **also known as 'Mountain Violet'**
> **a standard variety of the Garden Pansy**
> **fragrant flowers**

Gardeners cultivated the Mountain Pansy from the 16th century onwards. Nowadays, the flower rarely grows in gardens, although at first sight, it resembles the Horned Pansy, which is available in all kinds of brightly coloured varieties in nurseries during springtime. Originally, the the Horned Pansy is native to the Pyrenees.

stipules with slender sections

flower 2–4 cm in size with spur

stems mostly unbranched

leaf longer than it is wide

in many locations also with violet flowers

side petals pointing upwards

3 petals with darker stripes

Wild Pansy

Viola tricolor (violet family)

H 10–40 cm   April–Sept   annual, perennial

The German name for the Wild Pansy is 'Stiefmütterchen' ('little stepmother), from a fairytale of a stepmother. The outer petals represent her two natural daughters and the violet upper petals her two stepdaughters.

Habitat Embankments, woodland and meadow margins, wayside verges, grassy slopes, fallow and wasteland. Almost everywhere in Europe.

Did you know?

Garden pansies were created from a cross with the Wild Pansy and Mountain Pansy as well as other varieties. Many trends have been fashionable since cultivars were first propagated in the 18th century. Currently, larger flowers are more popular.

> flowers can also be entirely yellow or yellowish white
> the similar Field Pansy has smaller petals with a larger sepal

upper two petals mostly blue-violet

side petals upwards-pointed

sepals markedly shorter than flower corolla

lower petals yellow, with stripy pattern

269

flowers 1.5–3 cm in size

solitary on long, 3–8 cm stalks

numerous spherical seeds

fruit opens in three sections

spur on lower petal

leaf margin slightly notched

Dyer's Greenweed
Genista tinctoria (pea family)
H 30–60 cm   June–Aug   shrub

Habitat *Rough pastures, moorland meadows, woodland margins, open forests. Almost everywhere in Europe.*

> can be haired or without hairs
> attracted to poor, slightly damp locations
> intolerant of fertiliser

Dyer's Greenweed used to be one of the most important sources of yellow colour pigments and was once crucial for the English dye industry. The flowers, leaves and thin twigs all contain colour pigments. Depending on the additional treatments applied, the colours that are created range from lemon yellow to dark brown or olive green.

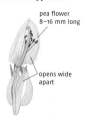

pea flower 8–16 mm long

opens wide apart

smooth margin

leaves 0.5–4.5 cm long, lanceolate

dense flower racemes at end of stems

twigs fairly rigid, without thorns

Gorse
Ulex europaeus (pea family)
H 60–120 cm   May–June   perennial

Habitat *Heathland areas, woodland and meadow margins, embankments, shrubberies. On soil with low lime content. Mainly in west and northern Europe.*

> colonising plant
> requires mild winters
> very sparse and thorny growth

In harsh winters, Gorse bushes tend to suffer frost damage. In west Europe, Gorse has partly become a nuisance weed. The drive to curb the rabbit population partly exacerbated this situation in the English countryside, as the plant's most frequent predators were severely depleted in numbers. Grazing cattle avoid Gorse.

pea flower, 1.5–2 cm long

opens wide apart

leaves and short shoots reformed into thorns

thorns branched, rigid

2-part calyx, yellow

solitary flower

twigs, with ridges

Broom

Cytisus scoparius (pea family)

H 50–200 cm   May–June   shrub ☺

The ripe fruit cases burst open with a loud crack, especially on hot days. They then scatter the seeds far and wide. The ragged, tough twigs were once used to make hard-wearing sweeping brushes. The flowers and tips of the twigs contain similar yellow pigment to the Dyer's Greenweed (see facing page) and were once used for dyeing wool. When taken in the correct dosage, the plant can prove an effective medicinal treatment for heart conditions and poor circulation.

Habitat Heaths, spinneys, copses, wayside and roadside verges, embankments. On acidic soil. Almost everywhere in Europe.

> **twigs without thorns**
> **requires plenty of light**
> **suitable for anchoring slopes**

up to 1–2 flowers in leaf axils

golden yellow, 2–2.5 cm long pea flower

271

leaves alternate

upper leaves single

5-edged young twigs

fruit pod, haired

wings roll up after opening

3-part lower leaves

stalked

Did you know?

If a bumblebee lands on the flower, it depresses the keel. Then, the anthers and style spring upwards and hit the insect. Once they have opened in this explosive fashion, the flowers stay open.

Winged Broom
Chamaespartium sagittale (pea family)
H 15–25 cm   May–June   shrub   (🕷)

Habitat *Rough pastures and grassland, embankments, woodland margins, waysides, rows of cliffs. Especially in central Europe.*

> usually covers wide areas
> requires warm summers
> indicates poor-nutrient soil

The Winged Broom's green wings on the stem take on the function of early-falling leaves, thus producing life-giving carbohydrates. They lose less moisture than is otherwise the case for large-leaved plants, which is why this plant can easily survive in dry locations.

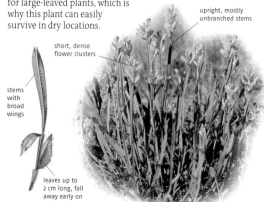

upright, mostly unbranched stems

short, dense flower clusters

stems with broad wings

calyx covered in short hairs

pea flower, 10–12 mm long

leaves up to 2 cm long, fall away early on

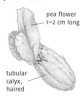

Kidney Vetch
Anthyllis vulneraria (pea family)
H 15–30 cm   May–Aug   perennial

Habitat *Sunny, dry grasslands, rough pastures, roadside verges and slopes, station embankments, stone quarries, cliff faces. Almost everywhere in Europe.*

> often grows in large groups
> intolerant of fertiliser
> dried flowers remain on flower head

Kidney Vetch was once regarded as an effective treatment for binding wounds. While the plant contains tannins, which have a cauterizing effect and can help stem blood flow, nowadays, it no longer has any role to play in herbal medicine. Perhaps a common belief was that the plant's medicinal powers derived from the red-tinged hue of the young flower buds.

flowers in dense, rich flower clusters

end leaflet often much larger

enclosed by palmately divided leaves

pinnate leaves

pea flower 1–2 cm long

tubular calyx, haired

Ribbed Melilot

Melilotus officinalis (pea family)
H 30–100 cm   June–Sept   biennial   (☺)

After it wilts or dries out, Melilot has a similar fragrance to hay or Woodruff (p. 98). It then contains coumarin and is a useful treatment for complaints of the arteries, burst blood vessels and bruising. If Melilot develops mould cultures, a different substance is produced, preventing blood clots, although this can cause fatal internal bleeding in cattle. The substance may be used as a rat poison and was also used as a base element for medication to thin out the blood.

Habitat *Sunny weedy areas on country paths, reservoirs, in quarries, on station sidings, scrub and wasteland. Throughout Europe.*

> *tolerates dryness*
> *often colonises wide areas*
> *fragrant flowers like honey, attractive to bees*

slender flower racemes, 4–10 cm long

pea flower, 5–7 mm long

273

nodding flowers

middle leaflet on longer stalk than two side leaflets

3-part leaves

toothed margin

Did you know?

White Melilot often grows in the same locations alongside the Ribbed Melilot and is primarily distinguished by different flower colours.

Black Medick
Medicago lupulina (pea family)
H 15–60 cm   May–Oct   annual to perennial

Habitat *Rough grass-land, dry meadows, arable fields, country paths, roadside verges, reservoirs. Almost everywhere in Europe.*

> colonising plant on exposed ground
> requires warm locations
> characteristic fruits

Black Medick has flowers, which resemble Hops, with curved seed pods. The flowers have an inbuilt explosive mechanism that catapults the stamens onto the insects' stomachs when they first visit the plant.

spherical flower heads, about 5 mm in size

fruit pod, 1.5–3 mm in size, kidney or sickle-shaped

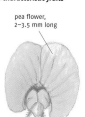

pea flower, 2–3.5 mm long

flower heads stalked in leaf axils

protruding tip

pinnate leaflets flattened or slightly indented at front

3-part leaves

Common Bird's-foot-trefoil
Lotus corniculatus (pea family)
H 5–40 cm   June–Aug   perennial   (🐝)

Habitat *Meadows, pastures, semi-dry grasslands, copses and wayside verges, embankments. From low plains up to altitudes of over 3,000 m. Throughout Europe.*

> roots reach up to 1 m deep
> good source of cattle fodder
> nutritious plant for many wild bees

The scientific name for the plant, 'Lotus' was commonly used in antiquity to refer to plants with a rich store of edible fruits. A bird's-foot-trefoil variety that was found growing in southern Europe was also consumed as a foodstuff. The Common Bird's-foot-trefoil, however, is only suitable as cattle fodder.

straight pods, 1.5–3 cm long

umbels with 3–8 flowers

with 5 pinnate leaflets

pea flower, 1–2 cm long

lower pinnate leaflets mostly clasping stem

buds especially often tinged red

Dragon's-teeth

Tetragonolobus maritimus (pea family)
H 10–30 cm   May–June   perennial

If an insect lands on a Dragon's-teeth flower, it activates a pump mechanism. Then, through a tiny opening at the tip of the lower, keel-shaped petal, a small amount of pollen is emitted that can cling to visiting insects. To observe the action, you can also press down on the petal with a small twig or piece of bark.

Habitat *Rough grassland on chalky ground, wet ground on slopes, moorland fens, wayside verges, riverbanks. Mostly in limestone areas. Central, eastern and southern Europe.*

> **tolerates salt**
> **requires plenty of warmth**

pod fruit, straight, 4–5 cm long

4 winged edges

lowest pinnate pair sessile on stem

leaf bluish green, with 5 pinnate sections

oversized upper petal

2.5–3 cm long, light yellow pea flower

275

solitary flowers, mostly pointing diagonally upwards

3-part leaf below flower

Did you know?

The Winged or Asparagus Pea is native to southern Europe. Their winged fruit pods are occasionally sold on markets and at delicatessens. If lightly sautéed, the fruits give a tasty vegetable a little like asparagus.

Horseshoe Vetch

Hippocrepis comosa (pea family)
H 8–25 cm   May–July   perennial

Habitat *Rough grassland and pastures on limestone, cliffs, reservoirs, waysides, embankments. Mostly on stony ground. Central and southern Europe.*

> **forms characteristic fruits**
> **often grows in larger groups**
> **prefers warm, dry locations**

A popular myth was that horses' shoes would fall off if they trotted over this plant. The idea emerged because, when ripe, the fruits fall into individual hoof-shaped sections.

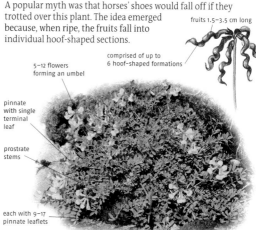

fruits 1.5–3.5 cm long

comprised of up to 6 hoof-shaped formations

5–12 flowers forming an umbel

pinnate with single terminal leaf

stalked petals

prostrate stems

pea flower, 8–12 mm long

each with 9–17 pinnate leaflets

276

Meadow Vetchling

Lathyrus pratensis (pea family)
H 30–100 cm   June–Aug   perennial   (🐝)

Habitat *Nutrient-rich and wetland meadows, hedgerows, woodlands, river and stream banks. Especially in loamy areas. Throughout Europe.*

> **clings to other plants with tendrils**
> **attracts bumblebees, bees and wasps**
> **characteristic meadow plant**

On warm sunny days, the black fruits heat up and dry out. In the process, enormous tension is created, which opens up the fruit at the seams. At top speed, the fruit curls inwards and the seeds are spun out far and wide.

branched tendril

1 pair of lanceolate, pinnate leaflets with parallel veins

pinnate leaf

2 stipules, almost pinnate

up to 12 flowers in a long, stalked cluster

pea flower, 1–1.5 cm long

Shrubby Milkwort

Polygala chamaebuxus (milkwort family)
H 10–20 cm   April–June   shrub

The scientific term *Polygala* means 'lots of milk', even though the plant does not contain any milky sap. Instead the extract of a related North American species, the Thinleaf Milkwort Root was once recommended to women who were breastfeeding to stimulate milk production. The Shrubby Milkwort was also reputed to have this effect.

Habitat Open pine forests, craggy rocks, rough grasslands on chalky ground. Mountains in central and southern Europe, in the Alps up to altitudes of over 2,000 m.

> *leaves green in winter*
> *flowers turn yellow to brownish-red to purple colour*
> *fragrance similar to violets*

flowers in leaf axils, 2–3 cm long

prostrate plant

leaves evergreen

flowers occasionally purple at start

leaves elliptical, leathery

2 white, wing-like petals

yellow petals, fused together, boat-like

277

Small Balsam

Impatiens parviflora (balsam family)
H 30–60 cm   June–Sept   annual   (☺)

bare leaf

margin with pointed teeth

Small Balsam was planted in gardens in Dresden around 1837. By the end of the 19th century, the plant was already distributed more widely throughout northern Germany. However its spinning mechanism (see next species) was not responsible for this. Rather, people unwittingly helped to disperse the seeds, which are wet, sticky and easily cling to places when ripe.

Habitat Originates from eastern Asia and Siberia. Naturalised in Europe in forests with herbaceous undergrowth, on wayside verges, in parks and gardens.

> *requires high humidity*
> *plants wilt as soon as they are in sunshine*
> *seeds can fly distances of over 3 m*

upright stem

few flowers, in upright clusters

pale yellow, trumpet-shaped flower, about 1 cm long

straight spur

inner ring with red pattern

Touch-me-not Balsam

Impatiens noli-tangere (balsam family)
H 30–100 cm July–Aug annual (🐝)

Habitat Riverside woodlands and ravines, woodland springs, damp forest margins. Almost everywhere in Europe.

> **found throughout Great Britain**
> **requires shade and damp conditions**
> **often growing in groups**

Balsam species have specially constructed fruit capsules. While they mature, considerable tension builds up inside. If the tension is great enough, the fruits explode at the slightest touch and scatter seeds for distances of over 3 m.

opened fruit with rolled up lid

fruit 2–3 cm long

often with droplets on toothed leaf

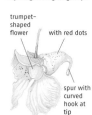

flowers pendent, in leaf axils

trumpet-shaped flower

with red dots

spur with curved hook at tip

flowers 2.5–3 cm long

278

Ground-pine

Ajuga chamaepitys (dead-nettle family)
H 5–15 cm May–Sept annual

Habitat Arable fields, vineyards, dry grass-land, fallow land and gravel areas. On dry, often stony ground. In southern Germany and southern Europe.

> **entire plant with long hairs**
> **requires plenty of heat**
> **aromatic fragrance when crushed, slightly resinous**

The attractive marking on the flower's lower lip guides pollinator bees to the nectar that is concealed deep within the flower. Ground-pine is more commonly found in the Mediterranean and was once thought to be effective against brain haemorrhages.

leaf deeply cleft, in 3 parts

labiate flowers, solitary in leaf axils, 7–15 mm long

leaves protruding above flowers

linear sections, 1–2 mm across

upper lip appears absent

plant with dense foliage

lower lip with reddish marking

Large-flowered Hemp-nettle
Galeopsis speciosa (dead-nettle family)
H 50–100 cm   June–Oct   annual

The hollow teeth on the flower's lower lip serve as a beacon to insects, especially bumblebees. To reach the nectar at the base of the flower tube, the bees must stick their head between the teeth and into the flower's throat. This is how they come into contact both with the stigma as well as stamens and pollinate the flower.

with bristly hairs

leaves decussate

angular stem

violet marking

flowers appear in whorls in leaf axils

labiate flowers, 2.2–3.5 cm long

Habitat Weedy patches in woodland clearings and on arable land, along waysides, riverbanks. Almost everywhere in Europe.

> attracted to nitrogen-rich soil
> requires plenty of moisture
> also flowers in shade

helmet-shaped upper lip

lower lip with 2 conically shaped, hollow teeth

sepal with awn-like tips

279

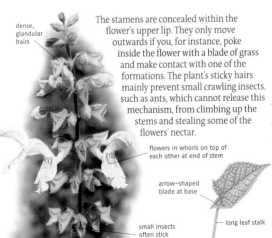

Sticky Clary
Salvia glutinosa (dead-nettle family)
H 40–80 cm   July–Oct   perennial

dense, glandular hairs

The stamens are concealed within the flower's upper lip. They only move outwards if you, for instance, poke inside the flower with a blade of grass and make contact with one of the formations. The plant's sticky hairs mainly prevent small crawling insects, such as ants, which cannot release this mechanism, from climbing up the stems and stealing some of the flowers' nectar.

Habitat Mountain woodlands with herbaceous undergrowth, woodland ravines and margins. On damp, mostly stony soil. Most of Europe, excluding Scandinavia.

> upper parts of plant especially sticky
> fragrant aroma when crushed
> especially attractive to bumblebees

flowers in whorls on top of each other at end of stem

arrow-shaped blade at base

long leaf stalk

small insects often stick to plant

tall upper lip, pressed sideways

light yellow labiate flower, 3–4 cm long

Yellow Archangel

Lamium galeobdolon (dead-nettle family)
H 15–80 cm   May–July   perennial

Habitat In forests with herbaceous undergrowth. On nutrient-rich soil in shady or partially shady locations. Throughout Europe.

> forms long runners, above ground
> may be cooked as a vegetable, like Spinach
> often green in winter

The variety found in gardens is usually the Garden Yellow Archangel with mottled, silvery white patches on the foliage. These plants are often naturalised near towns or villages. The spots appear because the outer leaf membrane is not in direct contact with the leaf's fibrous structure. Air is trapped between the two and reflects the light. Archangel is also suitable as an indoor pot plant.

leaves decussate

helmet-shaped upper lip

3-part lower lip, with striped pattern

leaves often with silvery white patches

margin toothed

flowers arranged whorl-like in leaf axils

light to golden yellow labiate flowers, 1.5–2.5 cm long

280

Perennial Yellow-woundwort

Stachys recta (dead-nettle family)
H 20–60 cm   June–Oct   perennial

Habitat Margins of copses and woodlands, rough grassland. Preferably on dry, mostly chalky soil in warm, summer locations. Central and southern Europe.

> flowers light yellow or almost whitish
> mostly grows in bright sunshine
> roots up to 2 m deep

In 16th century herbals, the plant was known as 'Heal-all'. It was regarded as an effective vulnerary especially for injuries to the limbs. Instead of this plant, in the Mediterranean, the Hairy Rock-cress was used, which is very closely related to Ironwort (see facing page).

labiate flowers, 1–2 cm long

whorl-like arrangement

sepal with 5 spiky, awn-like teeth

4-edged stem

lower lip with brown pattern

margin toothed

many whorls, loosely above each other at end of stem

leaves opposite

rough hairs

Ironwort

Sideritis syriaca (dead-nettle family)
H 20–60 cm   May–Aug   perennial

flower clusters
at end of stems

The plant is adapted to dry
locations with roots reaching
2 m into the ground and
downy hairs. Teashops
and markets offer dried,
flowering stems, mainly
finely ground, by the name
of 'Greek Mountain Tea'. These
make a pleasant herbal tea
with a faint hint of cinnamon.

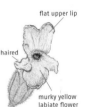

***Habitat** In shrubberies
and exposed
locations around the
Mediterranean from
Crete to Syria.*

> *pleasant fragrance when
  crushed*
> *can also be cultivated in
  northern Europe*
> *similar varieties growing
  in the Mediterranean*

flat upper lip

haired

leaf blade longish
to slender, oval

entire plant with
downy hairs

murky yellow
labiate flower

leaves opposite

Jerusalem Sage

Phlomis fruticosa (dead-nettle family)
H 50–130 cm   April–July   shrub

conspicuous whorls
with up to more
than 30 flowers

Only very heavy insects like
bumblebees or carpenter bees
can depress the flower's lower
lip and reach the nectar at the
base. The plant can develop
in mass colonies inside fire
cordons. The fruits have a
firm casing, which is fire-
resistant.

***Habitat** Bush and
shrubberies, rocky areas,
exposed locations, forest
clearings. Also in gardens
as ornamental plant and
naturalised there. Around
the Mediterranean.*

> *evergreen flowering
  shrub*
> *shunned by cattle*
> *other similar varieties in
  the Mediterranean*

helmet-shaped upper lip

very firm flower
formation

leaves opposite

grey hairs,
wrinkled

labiate flower,
2.5–3.5 cm long

Common Toadflax

Linaria vulgaris (figwort family)
H 20–75 cm   June–Oct   perennial

Habitat *Exposed, sparse weedy areas, stony river beds, station embankments, arable and wasteland, road-side verges. Throughout Europe.*

> *leaves resemble Flax (p. 159)*
> *requires plenty of sunshine*
> *attractive plant for wild flower gardens*

The orangey yellow 'mask' that encloses the flower opening looks at first sight like a single, large stamen. The plant simulates the appearance of an easily accessible store of food for insects. However in order to find nutrients, visiting insects must reach deep within the flower's spur. Strong bumblebees do so by separating the lips of the flowers.

leaf linear to lanceolate, 2–4 cm long, bluish green

flowers in dense clusters

flower enclosed by orangey-yellow swollen formation

long spur

282

flowers 2–3.5 cm long

upright stem

dense foliage

Did you know?

Alternative names for the plant are 'Bride-wort' or 'Brideweed', which may refer to the fact that flowering stems are located in many regions where herbal bundles are dedicated to the Virgin Mary on Ascension Day.

Wald-Small Cow-wheat

Melampyrum sylvaticum (figwort family)

H 10–35 cm   June–Sept   annual   (⚘)

flowers mostly
in pairs,
pointing to
one side

flower
up to
1 cm
long

The seeds are popular with ants as they have a nutritious, oily structure and also their size and shape resemble ant larvae. It is not surprising that ants transport the seeds to their nest, thus ensuring their dispersal. The seeds frequently germinate back in the ant hills.

Habitat *Open forests, heaths, woodland margins, upland moors. On acidic soil, often with mildew. Throughout Europe.*

> **mostly growing in groups**
> **rests with roots near pine**
> **trees or in bilberry fields**
> **and absorbs valuable**
> **nutrients**

smooth
margin

leaves opposite,
lanceolate

attachment contains oil

seeds about
0.5 cm in
size

upper lip with
downy hairs

4-part calyx

lower lip with 3 points

Monkeyflower

Mimulus guttatus (figwort family)

H 25–60 cm   June–Oct   perennial

solitary flowers in
upper leaf axils

The flowers are reminiscent of jugglers' or clowns' masks. Their special feature is the highly sensitive stigma, which initially opens like two lips. However if touched on the inside, the stigma recoils within seconds. The pollen brought by any insect visiting the flower is therefore not lost.

Habitat *Native to North America. In Europe as an ornamental plant, naturalised along banks of streams, rivers and ditches.*

> **requires wet soil**
> **attracts bees**
> **garden varieties also**
> **with red flowers**

open,
lip-shaped
stigma

stigma
folded
together

anthers
visible
beneath

upright
stems

leaves
roundish to
longish and
oval

leaves opposite

upper
leaves
sessile

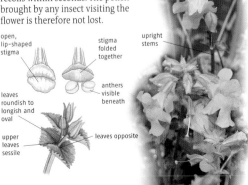

broad, trumpet-
shaped tube

double-
lipped
flower,
3–4 cm
long

mostly with red-brown dots

Greater Yellow Rattle
Rhinanthus alectorolophus (figwort family)
H 10–80 cm   May–Aug   annual   (☠)

Habitat Meadows with low fertiliser content, semi-dry grassland. On mostly chalky ground. Especially in central Europe.

> requires some heat
> often growing in large, loose groups
> mostly turns black when dried

The longish, lentil-shaped winged seeds make a loud rattling sound inside the ripe fruit capsules in the wind and when people walk past the plant or shake it. *Rhinanthus*, the plant's scientific name, refers to the nose-like shape of the flower's upper lip.

blue tooth, up to more than 2 mm long

helmet-shaped upper lip

densely haired calyx

solitary flowers, 1.8–2.2 cm long in axils of light leaves

densely haired plant

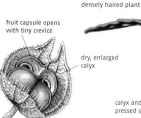

fruit capsule opens with tiny crevice

dry, enlarged calyx

calyx and corolla pressed sideways

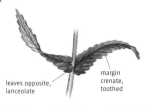

leaves opposite, lanceolate

margin crenate, toothed

Did you know?

The Greater Yellow Rattle is a semi-parasitic plant that absorbs moisture and nourishing minerals from the roots of other plants. If it grows in mass colonies, it weakens these host plants and therefore reduces the hay crop.

Leafy Lousewort

Pedicularis foliosa (figwort family)
H 20–50 cm   May–Aug   perennial

cluster with 20–30 flowers, up to 3 cm long

As with the Greater Yellow Rattle, (see facing page) the Leafy Lousewort is a semi-parasitic plant and grafts onto other plants with its roots, thus depriving them of moisture and essential minerals. To do so, it has to be hardier than if its roots only penetrated the soil and so it loses a lot of moisture in order to produce substantial powers of suction. This is why if you pick the stems, they wilt very rapidly.

Habitat Mountain grassland on limestone, stream banks, copses near the tree line. Mountains in central and southern Europe.

> previously used to prevent lice
> leaves resemble fronds

long foliage between flowers

helmet-shaped upper lip

dense, woolly hairs

leaves double pinnate

Yellow Asphodel

Asphodeline lutea (lily family)
H 40–100 cm   April–June   perennial

The plant's specific name, *lutea*, means 'yellow' and refers both to the flower colour as well as the plant's roots. When the plant first arrived from the Mediterranean in northern Europe during the Renaissance, it was first known as *Hastula regia* or 'King's Spear'. Another name for the plant is also 'Jacob's Rod'.

dense flower cluster, 10–15 cm long

flowers 2–3 cm in size

Habitat Mediterranean region on rocky areas and in shrubberies. Also cultivated in central Europe as ornamental plant.

> fragrant flowers
> tolerates dry conditions
> also known as 'Flower of the Dead'

6 slightly unequal petals

pointed leaf

linear leaves

extremely broad base

central vein green

Greater Bladderwort

Utricularia vulgaris (bladderwort family)
H 15–35 cm   June–Aug   perennial

flowering stems protruding out of water

The trap-like bladders have a flap with stiff bristles. If a small water insect, such as a water flea, makes contact with the bristles, the flap opens. A current of water then draws the insect inside the bladder. The flap then closes and the plant digests the insect. This is how the plant absorbs additional nutrients.

4–25 flowers on each stem

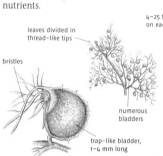

leaves divided in thread-like tips

bristles

numerous bladders

corolla 13–30 mm long, golden yellow

lower lip, saddle-shaped

trap-like bladder, 1–4 mm long

Coralroot Orchid

Corallorhiza trifida (orchid family)
H 8–25 cm   May–July   perennial

each stem with up to 11 flowers

The Coralroot Orchid has no or only sparse foliage and no roots. It finds nutrients solely with the aid of fungi that penetrate the coral-like branched, prostrate plant structure with fibrous networks and the plant consumes them.

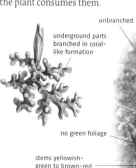

unbranched

underground parts branched in coral-like formation

other petals greenish-yellow, slender

no green foliage

lip 5–7 mm long, with red dots and stripes

stems yellowish-green to brown-red

Lady's Slipper

Cypripedium calceolus (orchid family)

H 15–50 cm   May–June   perennial

The flower's lower lip is like a trap. Insects tumble into the flower in search of nectar. To escape the slippery interior, they have to squeeze through a tight opening. In doing so, they offload pollen, which they bring along, or else take away new pollen. The flower's lip has light 'windows' guiding the insects to the exit.

Habitat *Woodlands with grassy or herbaceous undergrowth, shrubberies. In partial shade. Rare. Central and northern Europe.*

> has the largest flowers of any native European orchid
> flowering plants only from 16 years old
> rare and protected species

leafy stem

1–3 flowers on each stem

purple-brown petals, up to 6 cm long

globular, swollen lip, 3–4 cm long

287

leaf broad to spear-shaped

parallel leaf veins

Did you know?

Florists sell hybrid varieties of lady's slipper orchids as pot plants that actually originate from Asia and have been cultivated in many different varieties.

Asarabacca

Asarum europaeum (birthwort family)
H 5–10 cm   March–May   perennial

Habitat Deciduous and mixed coniferous forests with herbaceous undergrowth. On damp, mostly chalky soil. Mainly central and eastern Europe.

> leaves green in winter
> pepper-like fragrance when crushed
> flowers mostly concealed beneath foliage

Asarabacca was used as a snuff and to prevent bronchitis. The flowers attract fungus gnats. These small insects normally lay their eggs in fungi. However they are confused by the Asarabacca's fragrance and lay their clutches inside the flowers instead and so pollinate them.

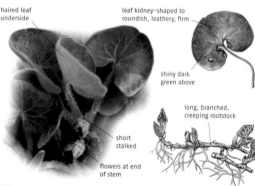

haired leaf underside

leaf kidney-shaped to roundish, leathery, firm

shiny dark green above

flower greenish outside, red-brown inside

long, branched, creeping rootstock

short stalked

flowers at end of stem

3–4 firm tips

Eastern Pellitory-of-the-wall

Parietaria officinalis (nettle family)
H 30–100 cm   June–Oct   perennial

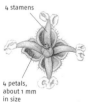

Habitat Open lowland woodlands, cliffs, walls, wasteland. On nutrient-rich soil. Central and southern Europe.

> requires heat and warmth
> reminiscent of a Stinging Nettle, without stinging hairlets
> brittle stems

The leaves of Eastern-Pellitory-of-the-wall gleam with a glassy lustre and turn translucent when dried. The plant's ash was once used to clean glass and crockery. Herbalists used the plant as a cure for urinary infections and to treat gall and kidney stones.

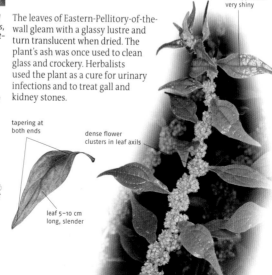

leaf upperside very shiny

dense flower clusters in leaf axils

tapering at both ends

4 stamens

leaf 5–10 cm long, slender

4 petals, about 1 mm in size

Common Stinging Nettle

Urtica dioica (nettle family)
H 30–150 cm   July–Oct   perennial

Stinging Nettle is regarded as a weed, although it can prove useful. You can gather the young plants bearing shoots early in the year and prepare them as you would Spinach. Pressing the leaves for juice can help prevent lethargy and tiredness in springtime. As a medicinal plant, it may be effective against arthritis and rheumatism as well as urinary and prostrate conditions. Fibres from the stems were used from the 12th century onwards to produce sails and fishing nets, until cotton became more popular.

Habitat *Country paths, frequently in villages or towns, shrubland, ditches, woodland margins, over-fertilised meadows. Throughout Europe.*

> **male and female plants**
> **one of the best indicators of nitrogen**
> **often colonises vast areas**

female flower with whitish, paintbrush-like stigma

male flower with 4 stamens

flowers in racemes in leaf axils

289

leaf mostly over 5 cm long

many short bristly hairs and long stinging hairs

leaves opposite

leaf roughly serrated

stinging hair with tip, easily broken

upright stem, unbranched

Did you know?

Stinging Nettles are food for some caterpillars of the butterfly family Nymphalidae. Caterpillars of these butterflies are especially conspicuous because until their last moult, they live in large groups in a cocoon.

Monk's Rhubarb
Rumex pseudoalpinus (knotweed family)
H 70–200 cm   June–Aug   perennial   (☠)

Habitat Mostly by mountain huts near cattle sheds. Also on former settlement habitats. Mountains in central and southern Europe.

> extremely large leaves
> indicates nitrogen and overgrazing
> leaves resemble those of the Butterbur (p. 56)

6 greenish to brown petals, about 0.5 cm long

red stigmas   6 stamens

dense flower head

leaf heart-shaped at base

Monk's Rhubarb is an Alpine weed that often colonises large areas near huts on mountain pastures and uplands. Grazing cattle shuns the plant, which contains oxalic acid that is poisonous if consumed in larger quantities. Farmers on the mountain uplands once used the large leaves to wrap cheese or butter or cooked them in a similar way to sauerkraut.

mostly wavy margin

lower leaves up to 50 cm long

French Sorrel
Rumex scutatus (knotweed family)
H 20–40 cm   May–Aug   perennial

stalked

spear-shaped leaf, blue or grass green

Habitat Stony rubble and scree, walls, quarries, station gravel. On disturbed, open rubble. Central and southern Europe.

> often with bluish-green appearance from a distance
> sorrel that is easily recognisable by leaves
> sour taste

In Roman times, the 'scutum' was the large, square-shaped insignia for the infantry. The shape is less strictly defined in reference to the botanical name (*scutatus*). French Sorrel has a more pleasant taste than Patience or Spinach Dock that is cultivated nowadays, albeit mainly by connoisseurs.

long, upright fruit stems

roundish fruits

petals pressed together

protruding anthers

stems spreading to climbing

Common Glasswort
Salicornia europaea (goosefoot family)
H 5–30 cm   Aug–Oct   annual

Common Glasswort is among the few plants that require salt for germination and optimal growth. The plant's fleshy appearance is due to deposits of salt and moisture. Occasionally, the plant is now used as a salty, tangy addition in salads. The plant's salty ash was once used in glass smelting, since it helped the glass to liquefy at lower temperatures. The name 'Glasswort' is derived from this earlier usage.

Habitat First to colonise salt mudflats around European sea coasts. Rare inland.

> most pioneering flowering plant on tidal mudflats
> frequently in loose groups
> mud forms around plants

flowering branch-ends swollen, cone-like

protruding stamens

flowers sunken into branchlets

291

knot-like stems, leafless

stems and branchlets thick and fleshy

Did you know?
The salt content of this Glasswort increases during the summer, so that the plant grows profusely. In autumn, shortly before the plants wither and die they turn a red colour.

Spear-leaved Orache

Atriplex prostrata (goosefoot family)
H 30–90 cm   July–Sept   annual

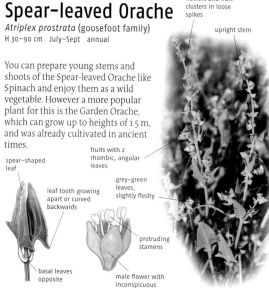

flowers and fruit clusters in loose spikes

upright stem

Habitat *Weedy patches along ditches, wayside verges, riverbanks, along sea coasts, on rubbish and shrubland. Everywhere in Europe.*

> **leaves often covered with membrane-like, detachable crust**
> **tolerates salt**
> **often grows in groups**

You can prepare young stems and shoots of the Spear-leaved Orache like Spinach and enjoy them as a wild vegetable. However a more popular plant for this is the Garden Orache, which can grow up to heights of 1.5 m, and was already cultivated in ancient times.

fruits with 2 rhombic, angular leaves

grey-green leaves, slightly fleshy

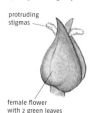

protruding stigmas

spear-shaped leaf

leaf tooth growing apart or curved backwards

protruding stamens

female flower with 2 green leaves

basal leaves opposite

male flower with inconspicuous flower casing

292

Salad Burnet

Sanguisorba minor (rose family)
H 15–40 cm   May–Aug   perennial

Habitat *Rough grassland, embankments, wayside verges, dry meadows, sheep grazing pastures, walls. On moderately dry, chalky soil. Almost everywhere in Europe.*

> **pollination on the wind**
> **attracted to poor soil**
> **also known as 'Pimpernelle'**

The Salad Burnet is a source of a slightly bitter, nutty tasting herb and salad ingredient. Nurseries therefore offer the herbaceous perennial as pot plants for herb gardens. However, another variety of the Salad Burnet is related to the Wild Carrot (p. 121) and is used in herbal remedies.

flower heads at end of stems and branches

male flower with many long, pendent stamens

leaves pinnate, with single terminal leaflet

flower heads, 1–3 cm in size

upper leaves female

female flower with 2, red stigmas, like paintbrushes

4 greenish leaves

roundish leaflet, roughly toothed

lower leaves male

Castor Oil Plant
Ricinus communis (spurge family)
H 50–400 cm   Feb–Oct   annual or shrub ☠

Archaeologists discovered the oldest seeds from the Castor Oil Plant in ancient Egyptian tombs dating from around 4,000 BC. Castor Oil seeds are, however, quite dangerous. They contain the deadly poisonous ricin, which must be carefully extracted and separated when the fatty oil is pressed. Castor oil is still recommended today as a cure for constipation.

Habitat Around the Mediterranean on roadside verges, on scrubland, wasteland. In central Europe as annual ornamental plant in parks and gardens.

> conspicuous leaf form
> naturalised from tropical Africa in Mediterranean
> grows rapidly, also known as 'Steadfast'

with attachment

seeds about 1 cm in size

blade with hand-like lobes

long leaf stalk

patterned

ovary with soft spines

red stigmas

upper flowers female

upright flower racemes

lower flowers male

293

male flowers with branched stamens

also as red-coloured variety in gardens

Did you know?

The scientific name Ricinus *is an allusion to the similarity of the seeds' appearance with ticks (Ixodes ricinus). The plant is sometimes also known as the 'Castor Bean'.*

Dog's Mercury
Mercurialis perennis (spurge family)
H 15–30 cm   April–Mai   perennial

Habitat Woodlands with rich herbaceous undergrowth, copses. Preferably in shady locations. Almost everywhere in Europe.

> often growing in large groups
> usually many male and few female plants
> indicator of water drainage

Dog's Mercury acts as a diuretic. If grazing cattle eat the plant, their urine turns a reddish-blue colour and may prove mildly poisonous. The plant changes colour from green when dried to a metallic, glimmering blue-black tone. In the Middle Ages, alchemists believed that the plant could help turn mercury ('quicksilver') into gold.'

leaf margin with rounded teeth

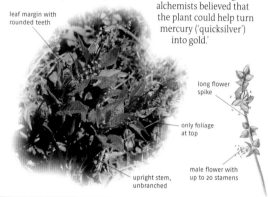

long flower spike

only foliage at top

2 stigmas

female flower with globular ovary

upright stem, unbranched

male flower with up to 20 stamens

Ribwort Plantain
Plantago lanceolata (plantain family)
H 10–50 cm   May–Sept   perennial

Habitat Pastures, meadows, park grassland, wasteland, pathways, arable fields. Mostly on low-lying ground. Almost everywhere in Europe.

> slightly bitter taste
> seeds become sticky when wet
> crushed leaves sooth insect bites

In medieval times, Ribwort Plantain was already a tried and tested cough tincture. Nowadays, tea or juice with extracts of this plant are still suitable as medication for dry, irritable coughs. In contrast to other plant juices, the pressé from this plant does not go mouldy and requires no additives. The juice contains substances that suppress the growth of micro-organisms.

stem with 1 terminal flower spike

many flowers forming an oval spike

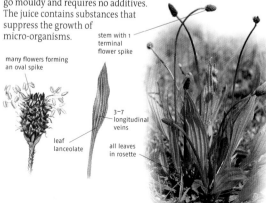

stamens yellowish, protrude far out

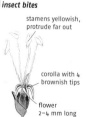

corolla with 4 brownish tips

flower 2–4 mm long

leaf lanceolate

3–7 longitudinal veins

all leaves in rosette

Buck's-horn Plantain

Plantago coronopus (plantain family)

H 5–15 cm   June–Sept   annual

up to over 4 cm long, slender flower spike

stem with 1 terminal flower spike

Italians and the French savour tender plantain leaves as a wild vegetable or for use in mixed salads. The plant is also cultivated for this purpose. On Italian menus, the vegetable is known as 'Minutina o erba stella'. The name 'Erba stella' (or 'star herb') for this plant dates back to the 17th century and refers to the shape of the leaf rosette.

Habitat Saline meadows along sea coasts, inland occasionally on salty ground. Central and southern Europe.

> very varied form
> also known as 'Hart's Horn Plantain'
> tolerates flooding

stamens protruding far out

leaf with 4–8 slender sections on each side

all leaves in a rosette

4 corolla tips with brown strips

flower about 0.2 cm long

295

Common Mare's Tail

Hippuris vulgaris (plantain family)

H 10–50 cm   May–Aug   perennial

Common Mare's Tail is sensitive to water pollution and disappears in heavily affected water. The plant's name possibly refers to the form of growth, which resembles small fir trees. Older names refer to the similarity with the Field Horsetail that is just as different to the Common Mare's Tail as a fir tree.

Habitat Floating plant in standing or gently flowing water with a maximum depth of 2 m. Also along riverbanks. Throughout Europe.

> very inconspicuous flowers
> mostly grows in larger groups
> requires clean, cool, nutrient-rich water

stem unbranched

leaves in whorls of up to 8–12, stiff, growing apart

minute flowers, sessile in leaf axils

leaves about 1 mm across

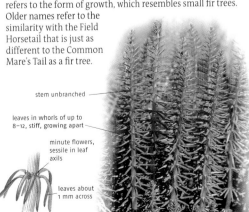

1 stamen

1 stigma

swollen, sac-like petal-like bract

Broad-leaved Pondweed

Potamogeton natans (pondweed family)
H 60–150 cm   June–Aug   perennial

Habitat *Meres, tarns, sea inlets or bays, back-waters. Often between other floating plants such as water-lilies. Throughout Europe.*

> grows fairly rapidly
> leaves float on water's surface
> can cover wider stretches of water

The surface of the floating leaves is covered in an oily film and so water trickles off them. Farmers used to collect the swollen rootstocks, which are rich in starch, and use them to fatten pigs. The plant grows in dense groups in garden ponds, which have to be thinned out, otherwise water can hardly penetrate the water's surface.

flower stems protruding upwards

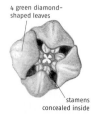

4 green diamond-shaped leaves

stamens concealed inside

flowers pointing to all sides

dense spike, up to 8 cm long

broad, elliptical to almost round leaves

296

Sweet Flag

Acorus calamus (calamus family)
H 60–120 cm   June–July   perennial (☒)

Habitat *Bogs, along banks of standing or gently flowing, nutrient-rich water in warmer locations. Almost everywhere in Europe.*

> reed-like leaves
> rootstock with aromatic scent when rubbed
> in Europe, a garden escape dating from the 16th century

Sweet Flag originates from south-eastern Asia. Nowadays, it is a common plant in Asia, America and Europe and comes in a variety of different species. European varieties supply a seasoning that is popularly used in liqueurs and drinks. Taken as medicines, it helps digestive problems and gastroenteritis.

patterned with green ovaries and yellowish stamens

spikes 4–10 cm long, growing sideways

leaves perfoliate (clasping) at base

rootstock up to 3 cm thick

inconspicuous flowers form a spike

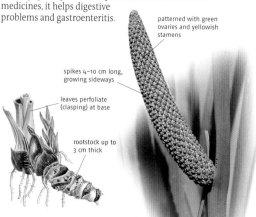

Cuckoo Pint

Arum maculatum (lords-and-ladies family)

H 15–40 cm   April–June   perennial

The sheath-like leaf forms a pitcher-shaped spathe that acts as a trap, albeit not meant as a death trap. This unfurls during the evening and the spadix gives off a urine-like odour to attract small moth flies. The insects then slide into the trap and help pollinate the female flowers. The anthers of the male flowers only open later on. The spathe flowers keep the gnats trapped inside the spadix and release them – dusted in pollen – in the evening. That is just in time for the gnats to fall into a new pollination trap.

Habitat *Deciduous woodlands with rich herbaceous under-growth, riverside wood-lands, hedgerows. On nutrient-rich soil in shady locations. Central and southern Europe.*

> each flower head only flowers for 1 day
> pungent, unpleasant odour
> leaves only in spring

sheath-like leaf curved inwards

leaves broad, arrow-shaped, glossy

bristly, sterile spathe flowers

male flowers, still closed

section with female flowers

297

club-shaped spikes (spadix)

flower head with brilliant red berries

flowers concealed in spathe

Did you know?

The plant used to be regarded as an oracle, with the different parts of the flower thought to represent different kinds of crop. Well-developed parts promised a good harvest, whereas those in decline heralded failed crops.

Friar's Cowl
Arisarum vulgare (lords-and-ladies family)
H 10–40 cm   Oct–May   perennial   🖾

Habitat In copses, Olive groves, on fallow land and by walls. Requires shady locations, not too dry. Around the Mediterranean.

> often flowers in spring-time and autumn
> mostly grows in groups

The spicy fragranced flower heads attract small flies and midges. In contrast to the closely related Cuckoo Pint (p. 297) pollinators can crawl unhindered inside and out of the tube of leaves. The green berries can also develop without insects' visits. The sharp taste helps protect the plant from hungry predators.

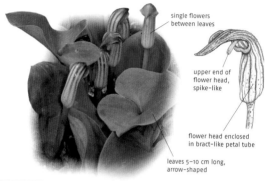

single flowers between leaves

upper end of flower head, spike-like

flower head enclosed in bract-like petal tube

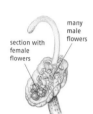

section with female flowers

many male flowers

leaves 5–10 cm long, arrow-shaped

Branched Bur-reed
Sparganium erectum (bur-reed family)
H 30–50 cm   June–Aug   perennial   (🖾)

Habitat In reeds of standing or flowing, nutrient-rich water, on humus-rich, muddy ground. Throughout Europe.

> named after shape of fruits
> also colonises heavily polluted water
> requires plenty of light

The ripe fruits in the round, spiky fruit burrs can float on water for up to 12 months and so arrive in faraway locations. The leaves contain an abundance of pointed, needle-shaped crystals, which serve as an effective deterrent against predators foraging for food.

female flower with protruding stigma

above spherical male flower heads

branched flower head

female flower heads below

male flower with 3 stamens

minute petals

female flower head round and spiky

leaves grass-like, 1–1.5 cm across

Bulrush

Typha latifolia (bulrush family)
H 100–200 cm   July–Aug   perennial

Nowadays, the dried fruit stems of the Bulrush are widely used for dried flower arrangements. Previously, however, farmers fed the rootstocks, which are rich in starch, to pigs or ground them up for use in times of shortage to increase the quantity of flour. In the late 19th and early 20th century, fibres from the leaves and stems were used as a substitute for jute. Cellar keepers used the leaves to insulate barrel joints up until the 20th century.

Habitat In reed beds in standing to gently flowing, nutrient-rich water. Can form large, dense groups. Almost everywhere in Europe.

> in moderate climates, dispersed almost worldwide
> cellar owners especially used to cultivate plants
> mature flower spikes wither away

male flower with stamens

miniscule solitary flower

thin, fibrous threads on stalk

299

remainder of male spike

female fruit spike, brown, 2–3 cm thick

leaves 1–2 cm across, rigid, upright, grey-green

large stigma

female flower with ovary

Did you know?

The fibrous fruit hairs used to be gathered as filling material for pillows or for bandages. However they are not suitable for spinning into longer threads.

Stinking Hellebore

Helleborus foetidus (buttercup family)
H 30–80 cm March–May perennial 🐝

The flower buds are already developed in autumn, but they only open in springtime. Stinking Hellebore leaves progressively evolve into flower petals, thus the plant serves as a model example for this type of long-term process. In many winegrowing areas, vintners hoped for a good vintage if the plant produced a profusion of flowers.

often with many pendant flowers

upper leaves lighter

leaf blade small or missing

spreading stalk

bell-shaped flower

green petals, often red at front edge

lower leaves with 3–9 lanceolate sections

abundant stamens

Yellow Bird's-nest

Monotropa hypopitys (bird's-nest family)
H 10–25 cm June–July perennial

flower cluster initially nodding

unbranched stem

The pale shoots are slightly reminiscent of Asparagus, although they are not edible. The roots of Yellow Bird's-nest are fused with a fungus that, in turn, cohabits with tree roots. This is how Yellow Bird's-nest absorbs lactose and other substances. It therefore counts among parasitic flowering plants that do not require any light.

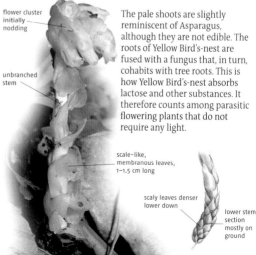

conspicuous stigma

scale-like, membranous leaves, 1–1.5 cm long

scaly leaves denser lower down

5 translucent, yellowish, slender petals

lower stem section mostly on ground

Fat Hen

Chenopodium album (goosefoot family)
H 20–150 cm   July–Oct   annual

Nowadays, Fat Hen is regarded as a weed. The seeds can germinate for up to several centuries. As each plant can produce up to 100,000 seeds, these can populate the ground and grow into mass colonies. In the Neolithic age, people used the seeds to make flour, as findings from pile dwellings have proven. The leaves and tips of shoots give a mild-tasting, Spinach-like wild vegetable or make a good soup.

Habitat *Weedy patches on scrubland, in gardens, on pathways, roadside verges. On nutrient-rich soil. Throughout Europe.*

> *often appears coated with a light dusting of flour*
> *very variable leaf form*
> *first to colonise wasteland*

flowers in clusters

tiny flowers

plant grey-green, more or less dense covered in white coating

5-part bract-like sepal, green, with white coating

301

leaves often coarsely and irregularly toothed

leaves also lanceolate, with smooth margin

leaves alternate

Did you know?

Good King Henry is a closely related plant and usually grows near residential areas. Folklore compared the plant to the good Samaritan or saint, as it was an important medicinal herb and vegetable. It supplies 'Wild Spinach' and was used against skin ailments.

Navelwort

Umbilicus rupestris (stonecrop family)
H 10–50 cm   May–July   perennial

Habitat *Dry cliff crevices and walls, mostly in the shade, shady slopes. South and west Europe.*

> also called 'Venus's Navelwort'
> name derives from characteristic leaf shape
> also colonises high wall crevices

In antiquity, Navelwort was used as an aphrodisiac. It was also thought to help treat epilepsy. Later on, herbalists recommended the soft leaves be applied to soothe and cool burns. The fleshy, moisture-storing leaves and a unique metabolism help the plant colonise even dry locations with poor humus, e.g. on rocky crevices.

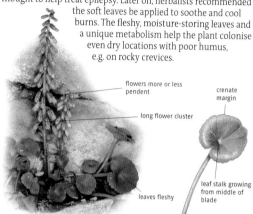

flowers more or less pendent

long flower cluster

crenate margin

flower about 1 cm long

corolla forming a tube

pointed tip

leaves fleshy

leaf stalk growing from middle of blade

Hound's-tongue

Cynoglossum officinale (borage family)
H 30–80 cm   May–July   biennial

Habitat *Weedy patches, scrubland, wayside verges, wasteland. Preferably on dry soil in sunny locations. Almost everywhere in Europe.*

> fruits more conspicuous than flowers
> attracted to nitrogen in soil
> mouse-like odour when bruised

The round, almost tongue-shaped leaves are probably why the plant is named Hound's-tongue. The fruit burrs cling to passing animals and are dispersed. The plant is regarded as an effective means of keeping away rats and mice due to its unpleasant odour. Occasionally, it is still planted today in gardens for this reason.

flower heads inrolled after flowering

4 fruitlets with reversed-curving spines

corolla murky, reddish-brown, 5–6 mm long

5 tips

5 enlarged, velveteen scales at entrance to tube

calyx enlarged after flowering

entire plant with dense hairs

leaves lanceolate

Deadly Nightshade
Atropa belladonna (nightshade family)
H 50–150 cm   June–Aug   perennial   ☠

Three of the sweet-tasting fruits that look tantalizingly like cherries are enough to prove fatal for a small child. Mild cases of poisoning produce a dry mouth, racing pulse and dilated pupils. If consumed in larger quantities, the symptoms include hallucinations and even death by respiratory paralysis. Birds, for instance, song thrushes can eat the berries without any problem and thus disperse the seeds. Deadly Nightshade was used as arrow poison in the Stone Age period.

Habitat Forest clearings, woodland paths, spinneys. Mostly on chalky soil in light or partly shaded locations. Central and southern Europe.

> flowers and fruits often appear simultaneously
> flowers with unpleasant aroma
> deadly poisonous

Did you know?

Scopolia is also equally as poisonous Deadly Nightshade and grows in deciduous forests in rural regions of southern and south-eastern Europe.

1 large and 1 small leaf, seem opposite, near flowers

sepal with 5 tips

5 short lobes, bent backwards

corolla, 2.5–3 cm long, bell-shaped, violet-brown, murky yellow inside

spherical, up to cherry-sized berry, gleaming black

sepals remain around berry

303

oval leaf, pointed at tip

smooth margin

flowers pendant in leaf axils

Ragweed
Ambrosia artemisiifolia (daisy family)
H 50–150 cm   Aug–Oct   annual

Habitat *Weedy patches on scrub, harbours and gardens. On warm, nutrient-rich soil. Central and southern Europe.*

> originates from North America and Mexico
> common spreading plant
> causes hay fever

The fruits were included for many decades in birds' winter food mixtures. This species is one of the few members of the daisy family to be pollinated on the wind. Its profusion of pollen causes hay fever or asthma in about 10 per cent of the population in those countries where the plant has its native habitat. Scientific research therefore recommends that the plant should be eradicated.

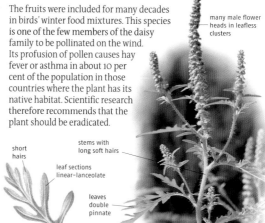

many male flower heads in leafless clusters

semi-spherical casing

short hairs

stems with long soft hairs

leaf sections linear-lanceolate

leaves double pinnate

5–12 disc flowers

male flower heads nodding

Herb Paris
Paris quadrifolia (lily family)
H 10–30 cm   May–June   perennial

Habitat *Damp woodlands mostly with rich herbaceous undergrowth, riverside woodlands. On nutrient-rich soil. Throughout Europe.*

> mostly identifiable by 4, occasionally 5 or 6 leaves
> indicator of ground or drainage water
> requires shade

In Greek mythology, Paris was the human judge in a beauty contest between the goddesses. They are represented by the four leaves surrounding the Herb Paris berry. In medieval times, people thought that the fruit, which is reminiscent of a boil that is a symptom of the Plague, could cure this disease and other contagious illnesses.

1 flower at end of stem

black-blue, pruinose berries, up to 1 cm thick

mostly 4 leaves in a whorl

surrounded by petals

yellow, long anthers

8 green 2–3.5 cm long petals

Common Figwort

Scrophularia nodosa (figwort family)
H 40–120 cm   June–Sept   perennial

The Common Figwort has a characteristic throat-shaped flower and people often imagine looking into the throat of a yawning animal. The plant especially attracts wasps as pollinators. In North America, even hummingbirds have been observed hovering above the flowers. In the Middle Ages, the tuberous rootstock was often compared to lumps on the lymph glands and other glandular swellings and people thought that the plant could therefore act as a healing herb.

Habitat Woodlands with herbaceous undergrowth, wayside verges. On well drained or damp soils. Throughout Europe.

> *usually only a few flowers opened simultaneously*
> *unpleasant aroma when crushed*
> *mostly flowers in shade or partial shade*

corolla 7–9 mm long, spherical

inside reddish brown

305

inconspicuous flowers

raceme at end of stems

irregularly toothed

leaf oval

leaves opposite

tuberous, swollen rootstock

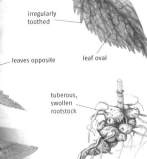

Did you know?

The distinctive caterpillars of the Water-betony moth and the very similar Mullein moth prefer the plants as summer fodder. These inconspicuous caterpillars pupate the following year, at the earliest.

Bird's-nest Orchid

Neottia nidus-avis (orchid family)
H 20–50 cm   May–June   perennial

Habitat Woodlands. In shady locations in humus or on mildew-covered wood. Almost everywhere in Europe.

> flowers with honey-like fragrance
> named after the shape of the roots
> without any chlorophyll

Unlike green plants that gain carbohydrates by using the sun's rays and carbon dioxide and water (via photosynthesis), the Bird's-nest Orchid does not photosynthesise. This means that the plant can flourish in the deepest and darkest forest locations. The plant gains nourishment purely from fungus threads penetrating its roots, which are interwoven like a bird's nest. Usually about nine years elapse from germination until the first flowers appear.

other petals pressed together

2-part lip, about 1 cm long

cluster with up to 60 light brown orchid flowers

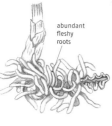

abundant fleshy roots

entire plant light brown

Did you know?

Fruit capsules open along longitudinal sections and release dusty fine seeds, each weighing only 0.000008 g. The dried fruit often remains visible for several years.

Common Twayblade

Listera ovata (orchid family)
H 20–50 cm   May–June   perennial

long cluster
with 20–40
Orchid petals

Common Twayblade has developed an unusual method to ensure pollination. If an insect comes into contact with a particular zone of the flower, a droplet of sticky fluid is sprayed onto it. Sacs of pollen are then caked onto the insect.

Habitat *Deciduous forests, riverside woodlands, copses, mountain meadows. On damp, preferably nutrient-rich ground in partial shade. Almost everywhere in Europe.*

> *also without flowers on 2 leaves*
> *lip often gleaming with nectar*
> *easily overlooked*

haired
stems

broad, oval, rough, with several longitudinal veins

2 almost opposite leaves, similar in size

other petals green, often with red margin

yellow-green lip, 6–8 mm long

Fly Orchid

Ophrys insectifera (orchid family)
H 15–40 cm   May–June   perennial

The flowers mimic the shape, colour and hairs of tiny female insects. They also produce sex hormones that female digger wasps usually produce in order to attract their mates. Male digger wasps then try to mate with the flowers, thus transferring pollen from one flower to another.

Habitat *Rough grassland, open, dry pine forests. On moderately dry, chalky soils. Almost everywhere in Europe.*

> *2 of the petals look like insects' antennae*
> *flowers trick insects and look like mates*
> *flower often overlooked*

2–20 orchid petals in slender flower head

yellow-green stem, upright

2 thread-like petals

3 yellow-green petals

lip about 1 cm long, short, velveteen hairs

large, blue-grey blotch

Bee Orchid

Ophrys apifera (orchid family)
H 20–40 cm   May–June   perennial

The flowers of the Bee Orchid mimic female insects, just like the Fly Orchid (p. 307). Scientists have observed how, especially since the early 1990s, the plant frequently colonises new habitats. Climate change has probably contributed to this development, but also the fact that the plant forms seeds even without pollination (see box). The plant can flower in favourable conditions for up to three to four years.

Habitat Rough grassland, semi-dry grassland, open oak or pine forests. On chalky soil in warm locations. Central and southern Europe.

> one of the most beautiful orchids
> green leaf rosette during winter
> flowers do not appear every year

3 whitish petals, pink or purple

lip light, patterned

lip about 1 cm long, globular, curved, with velveteen hairs

2–9 orchid flowers on elongated flower head

parallel leaf veins

bluish green leaves clasping stem

308

sacs with pollen

Did you know?

In central Europe, there are not enough bees to pollinate the plant. The flowers frequently tend to be self-pollinating. This is why shortly after the pollen sacs are filled, they protrude outwards and finally bend downwards as far as the stigma.

Lizard Orchid

Himanthoglossum hircinum (orchid family)
H 30–80 cm   May–June   perennial

The seeds are capable of germinating over many years. Flowers are mainly visited by wild bees that are attracted by the scent and sweet nectar contained in the flower spur. In contrast to most other orchids, this tall, robust plant can also grow among bushes.

Habitat *Rough grass-land, embankments, open, sunny copses, former vineyards. On warm chalky soil. In the western part of south and central Europe.*

> *unmistakeable due to characteristic ribbon-like laces*
> *sensitive to late frosts*
> *odour of billy goat, especially at night*

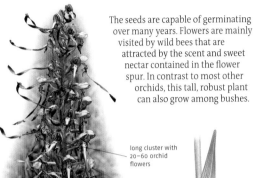

long cluster with 20–60 orchid flowers

leaves oval to lanceolate

leaves clasping stem

helmet-shaped upper petals

lip up to 6 cm long, inrolled or twisted

309

Black Vanilla Orchid

Nigritella nigra (orchid family)
H 5–20 cm   May–Aug   perennial

Hardly a mountaineer alive fails to sink to his knees to drink in the fragrance of this tiny Orchid. This flower is a miracle of fragrant delicacy. Cows generally avoid chewing on the plant, but if this does happen, it taints the cow's butter and cheese with a faint aroma of vanilla.

dense, pyramid-shaped flower head

Habitat *Sunny mountain meadows, dry grassland from 1400–2400 m. Mostly on chalky soil.*

> *mountains in central and southern Europe*
> *intense vanilla fragrance*
> *intolerant of fertiliser*

leaves directed diagonally upwards

leaves slender, grass-like

lip of petal pointing upwards

petals up to 7 mm long, blackish-red

Index of Species

Illustrations and Photographs

Illustrations
Golte-Bechtle/Kosmos (488); Haag/Kosmos (74); Hofmann/Kosmos (10); Kohnle/
Kosmos (11); Söllner/Kosmos (4); Spohn/Kosmos (456)

Photographs
Albers/Hecker 254H, Bellmann 101B; Hecker 72tP, 72tH, 87tP, 87bP, 87bH, 129tP, 131B,
132tH, 139tP, 158bH, 171bP, 171tH, 177bH, 181bH, 186P, 187bH, 195P, 288tP, 294tH, 294bH,
295tH, 297H; König 293H; Laux 79tH, 288tH; Mertz/Hecker 146tH; Pforr 18tP, 18tH, 23bP,
23bH, 25tP, 25tH, 27tH, 27bH, 29bP, 30tP, 30bP, 30tH, 30bH, 34tP, 34bP, 34bH, 36H, 40tP,
42bP, 45tP, 46tP, 46bH, 46bH, 48bP, 55tP, 55tH, 57tP, 57bP, 57tH, 58tP, 58bP, 58tH, 58bH,
60H, 61tP, 61bP, 61tH, 61bH, 62bP, 62bH, 63P, 63H, 63B, 64tP, 64bP, 64bH, 90bH, 97P, 100tP,
100tH, 103bP, 103tP, 103bH, 103tH, 107bH, 108bP, 110P, 113P, 113H, 115tH, 120bP, 125bP, 125tP,
125bH, 129bH, 137tP, 139bP, 139bH, 139tH, 141tP, 141tH, 142tP, 143P, 148bP, 148tP, 148bH,
151tP, 152H, 154tP, 154tH, 155H, 158tH, 166tP, 170bP, 171tH, 171bH, 174H, 177bP, 178bH, 179P,
187bP, 200P, 201bP, 202P, 203bP, 209tP, 210P, 214P, 216tP, 216tH, 218tP, 218bP, 219bP, 223H,
225tP, 226P, 231H, 237tP, 237tH, 245tP, 245bP, 245tH, 246bP, 250tP, 250bP, 254P, 256tP, 256tH,
256tH, 259tP, 259bP, 260bP, 261tP, 261bP, 264bP, 267tP, 267bP, 268tP, 277bP, 280tP, 282P,
282H, 285bP, 285tH, 285bH, 286tH, 287P, 293B, 300tH, 305P, 307tP, 307bH, 309bP, 1004tP;
Reinhard-Tierfoto, Hans Reinhard Heilgkreuzsteinach-Eiterbach 25bP, 25bH, 71tH, 76H,
85tP, 85tH, 89H, 119tP, 142bH, 161H, 286tP, 292tH, 298bH; Sauer/Hecker 55bP, 68bP, 77bP,
87tH, 88bH, 160bH, 188tP, 193bP, 308H; Schönfelder 19P, 20bP, 20bH, 27tP, 27bP, 36P, 40tH,
48tH, 50bP, 50bH, 56P, 60P, 95H, 96bP, 96tH, 96bH, 132bH, 136H, 137tH, 147tH, 152B, 155P,
158tP, 160bP, 164tP, 164tH, 164bH, 166tH, 168bH, 169P, 181bP, 185tP, 190H, 213tP, 219tP, 227tP,
230bP, 230bH, 232tP, 232bP, 232tH, 232bH, 243H, 245bH, 251bP, 252tP, 252tH, 253H, 264tH,
264bH, 270bH, 281tH, 295tP, 297P, 298tP, 298H, 300bP, 302bP, 302bH; Spohn 18bP, 18bH,
19H, 19E1, 19B, 20tP, 20tH, 21tP, 21bP, 21tH, 21bH, 22P, 22H, 23tP, 23tH, 24tP, 24H, 24B, 26P,
26H, 26B, 28P, 28H, 28B, 29tP, 29tH, 29bH, 31P, 31H, 32tP, 32bP, 32tH, 32bH, 33tP, 33bP, 33tH,
33bH, 34tH, 35P, 35H, 36B, 37tP, 37bP, 37tH, 37bH, 38P, 38H, 39tP, 39bP, 39tH, 39bH, 40bP,
40bH, 41P, 41H, 41B, 42tP, 42tH, 42bH, 43tP, 43bP, 43tH, 43bH, 44P, 44H, 44B, 45bP, 45tH,
45bH, 46tH, 47P, 47H, 47B, 48tP, 48bH, 49P, 49H, 50tP, 50tH, 51P, 51H, 52P, 52H, 53tP, 53bP,
53tH, 53bH, 54P, 54H, 54B, 55bH, 56H, 57bH, 59P, 59H, 59B, 62tP, 62tH, 64tH, 65P, 65H, 66tP,
66bP, 66tH, 66bH, 67P, 67H, 67B, 68tP, 68tH, 68bH, 69P, 69H, 69B, 70tP, 70bP, 70tH, 70bH,
71bP, 71tH, 71bH, 72bP, 72bH, 73P, 73H, 73B, 74P, 74H, 75tP, 75bP, 75tH, 75bH, 76P, 76B, 77tP,
77tH, 77bH, 78tP, 78bP, 78tH, 78bP, 78bH, 79tP, 79bP, 79tH, 79bH, 80P, 80H, 80B, 81tP, 81bP,
81tH, 81bH, 82P, 82H, 82B, 83tP, 83bP, 83tH, 83bH, 84tP, 84bP, 84tH, 84bH, 85bP, 85bH, 86P,
86H, 86B, 88tP, 88bP, 88tH, 89P, 90tP, 90bP, 90tH, 91P, 91H, 92P, 92H, 93bP, 93tP, 93bH,
93tH, 94bP, 94tP, 94bH, 94tH, 95P, 96tP, 97H, 97B, 98bP, 98tP, 98bH, 98tH, 99P, 99H,
100bP, 100bH, 101P, 101H, 102P, 102H, 102B, 104bP, 104tH, 104bH, 105P, 105H, 106P, 106H,
107tP, 107bP, 107tH, 108tP, 108bH, 108tH, 109P, 109H, 109B, 110H, 110B, 111tP, 111bP, 111tH,
111bH, 112tP, 112bP, 112tH, 112bH, 114P, 114H, 114B, 115tP, 115bP, 115bH, 116P, 116H, 116B, 117P,
117H, 117B, 118bP, 118tP, 118bH, 118tH, 119bP, 119bH, 119tP, 119tH, 120tP, 120bH, 120tH, 121P,
121H, 121B, 122tP, 122bP, 122tH, 122bH, 122bE2, 123P, 123H, 124bP, 124tP, 124bH, 124tH, 125tH,
126tP, 126bP, 126tH, 126bH, 127tP, 127bP, 127tH, 127bH, 128P, 128H, 128B, 129bP, 129tH, 130P,
130H, 130B, 131P, 131H, 132tP, 132bP, 133P, 133H, 133B, 134tP, 134bP, 134tH, 134bH, 135P, 135H,
135B, 136P, 136B1, 136B2, 137bP, 137bH, 138tP, 138H, 138B, 139E, 140P, 140H, 140B, 141bP, 141bH,
142bP, 142tH, 143P, 143B1, 143B2, 144tP, 144bP, 144tH, 144bH, 145P, 145H, 146bP, 146tP,
146bH, 147bP, 147tP, 147bH, 148tH, 149P, 149H, 150P, 150H, 150B, 151bP, 151bH, 151tH, 152P,
153P, 153H, 153B, 154bP, 154bH, 156tP, 156bP, 156tH, 156bH, 157P, 157H, 157B, 158bP, 159P, 159H,
159E3, 159B, 160tP, 160tH, 161P, 161B, 162tP, 162bP, 162tH, 162bH, 163tP, 163bP, 163tH, 163bH,
164bP, 165P, 165H, 165B, 166bP, 166bH, 167tP, 167bP, 167tH, 167bH, 168tP, 168bP, 168tH,
169H, 169B, 170tP, 170tH, 170bH, 172tP, 172bP, 172tH, 172bH, 173tP, 173bP, 173tH, 173bH, 174P,
174B, 175P, 175H, 175B1, 175B2, 176tP, 176bP, 176tH, 176bH, 177tP, 177tH, 178tP, 178bP, 178tH,
179H, 180P, 180H, 180B1, 180B2, 181tP, 181tH, 182P, 182H, 182B, 183P,

183H, 184P, 184H, 184B, 185bP, 185tH, 185bH, 186H, 186B, 187tP, 187tH, 188bP, 188tH, 188bH, 189P, 189H, 189B, 190P, 190B, 191tP, 191bP, 191tH, 191bH, 192P, 192H, 193tP, 193tH, 193bH, 194tP, 194bP, 194tH, 194bH, 195H, 195B, 196tP, 196bP, 196tH, 196bH, 197P, 197H, 198P, 198H, 199tP, 199bP, 199tH, 199bH, 200H, 201tP, 201tH, 201bH, 202H, 203tP, 203bH, 203tH, 204P, 204H, 204B, 205bP, 205tP, 205bH, 205tH, 206P, 206H, 206B, 207tP, 207bP, 207tH, 207bH, 208P, 208H, 208B, 209bP, 209bH, 209tH, 210H, 211P, 211H, 211B, 212P, 212H, 212B, 213bP, 213bH, 213tH, 214H, 215P, 215H, 215B1, 215B2, 216bP, 216bH, 217P, 217H, 218tH, 218bH, 219bH, 219tH, 220P, 220H, 221bP, 221tP, 221bH, 221tH, 222tP, 222bP, 222tH, 222bH, 223P, 223B, 224bP, 224tP, 224bH, 224tH, 225bP, 225bH, 225tH, 226H, 227bP, 227tH, 227bH, 228bP, 228tP, 228bH, 228tH, 229tP, 229bP, 229tH, 229bH, 230tP, 230tH, 231P, 231B, 233P, 233H, 233B1, 233B2, 234tP, 234bP, 234tH, 234bH, 235P, 235H, 236P, 236H, 236B, 237bP, 237bH, 238tP, 238bP, 238tH, 238bH, 239P, 239H, 239B, 240P, 240H, 241tP, 241bP, 241tH, 241bH, 242tP, 242bP, 242tH, 242bH, 243P, 243B, 244P, 244H, 244E1, 246tP, 246tH, 246bH, 247P, 247H, 247E2, 248P, 248H, 249tP, 249bP, 249tH, 249bH, 250tH, 250bH, 251tP, 251tH, 251bH, 252bP, 252bH, 253P, 255tP, 255bP, 255tH, 255bH, 256bH, 257P, 257H, 257E1, 257B, 258P, 258H, 258B, 259tH, 259bH, 260tP, 260tH, 260bH, 261tH, 261bH, 262P, 262H, 263P, 263H, 263B, 264tP, 265P, 265H, 265B, 266P, 266H, 266B, 267tH, 267bH, 268bP, 268tH, 268bH, 269P, 269H, 269B, 270tP, 270bP, 270tH, 271P, 271H, 271B, 272tP, 272bP, 272tH, 272bH, 273P, 273H, 273B, 274tP, 274tH, 274bP, 274bH, 275P, 275H, 275B, 276tP, 276bP, 276tH, 276bH, 277tP, 277tH, 277bH, 278tP, 278bP, 278tH, 278bH, 279tP, 279bP, 279tH, 279bH, 280bP, 280tH, 280tH, 281tP, 281bP, 281bH, 283tP, 283bP, 283tH, 283bH, 284P, 284H, 285tP, 286bP, 286bH, 287H, 287B, 288bP, 288bH, 289P, 289H, 289E3, 289B, 290tP, 290bP, 290tH, 290bH, 291P, 291H, 291B, 292tP, 292bP, 292bH, 293P, 293E3, 293E3, 294tP, 294bP, 295bP, 295bH, 296tP, 296bP, 296tH, 296bH, 297E1, 298bP, 299P, 299H, 299B, 300tP, 300tH, 301P, 301H, 301B, 302tP, 302tH, 303P, 303H, 303B, 304tP, 304bP, 304tH, 304bH, 305P, 305B, 306P, 306H, 306B, 307bP, 307tH, 308H, 309tP, 309tH, 309bH

P = main photograph, H = habitat, E = Extra detail (from top to bottom or left to right), B = box, b = bottom, t = top

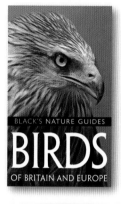

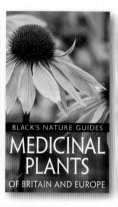
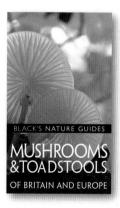
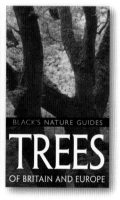

Discover nature
with A&C Black

ISBN 978 07136 8666 1

ISBN 978 07136 7237 4

ISBN 978 07136 7560 3

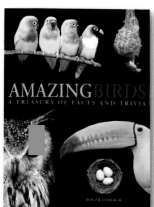

ISBN 978 07136 8666 1

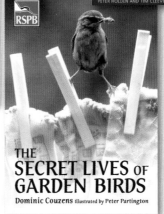

ISBN 978 07136 6616 8

About the Authors

Authors

Margot and Roland Spohn, a husband and wife team, are keen researchers and biologists who devote their time to the study of nature. Their skills perfectly complemented each other's for this book. Margot Spohn wrote about the plants, while Roland Spohn took photographs and prepared the illustrations.

With 2,054 photographs and illustrations (see index of illustrations p. 316).

The photograph on page 2 shows a Garden Peony. Photos on page 3 show, from top to bottom: Common Poppy, Garden Star-of-Bethlehem, Chicory, Arnica, and Herb Paris. Pages 16/17 show images of Yellow Iris.

Published 2008 by A&C Black Publishers Ltd, 38 Soho Square, London W1D 3HB

www.acblack.com

First published 2007 by Franckh-Kosmos Verlags GmbH & Co. KG, Stuttgart, Germany

Copyright © 2008 by Franckh-Kosmos Verlags GmbH & Co. KG

ISBN 978-1-4081-0153-7

A CIP catalogue record for this book is available from the British Library

This book is produced using paper that is made from wood grown in managed sustainable forests. It is natural, renewable and recyclable. The logging and manufacturing processes conform to the environmental regulations of the country of origin.

Authors: Margot Spohn and Roland Spohn
Commissioning Editor: Nigel Redman
Project editor: Jim Martin

Translation by Suzanne Kirkbright (Artes Translations)
Design by Fluke Art, Cornwall

Printed in Italy

10 9 8 7 6 5 4 3 2 1

Cover photograph: poppies © Orientaly/Shutterstock